Advances in Applied General Equilibrium Modeling

This series has a companion series in *SpringerBriefs in Applied General Equilibrium Modeling*.

The series publishes advances in the theory, application, parameterisation and computation of applied general equilibrium (AGE) models. AGE analysis is now an essential input in many countries to the discussion of a wide range of economic topics relevant to public policy. This reflects the capacity of AGE models to carry extensive economic detail, their flexibility in accommodating new policy-relevant theory and data, and their capacity to project economic outcomes for a large number of macroeconomic and microeconomic variables.

Topics in AGE modeling addressed by the series include: macroeconomic forecasting and adjustment; public finance; economic growth; monetary policy and financial markets; environmental policy; energy policy; income distribution and inequality; global modeling; country-specific modeling; regional modeling; economic effects of natural disasters and other catastrophic events; productivity; demography; foreign direct investment; economic development; model solution algorithms and software; and topics in estimation, calibration and validation.

AGE applications are increasingly multi-disciplinary, spanning inputs from such diverse fields as engineering, behavioral psychology, energy modeling, land use modeling, demography, and climate modeling. The series allows for the comprehensive documentation and careful exposition of not only the AGE models themselves, but also the inter-disciplinary inputs to the modeling, and the interactions between each.

For AGE modelers, the series provides a format supporting: clear exposition of data work, attention to the theoretical modeling of relevant policy detail, and thorough discussion of simulation results. This aids both academic and policy readerships.

Academic readers will appreciate: the capacity to see details of the full complexity of relevant components of model equation systems; comprehensive documentation of data manipulation algorithms; supporting analysis and discussion of model input and closure assumptions; and careful discussion of results grounded in AGE theory, data and closure assumptions.

Policy readers will appreciate: a format that supports the reporting of the comprehensive set of model outputs of interest to policy makers; discussion of elements of the theory and data that exert a heavy influence on research findings; and nuanced and qualified discussion of the policy implications of AGE research.

More information about this series at http://www.springer.com/series/13860

Glyn Wittwer
Editor

Multi-regional Dynamic General Equilibrium Modeling of the U.S. Economy

USAGE-TERM Development and Applications

Springer

Editor
Glyn Wittwer
Centre of Policy Studies
Victoria University
Melbourne, VIC
Australia

ISSN 2520-8268 ISSN 2520-8276 (electronic)
Advances in Applied General Equilibrium Modeling
ISBN 978-3-319-58864-3 ISBN 978-3-319-58866-7 (eBook)
DOI 10.1007/978-3-319-58866-7

Library of Congress Control Number: 2017939616

Printed on acid-free paper

This Springer imprint is published by the registered company Springer Nature Switzerland AG
The registered company address is: Gewerbestrasse 11, 6330 Cham, Switzerland

Preface

The compilation of regional data so as to prepare an early version of USAGE-TERM did not seem at first to be a massive task. It soon became evident that proper documentation would be time-consuming. Detailed documentation, technical refinements, and model applications have taken a number of years.

USAGE-TERM follows in the footsteps of the dynamic USAGE model of the US economy developed by Peter Dixon and Maureen Rimmer over many years. Many of the research memoranda, working papers, and publications authored by Peter and Maureen in devising the USAGE model are cited in the volume. Some of the model enhancements implemented in USAGE have been adopted in USAGE-TERM.

USAGE-TERM development has been the culmination of a team effort. Peter Dixon and Maureen Rimmer have brought the model to life through commissioned projects originating from various US federal departments. Mark Horridge pioneered the TERM approach to CGE modeling. The first application of TERM concerned drought in Australia late in 2002. More recently, Mark and other GEMPACK specialists, Michael Jerie, Florian Schiffmann, and Dean Mustakinov, have responded to the growing technical demands of model users as the theory and database of the model have grown.

Without clients, many of the enhancements of USAGE-TERM would not have been developed. The contributors to this volume are grateful to CREATE at USC, the MITRE Corporation, the Department of Homeland Security, and the US Department of Commerce for their commissioned projects using the model.

The Centre of Policy Studies (CoPS) moved to Victoria University early in 2014. We are grateful to Vice-Chancellor Peter Dawkins for the opportunity to continue research in a new setting.

The saddest recent event in CoPS has been the passing of Ken Pearson in May 2015. He was a selfless, devoted, brilliant colleague. His grand vision of GEMPACK software as a tool to spare the CGE modeler from the need to acquire specialist programming skills has enlarged the CGE community. Every working day at CoPS, we use the software that remains Ken's legacy.

Melbourne, Australia
January 2017

Glyn Wittwer

Contents

Contributors

Note: All authors are at the Centre of Policy Studies

Janine Dixon Centre of Policy Studies, Victoria University, Melbourne, VIC, Australia

Peter B. Dixon Centre of Policy Studies, Victoria University, Melbourne, VIC, Australia

Mark Horridge Centre of Policy Studies, Victoria University, Melbourne, VIC, Australia

John Madden Centre of Policy Studies, Victoria University, Melbourne, VIC, Australia

Maureen T. Rimmer Centre of Policy Studies, Victoria University, Melbourne, VIC, Australia

Glyn Wittwer Centre of Policy Studies, Victoria University, Melbourne, VIC, Australia

List of Figures

List of Tables

Chapter 1
Beyond Regional Input–Output Modeling

Glyn Wittwer, Janine Dixon and John Madden

Abstract Politicians and analysts are concerned with the economic health of regions. Sub-national economic modeling has relied heavily on input–output models. The absence of resource constraints in such models implies that they miss much of regional adjustment story in response to economic shocks. The Horridge approach enables the practitioner to represent small regions using a CGE model, based on the theory of national ORANI-style models. Dynamics are an invaluable enhancement to multi-regional CGE models, as the path of adjustment of a region is of policy interest. The dynamic, multi-regional USAGE-TERM model has relied heavily on the dynamics developed in the national USAGE model.

Keywords Regional CGE modeling · Dynamics · Paths of adjustment

1.1 Introduction

There is great interest in regional economies. Residents of one region may view that world quite differently from those in another. National data which point to a booming economy may mean little in a region that is suffering a local recession due to the closure of manufacturing plant that formerly employed a significant share of the region's workers.

During and after the global financial crisis (GFC), some U.S. regions benefited from an unusual confluence of a weaker dollar and rising commodity prices, which raised the prosperity of mining and agricultural regions. North Dakota boomed as the price of oil soared. Elsewhere, the picture was bleak. Lost jobs in the wake of the

G. Wittwer (✉) · J. Dixon (✉) · J. Madden (✉)
Centre of Policy Studies, Victoria University, Melbourne, VIC, Australia
e-mail: glyn.wittwer@vu.edu.au

J. Dixon
e-mail: janine.dixon@vu.edu.au

J. Madden
e-mail: john.madden@vu.edu.au

G. Wittwer (ed.), *Multi-regional Dynamic General Equilibrium Modeling of the U.S. Economy*, Advances in Applied General Equilibrium Modeling,
DOI 10.1007/978-3-319-58866-7_1

GFC resulted in vast swathes of U.S. suburbia being adversely impacted. The great American dream for many was lost, as banks foreclosed on their family homes. Many workers left their families behind to seek employment in booming regions. Others stayed, but had to accept lower wages or underemployment to do so.

People care about regions. They identify with where they grew up even as the world changes around them. For generations in local rural communities, parents and grandparents have despaired as the young have left their home region in search of better job opportunities elsewhere. But this change is not confined to small towns in rural regions. Medium-sized cities that were formerly manufacturing hubs may have peaked decades ago when manufacturing was the lifeblood of the nation. Over several generations, with ongoing structural change in the economy, the relative importance of individual states within the U.S. has changed dramatically. Within the working lifetimes of some veteran members of congress, New York State has declined from having four or five times as many congressional representatives as Florida to having the same number in the current congress.

Politicians are elected to a large extent by region. Regional rivalries come to the fore when it comes to substantial national public spending. Defense training bases and defense manufactures, for example, are important to regional economies. Changes in funding or strategic direction have political implications. Local politicians will fight hard to maintain defense spending in their region. Local jobs and votes depend on it.

Structural change has had dramatic impacts on the U.S. economy. In 1948, agricultural output accounted for 9% of GDP nationally (Fig. 1.1). For the past decade or so, this share has hovered around 1%. Much of the story of agriculture's decline reflects not the Dustbowl of the 1930s that impoverished tens of thousands of families. Rather, it reflects farm productivity gains that have resulted in labor

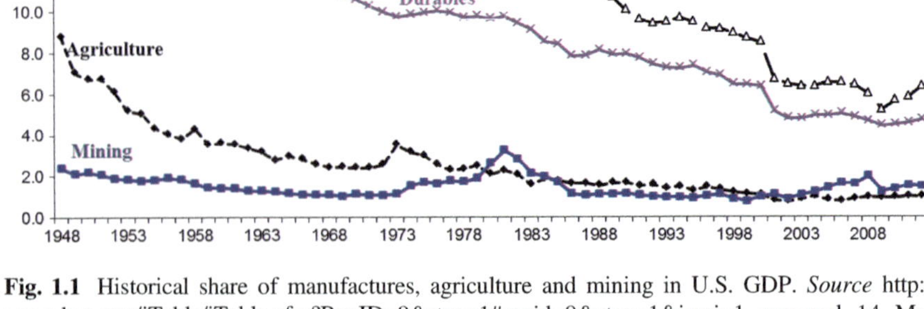

Fig. 1.1 Historical share of manufactures, agriculture and mining in U.S. GDP. *Source* http://www.bea.gov/iTable/iTable.cfm?ReqID=9&step=1#reqid=9&step=1&isuri=1 accessed 14 May 2015

savings on a relatively fixed area of farmland. Job opportunities grew first in manufacturing and ever more so in service sectors. Townships have shrunk as larger urban centers have become hubs for the services that are accounting for a continually growing share of GDP.

Turning to manufacturing, proud cities in the U.S. heartland have diminished as the nation's factories have been run ragged by rising international competition, most recently from China. Maybe Detroit is the best known casualty: its population peaked at 1.8 million at the 1950 census and is now the only U.S. city whose population has climbed above one million and subsequently fallen below. Part of Detroit's decline has arisen from the decline of manufacturing and, in particular, the declining importance of the automobile sector as a source of jobs. The picture of decline is not so dramatic if we consider the Detroit metropolitan area, which covers more than 3000 km^2. The population of the metropolitan area has hovered around 4.3 million over the past four decades, although it took a hit from the GFC, with a decline of 3.5% between 2000 and 2010.[1]

Buffalo presents a similar story with its population peaking at 580,000 in the 1950s. It has now fallen below 260,000, but the overall decline in the Buffalo-Niagara Falls metropolitan area has been smaller as the population stretches out to the suburbs. In addition to the diminishing role of manufacturing, Buffalo's decline stems from evolving transport modes. The Erie Canal and Buffalo's role as a railway hub have become less important over time.

Modeling of regional U.S. economies has been undertaken for several decades. Regional input–output databases have been compiled at the state and county levels, and more recently at the congressional district level. Input–output models have been extended to include inter-regional trade matrices so as to better depict the interactions between regions (Park et al. 2007). Yet the assumptions of input–output models raise doubts concerning the veracity of results generated by such models.

It would be remiss of multi-regional computable general equilibrium (CGE) modelers not to acknowledge that they have learnt from the data issues faced by input–output modelers. The task of the CGE modeler is to use the struts of input–output databases to devise models that improve the depiction of economic adjustment to scenario shocks.

The remainder of this chapter starts with an outline of Mark Horridge's path-breaking approach to preparing multi regional CGE databases. A summary of how the ORANI school of CGE modeling overcame computational limitations follows. Having identified a suitable computational approach, the discussion turns to resource constraints and local multipliers. The focus then turns to the limitations of input–output modeling, even in small regions. The context of small region booms opens us to the motivations for moving from comparative static to dynamic modeling. Inevitably, dilemmas arise in small region representation dealing with where people live rather than work.

[1]See http://en.wikipedia.org/wiki/Metro_Detroit.

1.2 A Dynamic CGE Approach

1.2.1 Database Estimation and Variable Aggregation

With modern computers, database processing software and ready access to regional data on the web, it is relatively straightforward to devise input–output tables for states or small regions. It is less straightforward to estimate inter-regional trade matrices. Typically, where estimation has been attempted, existing input–output tables are aggregated to a relatively small number of sectors. However, sectoral aggregation limits the potential applications of a given database. For example, a database may contain a sufficient number of sectors to depict a scenario that has impacts on a particular urban area. The same database is likely to be deficient in a scenario concerned with R&D in agriculture in a neighboring region, or the impacts of fracking in a given state or the regional impacts of growth in high-tech manufacturing.

1.2.1.1 Horridge's Approach to Multi-regional Model Problems

There are two major problems to overcome in a multi-regional model. The first concerns availability of regional data. The second concerns dimensionality. Mark Horridge revolutionized multi-regional CGE modeling by introducing TERM (The Enormous Regional Model), first used to evaluate the impacts of drought on regional Australia (Horridge et al. 2005). Chapter 9 outlines the Horridge approach in more detail than here.

Horridge's method is to start with a national input–output table, rather than to rely on regional tables (Horridge 2012). The first step in the Horridge approach is quite counter-intuitive. Instead of aggregating the national CGE database, processed from the available national input–output table, the national table is disaggregated. The motivation that other practitioners may have for relying on aggregated tables is a fear that regional data are less accurate than national data. Horridge's motivation for disaggregating the national table as a starting point is that often, we know much about industries that operate at the regional level. For example, we know specific crop outputs by state and even have information at the county level. This information is more disaggregated in the sectoral dimension than that in publicly available national input–output tables. Horridge's method assumes that a given industry in each region uses the same technology. Typically, agriculture is one of the main parts of the table that we split in order to make defensible the assumption of identical technologies across regions.

It is easy to think of examples in which the assumption of identical technologies breaks down if the initial national table is not sufficiently disaggregated. For example, we do not expect crops in Wisconsin to use the same technology as crops in Florida, due to marked differences in climate. However, to assume identical technologies for citrus production or corn production in different regions is reasonable. We would expect differences in climate to be reflected in differences in the composition of agricultural output across regions. Therefore, we split the published input–output table into more crop and livestock types. Then, we use available regional data on outputs of these types to estimate regional shares of national activity. Through this approach, we capture regional differences in agricultural technologies via regional differences in the composition of outputs.

The second main area of the national database that we split routinely is the electricity sector. Electricity generation in different regions tends to be dominated by different fuel types and technologies. For example, much of California's generation is hydropower, whereas West Virginia relies heavily on coal-fired generation. We split electricity supply into different types of generation, which feed into an electricity transmission/distribution sector. This enables us to utilize available small region data on electricity generation, notably Carbon Monitoring for Action data, downloadable from carma.org. Chapter 7 discusses regional electricity supply in greater detail.

We need to construct sub-national inter-regional trade matrices in a multi-regional CGE model. The absence or paucity of data has in the past been advanced as an impediment in multi-regional model development. Whereas international merchandise trade data are collected at customs posts, no such data are collected for sub-national trades. Even the most comprehensive of such data do little to fill the trade matrices, as they are patchy and often recorded in terms of somewhat generic volumes rather than commodity-specific values that align conveniently with input–output sectors. Prior to the Horridge approach, practitioners constructing multi-regional databases were content to aggregate the national database in an attempt to accommodate the limited inter-regional trade data.

Using the Horridge approach, some sectors, such as housing and hairdressers, are designated as non-traded, so that supply must equal demand in each region. In other sectors, at a high level of disaggregation in both the sectoral and regional dimensions, it becomes obvious that there are many zero activity cells in each dimension. For example, urban-based regions will have little or no activity in broadacre agricultural sectors. Whereas we may expect education services to be provided in all regions, no matter how small, once we split education into pre-school, elementary schooling, college education and university education, we will once again find many small regions with zero activities, at least at the university level.

The gravity assumption, in which trade volumes are inversely proportional to the distance between the origin and destination, is used to estimate inter-regional trades. Since the estimation process is undertaken at a maximum level of disaggregation, more zero supply activities appear in the database. This simplifies the task of estimating inter-regional trades.

The next issue concerns dimensionality. Section 1.2.1.2 outlines the use of linearized algebra and model condensation, implemented from the earliest days of the ORANI model, to ease the computational burden of solving a national model. As we move from a single region to multi-regional model, the database size increases rapidly. Therefore, when we move to a multi-regional model, we need to do more. The next steps are to replicate two techniques used in multi-county GTAP modeling (Hertel 1997). The first is to make use of the common sourcing assumption. This is explained in Sect. 9.1. A further step is to aggregate the master database, with the aggregation tailored to the requirements of each specific application. The implications of variable aggregation are discussed in Sect. 9.1.

1.2.1.2 Reducing Computing Requirements in CGE Modeling

There are several difficulties in moving from an input–output to CGE model. The first is that a CGE models requires greater computational power. Dixon et al. (1982) devised the ORANI model of the Australian economy with over 100 sectors. At a time when computing power was much scarcer than it is now, this was a significant advance. That solving a CGE model with over 100 sectors was possible in the late 1970s and early 1980s was due to innovations used to implement ORANI. First, the equations of the model were linearized. Second, a huge number of equations in the model were condensed by the use of substitution of a number of multi-dimensional variables. Substitution enables the modeler to reduce the number of endogenous variables and equations many-fold, turning a computationally limiting model into a model that can be solved with relative ease. Third, in order to reduce linearization errors to insignificant magnitudes, Dixon et al. (1982, Chap. 5) implemented a multi-step solution process. As is outlined later in this section, ORANI modelers also introduced flexible closures so that if the modeling environment of a scenario changes, the choice of endogenous and exogenous variables changes, eliminating the need to switch to a different model.

1.2.1.3 CGE Modeling for Policy Analysis

At this point, it is appropriate to acknowledge the contribution of Alan Powell to CGE model development. Powell's over-arching vision was that it should be possible to utilize real data to develop an economy-wide model for policy analysis. In the 1970s, this was a massive undertaking. This was long before the era of readily downloadable data, before the era of software which eased model development. Powell's vision emerged in the era of punch-cards and voluminous computer printouts for every task. Powell was appointed to director of the IMPACT project in 1975. The objective of the project was to develop models in order to provide policy advice to the Industries Assistance Commission. Of the four models developed as part of this project, the CGE model ORANI became the foundation for models used in Australia and elsewhere that remain in use today.[2]

[2]The TERM suite of models combines the core theory of an ORANI model with bottom-up regional detail.

Ongoing database and model development required a small army of contributors. The Australian Bureau of Statistics (ABS) provided much more than input–output detail. The requirements of the team led by Peter Dixon on ORANI model development included details of each margin involved in a transaction. To this day, the ABS releases margins as part of the input–output table. The ABS also provides details of commodity taxes and subsidies, and import duties, a legacy arising from the emphasis in early modeling efforts of estimating the impacts of removing distortions from the economy.[3] Work within the IAC included regular estimates of rates of effective protection, arising from binding import quotas that were more distortionary than explicit tariffs.[4]

Another major contributor to the IMPACT project was Ken Pearson. His vision was that CGE practitioners need not have specialist programming skills in order to run a model. Pearson developed the GEMPACK platform, which eased CGE model development and transferability. Pearson, in conjunction with Mark Horridge and later Michael Jerie, continued to enhance GEMPACK. The IMPACT/Centre of Policy Studies (CoPS) approach emphasizes to need to explain simulation results in terms of the data and theory of the model. AnalyseGE, for example, was developed by Pearson after he observed participants at an introductory course on CGE modeling struggling to bring together data and theory with existing software (see http://www.copsmodels.com/gpange.htm).[5]

1.2.2 Resource Constraints

Input–output modeling does not account for resource constraints in default applications. In the historic circumstance of Leontief's pioneering application of an input–output model to examine the impacts of the mobilizing of resources for the war effort, the assumptions of an input–output framework were quite defensible. This circumstance was that the levels of idle factories and unemployed workers were extraordinarily high. Therefore, increased demands for the war effort were accommodated by factor supplies which in effect were elastic. Unfortunately, input–output models have been applied routinely to scenarios ever since in which there are resource constraints.

---

[3]For an example of detail provided by the ABS, see http://www.abs.gov.au/AUSSTATS/abs@.nsf/DetailsPage/5209.0.55.0012013-14?OpenDocument. Product details (i.e., sales to disaggregated users) are downloadable from http://www.abs.gov.au/AUSSTATS/abs@.nsf/DetailsPage/5215.0.55.0012012-13?OpenDocument (accessed 12 July 2016).

[4]The research output of the IMPACT project from 1985 till 1987 is summarized in http://www.copsmodels.com/ftp/workpapr/r-07.pdf (accessed 12 July 2016).

[5]Pearson passed away in May 2015 after a long battle with cancer (see Dixon et al. 2015). The Ken Pearson Scholarship funded by CoPS and awarded at the annual Global Economic Analysis conference honors his contribution.

Before venturing further into the attributes of CGE modeling, some explanation of the nature of constraints may be helpful. In creating new capital, the funding of investment used to create capital must come either from domestic savings or foreign funds. If domestic savings are the source of investment, such savings are at the cost of current consumption. If foreign funds are the source of investment, we must pay foreigners at the expense of consumption in the long run.

In the labor market, one constraint is the pool of available national labor. During periods of high unemployment, we may be able to draw on the pool of unemployed labor to satisfy increases in demand for labor. Once we consider the skill composition or the regional distribution of the labor force, we find more constraints. As tastes and technologies change over time, some skills will become scarce while others fall out of favor. During a construction boom, we may observe shortages of skilled workers in the building industry. A more extreme example may arise from a disease outbreak in the population. A disease will increase demand for health workers. The supply of health workers will be a constraint in the short term. In addition, to the extent that they are affected by the outbreak, the supply of health workers may shrink temporarily.

In the context of regional modeling, an important constraint is the willingness of people to move between regions in response to changing relative regional economic circumstances. Inter-regional migration may entail separation from families and lifelong friends. There are transactions costs and stamp duties arising from selling and buying properties. There are travel costs. It is not unusual in a multi-regional CGE model to assume that inter-regional migration of labor is perfectly elastic. This implies that people will migrate in response to changes in regional labor markets until real wages are equalized across regions. In some modeling contexts, this labor market assumption is not important. In others, it may overstate resource mobility, at least in the short term.

In addition to the mobility of labor, we might need to examine the movement of goods and services between regions. For example, an important contribution was made to U.S. economic development in the twentieth century by electricity. Three electricity grids were developed across the nation, covering all lower 48 states, which have provided mains access for the vast majority of households and industries in the nation. The grids have enhanced greatly the availability and mobility of electricity across regions. In the Australian context, Adams and Parmenter (2013) formally model an electricity grid in states joined by contiguous supply, so that increased electricity demands can be satisfied in one region by diverting electricity from use in another. Inter-regional electricity demands are imperfectly substitutable, with different types of generation contributing to the electricity grid pool. Adams and Parmenter (2013) limit this form of substitution to those regions covered by the grid. Western Australia, for example, is not part of the national grid and therefore unable to purchase electricity from interstate in response to increasing demands. In the U.S. context, Texas is a standalone state at present, with its own electricity grid. When undertaking regional modeling, we need to be conscious that our assumptions concerning regional mobility, such as an electricity grid, do not contradict reality in scenarios in which these assumptions are relevant. That is, if we choose to model U.S. electricity, we should not allow electricity trading between Texas and other states in our base case.

1.2.2.1 Resource Mobility in Small Regions

A defense often mounted for input–output modeling is that the assumption of elastic supplies is reasonable in small regions. After all, workers migrate from other regions to take advantage of job opportunities. If input–output supply assumptions are indefensible at the national level, surely they provide a reasonable approximation of reality in small regions. Is this so? We can examine North Dakota's oil boom as an example. A closer inspection on the ground in a boom town may reveal a different story. Consider Williston, Williams County, at the epicenter of North Dakota's oil boom. It is evident that the prices of local services and amenities soared during the boom. The town had the distinction early in 2014 of having some of the steepest rents in the union (Newcomb 2014). This is because housing is non-traded, and in the short term has relatively inelastic supply. Therefore, accommodation prices rise steeply as the mining boom induces workers to the town. Depending on how high wages need to be to attract workers into mining, there is also a risk that employees in service industries in Williston become scarce. If prices escalate for inter-staters seeking accommodation in Williston, prices may also rise for locals. Long-time locals may own their Williston property and sense a windfall from rising real estate prices. But when they dine out or purchase a takeaway meal, they may be jostling for a seat in the diner or waiting in a queue with others who have come to town in search of a living from the oil fields. Prices for local services may rise as demands increase.

Regional input–output modelers show awareness of resource constraints by exogenously imposing negative impacts on a model. A bio-fuel industry, for example, may reduce the sales and output of other fuel types. Modelers may shock the lagging industries to reflect this. The advantage of CGE modeling is that price pressures are endogenous. There is no need to impose shocks on industries that may lose out, because resource constraints and price impacts will do this within the model. Many input–output modelers introduce price behavior so that in effect, their model behaves more like a CGE model.

Price movements diminish the magnitude of local multipliers. Similarly, to the extent that goods and services can be imported from other regions, local multipliers are diminished further. We must be skeptical of multiplier analysis that concludes that each dollar of additional direct activity in region results in several dollars of indirect additional activity in that region.

There is nothing unique about the Williston story. Port Hedland in Australia ships a significant share of global iron ore production to East Asia. The town is as remote any in the world, being more than 800 miles north of Perth, which is turn is the most isolated major city (i.e., population exceeding one million) in the world, separated from the rest of world by the breadth of the Indian Ocean on its western flank, and from the cities of eastern Australia by an expanse of desert that stretches across the continent. Port Hedland's housing prices and rents soared to extreme levels during the boom. The sale price of a modest family home often exceeded a million Australian dollars after the mining price boom gathered momentum around 2007. The squeeze on the cost of living of local health workers and teachers has been excessive. In addition to its isolation, Port Hedland has a harsh climate. High iron ore prices meant that mining companies were prepared to pay extremely high wages to attract workers to the region, as compensation for isolation and the harsh climate. Indeed, part of the labor demands during the prolonged construction phase was satisfied by workers flying in from Perth, the eastern state capitals of Australia and even Indonesia. Fly-in, fly-out (FIFO) employees typically work 10 days on, before returning home for 10 days off. During the peak of the boom, a truck driver in Port Hedland earned a salary closer to that of a surgeon than his or her truck-driving city colleague.

The examples of Williston in North Dakota or Port Hedland in Western Australia indicate that local price hikes, at least in the short- to medium-term, are a typical part of adjustment to a local boom. We can model such adjustment more naturally in a CGE than input–output framework. In a CGE model, we can impose constraints on capital adjustment and provide for imperfect mobility in the labor market. The assumption of capital adjustment fits our understanding of the local housing response to a boom better than the elastic supply assumption of an input–output model. Imperfect inter–regional labor mobility allows for the possibility of handsome wage premiums being paid in remote regions to attract people and to keep them as local prices rise.

It follows that with the end of a boom, we will not necessarily observe massive negative multipliers as demands for labor wind down. Much of the impact initially may be on prices rather than quantities. The long-time locals who enjoyed windfall gains in the value of their real estate may observe a falling of real estate values as dramatic as the earlier price rises when the boom started, as demand for labor in the mining region wanes with the drawing to a close of a construction boom. This is not to say that the local economy will go back to the way it was before the boom.

One issue that has arisen with the mining boom in Australia is that local communities should receive some of the benefit from mining royalties. This may mean that money is poured into local schools and health amenities. In addition, there may be private investment in services in the town that increase the attractiveness of the town for local inhabitants. It is possible, therefore, the local community will be left with more essential services, more restaurants and more recreational facilities and a bigger population than before the boom, even if the heady days of height of the boom have long passed.

There is a less optimistic alternate view. It is possible that local infrastructure investments are under-utilized once the boom is over. This may result in empty commercial premises, empty houses and emptying schools. Through geographic remoteness, many towns and cities are unable to move in tandem with changing economic structures. That is, some business services and services associated with government may be confined to a small subset of urban centers in a particular state. This leaves other centers without the diversification once the main economic activity in the local region declines.[6]

Whereas towns arising from mining are vulnerable to long-term decline, a collapse in tourism demand may result in a short-run downturn in local economic activity. In this short-run circumstance, employment and income multipliers calculated using input–output analysis may provide a better picture of the downturn than the default assumptions of CGE modeling. An improved short-run local depiction might arise within a CGE model from assuming that local capital operates temporarily with reduced capacity utilization. A precedent for this approach is in the modeling of idle capital used by Dixon and Rimmer (2010) to depict the national U.S. impacts of a global recession. In this national example, temporarily idle capital ensures that real exchange rate adjustments do not restore baseline employment levels. The analogy at the local level is in the context of a disruption such as a hypothetical terrorism incident which drives tourists away from the region. Capital is not restored to usual capacity until the aversion of tourists to the local area returns to base. As long as capital is under-utilized within the model, demand for workers remains below base and adjustment in local real wages can do little to restore employment.

1.2.3 The Need for Dynamics

The above comments indicate that a desirable multi-regional economic model requires more than the simultaneous price and quantity adjustments depicted in a comparative static CGE model. Such a model will be enhanced if it accommodates incremental adjustments in labor, capital, housing and other local markets over time. We might expect an increase in local employment to generate an increase in local demand for housing. In the early years, when perhaps the boom is not fully anticipated and investors are not entirely confident that adding to the local housing stock is prudent, much of the housing market adjustment will be via prices. Over a number of years, new housing will be built, though the supply response may be constrained by the relative remoteness of the region and a concern that the boom's duration will be much shorter than the typical lifetime of a house.

We can enhance our multi-regional CGE model by including a time dimension. Dixon and Rimmer (2002a) devised a CGE model with year-on-year recursive dynamics. The development of dynamic USAGE-TERM has piggy-backed on the

[6]Ker (2016) provides some insights into regional impacts on housing and fly-in, fly-out workers of the end of a boom.

innovations of Dixon and Rimmer, and more recently, in the context of the U.S. economy, Dixon et al. (2013).[7] The core dynamics include links between investment, driven by changes in rates of return, and capital stocks. The full adjustment to a shock, such as a rise in local demands induced by a mining boom, takes a number of years through successive annual partial adjustments. In the context of our boom, it may take a number of years for the housing supply response to reverse escalating housing prices.

There is evidence that dramatic price falls will occur eventually. The following is an example:

> A house in the mining town of Port Hedland has been passed in at auction for $360,000 after it was bought 4 years ago for $1.3 million.
>
> The three bedroom, one bathroom fibro and iron house, was built in the 1960s in the Western Australian town.
>
> Real estate agent Barry Walsh said it was a sign the mining boom's construction phase, which drove property prices to unrealistic levels, has tapered off.
>
> He said prices were also very high during that phase because there was a high demand for accommodation and a lack of available land to build property on.
>
> Mr Walsh said the real estate market, which had been attracting phenomenal rents of thousands a dollars a week, was unsustainable.
>
> A spectator at the auction said "it was an extraordinary event".
>
> Mr Walsh said the auction showed that people could now afford to buy homes in Port Hedland again, and the town might be able to rely on a local workforce and fewer fly-in, fly-out workers.
>
> ABC News (2015).

In implementing a dynamic model, the Dixon and Rimmer (2002a) approach is first to devise a forecast business-as-usual baseline. An important part of devising a forecast baseline is to choose a suitable closure for the model, that is, an appropriate choice of exogenous and endogenous variables. A CGE model containing n equations and $n+m$ variables will have n endogenous variables and m exogenous variables. One of the innovations of the ORANI school (Dixon et al. 1982) of CGE modeling was to use flexible closures to reflect various contexts of a CGE scenario. For example, in the short term in a comparative static national model, we assume routinely that capital stocks and real wages are fixed. This implies that rates of return on capital and national employment are endogenous. In the long run, we expect adjustment to capital so as to return rates-of-return to base case levels. We also expect all the adjustment in the national labor market to be via changes in real wages relative to the base case, without a change in employment relative to the national base case. The two different environments are created in the CGE model

[7]In addition to the theoretical basis of the national USAGE model, USAGE-TERM uses a national USAGE database as a starting point for the regional split. The preparation of the national database required a major effort over many years (Dixon and Rimmer 2002b, 2003). The USAGE baseline provides a template for the USAGE-TERM baseline in dynamic model runs.

not by using different models with different equations for the short and long runs. Rather, we change the choice of endogenous and exogenous variables, which deactivates one set of equations and activates another set.

Closure flexibility is extended in a dynamic CGE model to distinguish between a baseline forecast closure and a policy or scenario closure. As a starting point, we consider historical updating or forecasting of a CGE database. On the expenditure side of GDP, we usually have historical data for real growth in the macroeconomic aggregates, namely private consumption, investment, government consumption, exports and imports. In addition, macroeconomic forecasters may provide projections for these real economic variables a decade or so into the future.

The macroeconomic variables are of interest to us in scenario analysis and are therefore naturally endogenous. But in order to update and project a CGE model into the future, we shock these variables and therefore they must be exogenous. This implies that we require a particular forecasting closure. For example, in forecast, so as to fit an aggregation consumption target, we may make the average propensity to consume shifter endogenous.

On the income side, GDP is a function of primary factors and underlying technologies. That is, GDP = f(K,L,1/A), where K denotes capital stocks, L aggregate employment and 1/A the technology. We have historical data and forecasts of aggregate employment. The level of capital stocks is pre-determined by the link between present capital, previous period capital net of depreciation and previous period investment. From expenditure-side historical data and forecasts, we have real GDP growth. Therefore, in order to accommodate the GDP growth forecast, given forecasts of capital and labor inputs, the economy-wide technological change variable must be endogenous.

Our policy or scenario closure must differ from our forecast closure. When we run the policy scenario, variables such as the average propensity to consume and economy-wide technological change revert to their usual exogenous state. The variables that are switched from endogenous to exogenous in moving from the baseline to policy closure are shocked so at the match the changes of the baseline run. Therefore, if we run the model with the policy closure, but do not ascribe any policy shocks, the year-on-year changes in variables should be identical to those of the baseline run.[8] When we ascribe policy shocks, we report the year-on-year cumulative deviations of the policy run from the baseline run for key variables.

The environment in which a policy scenario proceeds will impact on the deviation of the policy scenario from the baseline scenario. In this respect, dynamic CGE modeling differs from comparative static CGE modeling in which there is no attempt to provide a forecast. For example, we can refer to the construction and operational phases of a large coal mine. Using detailed year-by-year construction costs and estimates of the value of output during the operational phase, driven by estimates of annual output multiplied by forecast coal prices (ascribed in the forecast run of the model), we might find that the welfare impact of the project is

[8]See Chap. 5 of Dixon and Rimmer (2002a) for a comprehensive explanation of closure swaps.

positive. If, in an alternative baseline, coal prices collapse several years into the operational phase, the welfare impact will diminish or even turn negative. There is no difference in the policy shocks: the difference in welfare impact arises from differences in the baseline. It is much more challenging to replicate this sort of story using a comparative static model.

In capital creation, we know intuitively that adjustment is rarely painless or costless. Capital that is immediately available for use tends to be the exception rather than the rule. If a road link is built to service increasing demands in a region, there may be years of planning and construction before the link is operational. In the time of construction, not only are growing demands over time likely to worsen congestion. Disruptions to business-as-usual operations associated with construction, such as temporary intersection closures, may add to short term costs. Clearly, there are adjustment costs which we should seek to capture in a formal model framework.

In the regional labor market within the theory of USAGE-TERM, workers are attracted to a booming region by local real wages that rise relative to real wages elsewhere.[9] Eventually, local labor supply rises to match the rise in local labor demand, at which point local real wages cease rising relatively to forecast. As the labor market weakens in later years when construction slows, labor demand falls below labor supply, imposing downward pressure on real wages. When labor supply adjusts sufficiently to match labor demand, real wages will cease falling.

An important flow and stock relationship in our regional model is that between the trade balance and net foreign liabilities. Consider an investment project. USAGE-TERM modeling of an investment project will show a real appreciation as net imports increase to accommodate the increased demands. The stock of net foreign liabilities will increase due to the increase in net imports. Therefore, additional interest payments to foreigners are required in the long term. USAGE-TERM can be a tool of project evaluation by summing the discounted marginal cost and marginal benefits of the project over time. Payments to foreigners need to be included in the calculation.

The Department of Homeland Security (DHS) has been an important client for regional modelers. Hypothetical scenarios commissioned by DHS include terrorist attacks on specific regions. A dynamic multi-regional CGE model is a better tool than an input–output model or a one region CGE model for this task. In a hypothetical attack which results in substantial capital destruction, the recovery phase is likely to provide a substantial regional and national economic stimulus. Clean-up operations and rebuilding are relatively labor-intensive activities that will increase regional and national employment relative to forecast in the short term.

[9]In the context of a mining boom that occurs after the GFC, the real wage hike necessary to induce workers to a mining region is lower than otherwise. In this circumstance, mining jobs may provide employment when the alternative for a worker displaced by the GFC is unemployment in their former place of residence.

The recovery phase may mask the true economic costs of an adverse event. A congressional representative might be surprised to see model results which show that his or her district could receive a local stimulus in the aftermath of a catastrophic event such as a terrorist attack. Indeed, during a restoration phase, labor and federal funds may flow into the district from others in the union, which is normally regarded favorably by congressional representatives. But in times of post-attack trauma and recovery, the context of resource inflows is markedly different from such inflows driven by other means such as a federal stimulus package.

Moreover, the increased demands arising from the clean-up and rebuilding phase are likely to be funded by a deterioration of the trade balance. The addition to net foreign liabilities relative to a business-as-usual forecast baseline arising from an increase in net imports may be in the tens of billions of dollars. An input–output model does not have a balance of payments constraint. The user of a single period CGE model will struggle to account for the impact of clean-up costs on net foreign liabilities from the national perspective. The importance of accounting for the impact of the scenario on net foreign liabilities within a dynamic model is that it contributes to estimating the economic costs of the event many years into the future.

1.2.4 Where We Live and Where We Work

The master database of the first TERM model (Horridge et al. 2005) represented 57 Australian regions. Within a few years, this had been extended to over 200 regions. The motivation for a further split from 57 to 200+ regions was that Australia's two largest cities, Sydney and Melbourne, contain 40% of the nation's population but are represented by only two regions in the original database. When dealing with one of the growing issues of the twenty first century, urban transport infrastructure, it appears highly desirable to split these cities into a number of regions.

It is apparent that once we split large cities, more people are going to live in one region and work in another. A response to this problem in putting a TERM database together is in the first instance to concentrate on where people live. This is based on the assumption that most household spending occurs in the region of residence. We can think of exceptions.

Section 1.2.2.1 mentions FIFO workers in the mining industry. If we use census data based on place of residence to estimate small-region economic activities, we will create mining activity in capital cities and elsewhere remote from the mines. This is an artifact of our abstraction that the industry is located where people live. When it comes to estimating regional household activity, this is the preferred assumption. However, the artifact of mining activity appearing in urban areas implies, under the assumption of identical technologies in each region for a given industry, that some mining inputs will also be recorded in these urban areas. If such inputs have a small magnitude, they are unlikely to create modeling difficulties.

But in some specific scenarios, using the place of residence to locate the industry may create problems. Rather than discard the place of residence assumption, we could in a specific scenario tailor the shocks to bypass the difficulties created by the assumption.

In some cases, modifications to deal with the place of work v. place of residence dilemma are relatively straightforward. In a typical city many more people work in a downtown area than live in it, as is discussed in Sect. 9.4. In such a circumstance, if we are modeling a downtown disruption, we should be careful to assign any labor market shocks to the regions in which downtown workers live. Census data on employment by zip code provide a basis for assigning the regional shocks.

1.3 Project-Specific Model Modifications

An important part of conducting policy-relevant modeling is in being prepared to make modifications to a model that are specific to an individual project. For example, Chap. 11 presents modeling of the impact of the Californian drought on irrigation regions. This required several modifications. First, the regions of the master database of USAGE-TERM were altered so as to represent the counties of the Central Valley and irrigation regions to the north separately. Second, using USDA data on crop acreage and irrigation water requirements, irrigation water accounts were devised for the application. Third, irrigation water requirements were modified so as to depict differences in average annual rainfall between different counties.

The theory of USAGE-TERM was modified for agricultural industries so as to distinguish between annual crops, with relatively mobile factors, and perennial crops, with relatively fixed factors of production. This was an essential step in preparing the model to depict large changes in water availability. As the main barriers to water trading between users in the irrigation regions are institutional rather than physical, the model was modified to enable water trading between irrigators. The objective of this modification was to depict hypothetical water trading scenarios as a response to extreme water stress.

Other projects require different modifications. As outlined in Sect. 10.2.1, the default TERM gravity assumption was modified so as to depict a higher degree of tradability between regions that are close neighbors, notably city-based congressional districts.

The modifications made for one project do not usually result in changes that will be carried over to the generic version of the model. No model is such a complete depiction of reality that it can accommodate the particular emphases of each and every project that is undertaken by the practitioner. Project-specific model modifications are a necessary part of policy relevant economic modeling.

1.3.1 Government and Household Spending in the National I–O Table

Statistical agencies in federal and state government departments may devote considerable resources to preparing input–output tables. CGE modelers and their clients invariably want more detail than is offered in default electronic and published data. Chapters 2–6 in this volume address sectoral detail in the regional dimension. It takes little effort to think of additional dimensions that may be useful in addressing policy questions.

Two chapters outline other enhancements to regional CGE detail. In Chap. 7, Janine Dixon looks at income attribution, an important indicator of regional welfare often overlooked in preference for regional GDP. In a world where increasingly both capital and labor are mobile, economic activity and household income may differ substantially at the regional and even national level, and may be impacted differently by changing economic circumstances. To this end, it is helpful to have a suitable structure in which to organize data on revenue as it accrues to regional households and government and the rest of the world through sales, factor income, tax collection and transfers. A format is introduced in which the balancing conditions are made explicit for commodity supply and usage and agent income, expenditure and savings. This format has potential to simplify the data requirements and validation of a CGE model with the capacity to deal with household income distribution, regional and foreign ownership of factors, and different tiers of government.

In Chap. 8, John Madden takes up the question of fiscal accounting in regional CGE models. He uses the income framework developed in Chap. 7 to show the data required at various levels of fiscal and regional disaggregation. The example of detailed government financial modelling being implemented for a single-region CGE model of Florida is then discussed. It is shown how fiscal modeling in the Florida State Model is designed to capture institutional features such as the state's legislative requirement to balance the budget by linking each areas of state government expenditure to income received from specified sources of revenue.

Madden then deals with certain issues that some U.S. national accounting conventions bring about for the construction of government-finance data sets in a form appropriate for CGE modeling. For instance, he notes that current government spending is restricted to no more than four commodities: Federal general government (defense), Federal general government (non-defense), and State and local general government (sometimes disaggregated to education and non-education). The non-defense and non-education commodities bundle together a range of diverse goods and services (e.g. hospitals, criminal justice, and general government administration). It is shown how these commodities can be disaggregated to yield an industry structure better suited to public sector analysis. Madden concludes with a discussion of extending detailed fiscal modelling to multiregional models, noting the considerable problem of data scarcity, particularly at the county level.

The U.S. convention is to confine current government spending to four commodities, "SLGOther", "SLGEduc", "NatlDefG" and "NonDefG". In the initial fully disaggregated national database, "GenGovInd" is sold to an array of industries. Practical modeling applications may require much more detail than this.

The Florida example reveals in the case of a single state that fiscal accounts dealing with multiple tiers of government require considerable data, much data processing and the addition of a substantial number of equations to a CGE model. An adventurous practitioner wishing to extend the methodology to more states will gain a better understanding of the magnitude of such a venture from this chapter.

References

ABC News (2015) Port Hedland house passed in at auction in million-dollar dive, sign mining boom over. http://www.abc.net.au/news/2015-02-07/house-passed-in-at-auction-after-million-dollar-price-dive/6077724. Accessed 31 May 2016

Adams P, Parmenter B (2013) Computable general equilibrium modeling of environmental issues in Australia: economic impacts of an emissions trading scheme. In: Dixon P, Jorgenson D (eds) Handbook of computable general equilibrium modeling. North-Holland, Amsterdam, pp 553–657

Dixon P, Rimmer M (2002a) Dynamic general equilibrium modelling for forecasting and policy: a practical guide and documentation of MONASH. North-Holland, Amsterdam

Dixon P, Rimmer M (2002b) USAGE-ITC: creating a 1992 benchmark input-output database, further developments. Centre of Policy Studies Mimeo. http://www.copsmodels.com/archivep.htm TPGW0157. Accessed 15 July 2016

Dixon P, Rimmer M (2003) Regional database for USAGE. Centre of Policy Studies Mimeo. http://www.copsmodels.com/archivep.htm TPGW0157. Accessed 15 July 2016

Dixon P, Rimmer M (2010) You can't have a CGE recession without excess capacity. Econ Model 28:602–613

Dixon P, Rimmer M, Hirst J (2015) Mathematician's 30-year winning tangent. http://www.smh.com.au/national/obituaries/mathematicians-30year-winning-tangent-20150617-ghqley.html. Accessed 12 July 2016

Dixon P, Parmenter B, Sutton J, Vincent D (1982) ORANI: a multisectoral model of the Australian economy. Contributions to economic analysis, 142. North-Holland, Amsterdam

Dixon P, Koopman R, Rimmer M (2013) The MONASH style of computable general equilibrium modeling: a farmework for practical policy analysis. In: Dixon P, Jorgenson D (eds) Handbook of computable general equilibrium modeling. North-Holland, Amsterdam, pp 23–103

Hertel T (ed) (1997) Global trade analysis: modeling and applications. Cambridge University Press, Cambridge

Horridge M (2012) The TERM model and its database. In: Wittwer G (ed) Economic modeling of water: the Australian CGE experience. Springer, Dordrecht, pp 13–36

Horridge M, Madden J, Wittwer G (2005) Using a highly disaggregated multi-regional single-country model to analyse the impacts of the 2002–03 drought on Australia. J Policy Model 27:285–308

Ker P (2016) Pampered FIFO workers come back to earth with a bump. http://www.theage.com.au/business/mining-and-resources/fifo-workers-face-leaner-times-as-downturn-eats-away-their-perks-20160522-gp164q.html. Accessed 8 July 2016

Newcomb A (2014) Costliest place for renters has Yellowstone River views. http://abcnews.go.com/US/life-williston-north-dakota-expensive-place-rent-apartment/story?id=22549192. Accessed 27 Jan 2017

Park J, Gordon P, Moore J, Richardson H, Wang L (2007) Simulating the state-by-state effects of terrorist attacks on three major US ports: applying NIEMO (National Interstate Economic Model). In: Richardson H, Gordon P, Moore J (eds) The economic costs and consequences of terrorism. Edward Elgar, Cheltenham, UK

Part I
Sectoral Detail in USAGE-TERM

Chapter 2
Agriculture and Mining in Regional United States

Glyn Wittwer

Abstract Agricultural sectors in USAGE-TERM are represented on a commodity basis. This requires converting available input–output tables from a farm-type basis. Agriculture's share of the national economy has declined with population growth and technological change. Farm lobbyists historically have wielded considerable influence in congress, so that for many decades, U.S. agriculture was highly distorted. In a new era of worsening global land and water scarcity, commodity prices may strengthen, boosting agriculture. A dramatic change in mining has arisen from the use of fracking techniques to extract coal seam gas.

Keywords Agriculture · Trade distortions · Mining

2.1 Overview of Regional Database Chapters

This is the first of four chapters that include a combination of background material on industries, information on data collection and processing of these data. When it comes to preparing a very detailed, multi-regional database for a CGE model, background information, data and policy issues often go together. The desirable extent of sectoral disaggregation depends on the policy issues. For example, modeling of the impacts of agricultural R&D may rely on a suitable representation of specific crops and types of livestock. From the outset, it is apparent that the default sectors in published input–output tables, regardless of how many sectors there are, do not necessarily give a sufficient representation of economic activities that are of interest to analysts. In agriculture, we require substantial database amendments to move the representation of agriculture from a farm-type basis in published input–output tables to a commodity basis for CGE analysis. This is discussed further in Sect. 2.2. In the electricity sector, discussed in Chap. 4, given the importance of carbon emissions in policy analysis, we wish to split electricity

G. Wittwer (✉)
Centre of Policy Studies, Victoria University, Melbourne, VIC, Australia
e-mail: glyn.wittwer@vu.edu.au

G. Wittwer (ed.), *Multi-regional Dynamic General Equilibrium Modeling of the U.S. Economy*, Advances in Applied General Equilibrium Modeling,
DOI 10.1007/978-3-319-58866-7_2

into generation and transmission/distribution sectors, and further into different types of electricity generation. A split of the electricity sectors will also help distinguish between types of generation suitable for base-load from those that are not.

While the approach of examining background and policy matters may provide a guide as to where in the database we could improve the sectoral representation, more deficiencies may emerge over time. In the mining sectors, Oil and gas is represented in USAGE-TERM as a single sector. In future database preparations, with the rise of fracking, separate oil and gas sectors would be more appropriate.

An important theme that emerges from the discussion of manufactures in Chap. 3 is that structural change in the economy has seen the broad sector move from a powerhouse of the U.S. economy several generations ago to a position of diminished importance now. The change is more dramatic at the regional than national level. Some cities have gone into long-term decline, due to their reliance on manufacturing in their heyday.

We devote an entire chapter to electricity (Chap. 4). The construction of major electricity grids in the 1930s provided a boost to rural regions at a time when there had been marked disparities between urban and rural access to electricity. The USAGE-TERM database is constructed from a register of every power station listed in the country compiled by Carbon Monitoring for Action (carma.org).

Health care in the U.S. is more expensive than in other OECD nations, to such an extent that direct comparisons of per capita income may overstate U.S. living standards, unless comparisons weigh health services carefully. Since health care involves large amounts of public expenditure, fiscal accounts may enhance the model. Health care, education, international trade and other services are covered in Chap. 5. Chapter 6 outlines modifications to improve the representation of tourism and transport in USAGE-TERM.

2.2 Introduction to Agriculture

Multi-regional computable general equilibrium (CGE) modeling has usually been undertaken with a small number of sectors. Without sectoral detail, CGE models become more abstract and less useful for scenario analysis. Many agricultural economists are driven by practical questions, such as returns to R&D, productivity, water management, market liberalization and risk management. Some of these issues have remained in the domain of partial equilibrium models, as they cover relatively small regions and specific agricultural activities. Such models capture details in production functions that may be relevant to a particular region. However, they lack detail on market conditions such as downstream demands, fluctuations in international demand and supply, and competition for land, labor and capital.

A CGE model can combine the detail of partial equilibrium models with market details that are external to an industry. The GTAP model (Hertel 1997) has opened up the field of CGE modeling to trade analysts by including 12 agricultural sectors in its representation of the global economy.

Data are available from the Food and Agricultural Organization of the United Nations (FAO) for almost 1,000 raw and processed agricultural commodities.[1] This indicates that there is scope for considerable expansion of representation of agriculture within a CGE database, be that in a single region model or multi-regional model. The TERM (The Enormous Regional Model) approach has revolutionized CGE modeling (Horridge 2012). Whereas the usual approach to devising a multi-regional database is to use more aggregated data than at the national level, so as to recognize the fall-off in data accuracy as one moves to smaller regions, the TERM approach usually involves splitting the available national input–output table into more sectors. This even applies in the U.S. case where the national database has more than 500 sectors.[2]

An important issue we may wish to model concerns the changing global food market and the consequent regional economic impacts of such changes. To investigate this further, we might require global demand and supply projections for individual farm commodities. From this, we would work out which commodities are most important in the U.S. context and what sort of representation we should include in the master database of USAGE-TERM.

In the context of agriculture, disaggregating the database further enhances the usefulness of the database. The national database with which we start represents agriculture by farm type. Data on farm types do not match data that are used in commodity analysis. Specific crop and livestock data on production, consumption and trade are readily available. Therefore, moving the sectoral representation from farm type to commodity output type is a priority in improving the representation of agriculture in a CGE database.

An objection to this approach is that farms exist as a type rather than being defined by a given commodity. A particular farm may produce a number of crops and also carry livestock. We can redress this objection by modifying the theory of the CGE model. Farm land, farm labor and farm capital can be made mobile between different outputs. If market conditions turn in favor of one crop over another, farm factors turn towards production of the relatively favorable crop. This movement from industry by farm type towards representation by output type enhances the model's capabilities. Moreover, relevant economic information such as output, export data and price data are available in detail at the commodity level.

---

[1]See http://www.fao.org/faostat/en/#data accessed 27 January 2017.

[2]The database from USAGE, a dynamic model of the national US economy, is the starting point for the USAGE-TERM database (Dixon and Rimmer 2012).

2.3 Splitting the National Database into More Types of Farm Outputs

Another advantage of a commodity representation of agriculture in the database is that the U.S. Department of Agriculture (USDA) produces agricultural census data that are based on specific crop and livestock outputs. The main source of county level agricultural data is the USDA website http://quickstats.nass.usda.gov/. The site provides data for individual crops and livestock activities. The split of the national database into more farm outputs is the first point at which USDA data are used. These data are available at the county level so that we can calculate county shares of state activity with relative ease. The only disadvantage of census data is that they tend to be dated relative to available state data. For example, we used 2007 census data to estimate county level farm outputs. However, these estimates are not the sole source of agricultural data. In particular, farm outputs are scaled so as to match state level value-added totals provided in national accounts data.

Table 2.1 shows agricultural classifications as they appear in NAICS (The North American Industry Classification System), the national USAGE database and in USAGE-TERM. The first objective of using USDA data is to split the commodities in the national CGE database further, in line with the right-hand column of Table 2.1. For example, the USDA data added across counties indicate that in 2007, among the food grain sectors, wheat sales totalled \$10.3 billion, rice sales \$1.9 billion and corn \$39.7 billion. The USDA data provided shares for an initial split of the food grains. Both the absolute numbers and the shares alter via adjustments through subsequent scaling, balancing and updating of the database.

A key assumption in devising a multi-regional CGE database is that a given industry uses an identical technology or cost structure in all regions. At an aggregated level, this could be a burdensome assumption. For example, a database with a single livestock sector would impose the same cost structure on a region predominantly producing dairy cattle as on a region that produces mainly turkeys. This appears not to be defensible, whereas if there are separate dairy cattle and turkey industries, the assumption that each region produces dairy cattle with one technology and turkeys with another technology, each identical across regions, is more reasonable. As is evident in what follows, the disaggregation we end up with in USAGE-TERM does not free us entirely from examples in which industry technologies may differ between regions. That is, we may choose a set of industry splits with the expectation that they will enhance policy modeling capability. By the time we have completed the process of preparing a multi-regional database, we may be aware of a litany of examples in which the assumption of identical technologies does not hold. Whether or not we need to act on possible differences may depend on the nature of proposed studies, as is discussed in Sect. 2.6. The struggle to choose an appropriate sectoral representation is one that practical CGE modelers cannot avoid.

Table 2.1 Industry classifications in agriculture

NAICS code	NAICS industry (1)	USAGE industry (2)	USAGE-TERM industry (3)
1111	Oilseed and grain farming	Food grains Feed grains Oil bearing crops	Wheat, rice, Corn Soybean (part) Oilseeds
1112	Vegetable and melon farming	Vegetables	Vegetables, Potatoes, Tomatoes
1113	Fruit and tree nut farming	Fruits Tree nuts	Apples, Grapes, Citrus, Strawberries, Other fruit Other fruit & nuts, Almonds
1114	Greenhouse, nursery and floriculture production	Greenhouse, nursery and floriculture production	Nursery
1119	Other crop farming	Crops miscellaneous	Hay and forage, sorghum, sugar cane, sugar beet, Soybean (part), Cotton, Tobacco, Other broadacre Miscellaneous agriculture
11191	Tobacco farming	Tobacco	Tobacco
11192	Cotton farming	Cotton	Cotton
1121	Cattle ranching and farming	Meat animals (part)	Beef cattle
11212	Dairy cattle and milk production	Dairy farm products	Dairy cattle
1122	Hog and pig farming	Meat animals (part)	Hogs
1123	Poultry and egg production	Poultry and eggs	Poultry and eggs Turkeys
1124	Sheep and goat farming	Meat animals (part)	Other livestock (part)
1129	Other animal production	Livestock miscellaneous	Other livestock (part)

2.4 The Multi-Regional Representation in USAGE-TERM

The assumption that identical technologies apply to a given industry in every region simplifies the task of preparing a multi-regional CGE database. The regional shares of national output we obtain from regional data are used to split the national CGE database. That is, we aim to use all of the information in the national database without contradicting it. By treating regional activities as shares of national activities, we avoid the circumstance that may arise from independent estimation of regional input–output tables in which a particular industry has a larger output than is shown in the corresponding national table.

Our regional output shares of national activity provide two lots of regional data in USAGE-TERM. The bottom-up core of the CGE database includes 70 regions, including all states plus a split of some larger states into additional regions. In addition, we utilize county level census data to prepare a top-down county module with 3142 regions. All shares obtained using USDA data are scaled so as to be consistent with state level totals for the national accounts crops and livestock sector. In "bottom-up" modeling, each industry in each region has its own production function. Each region has its own household and consumption function. Inter-regional trade matrices link the regions. "Top-down" results are derived from the bottom-up results, based primarily, in the context of USAGE-TERM, on county shares of state/region activities. "Top-down" results, being a module without separate prices, do not affect bottom-up results (see Chap. 9).

In practice, USAGE-TERM is never run with the full dimensions of the master database. Not only are 512 sectors and 70 regions impossible to solve with the usual memory of a PC. The results would be rather difficult to present. In typical applications, we aggregate the sectors to fewer than 100 and the regions to fewer than 10. In addition, we calculate top-down county level results for those counties in regions of interest in a particular study. In most applications of USAGE-TERM, there is a composite "Rest of USA" region from which we omit top-down county-level results. That is, if we are not interested in the individual bottom-up regions within a composite region in a particular study, it follows that the corresponding top-down results are also of no interest.

Table 2.2 shows the top five regions for each agricultural output. Some crops are concentrated in a handful of regions. The extreme case is that of almonds, produced almost exclusively in the Rest of California, namely the portion of the state excluding the counties of Los Angeles, Sacramento, Riverside or Orange, and excluding the conglomerate of counties that cover San Francisco and its surrounds. Rest of California also dominates production of grapes (66% of the national total), strawberries (61%) and other tree nuts (61%). Citrus production is confined to regions where winter is relatively warm. Other agricultural activities are widely dispersed, including hay and forage. With a diversified base in animal feed, certain livestock activities are also highly diversified. No region dominates turkey production, ensuring a diversified supply for Thanksgiving festivities. But the least concentrated of all agricultural activities is poultry and eggs, with only one state, Georgia, accounting for more than 10% of national production. The geographic dispersion of poultry and egg production is in keeping with an industry not limited to a narrow range of climates.

In cattle production, the national sales value indicated by USDA data is several-fold larger than value-added indicated by the national input–output table. This reflects a high reliance on feedlots rather than grazing on rain-fed pastures, the former using intermediate inputs, the latter a primary factor that forms part of

Table 2.2 Top 5 states/regions for each agricultural output

Output	Rank 1	%	Rank 2	%	Rank 3	%	Rank 4	%	Rank 5	%		%	National value-added c$m 2010
HayForage	RoTexas	11.7	Kansas	6.8	SouthDakota	6.3	Nebraska	6.0	Wisconsin	4.7	Rest	64.6	9924
Almonds	RoCalifornia	99.5	SanFranCtyCA	0.4									2337
Apples	Washington	45.1	RoMichigan	12.7	RoNewYork	12.5	RoPnnsylvnia	6.1	RoCalifornia	4.4	Rest	19.2	861
OthTreeNuts	RoCalifornia	61.5	RoTexas	12.4	NewMexico	8.5	Oklahoma	7.1	Georgia	4.2	Rest	6.3	2676
Vegetables	RoCalifornia	33.4	Arizona	8.5	Washington	7.6	Wisconsin	5.0	Idaho	4.5	Rest	41.1	8227
OthBroadAcre	RoTexas	10.0	RoCalifornia	8.9	Minnesota	8.2	NewMexico	5.0	Idaho	5.0	Rest	62.8	215
PoultryEggs	Georgia	12.4	NorthCarolin	9.9	RoTexas	9.0	Alabama	7.7	Mississippi	7.6	Rest	53.4	10939
SugarCane	Louisiana	58.2	PalmBeachFL	27.7	RoTexas	8.0	RoFlorida	6.2			Rest	0.0	365
OilSeeds	NorthDakota	60.8	SouthDakota	19.2	Kansas	6.3	Minnesota	6.1	Colorado	2.9	Rest	4.8	879
BeefCattle	Nebraska	16.9	RoTexas	16.2	Kansas	15.4	Iowa	6.1	SouthDakota	5.0	Rest	40.2	6238
MiscelAgri	RoCalifornia	11.0	Iowa	9.0	Nebraska	7.7	Minnesota	6.5	RoIllinois	6.2	Rest	59.6	107
Corn	Iowa	18.1	Nebraska	15.4	RoIllinois	12.6	Minnesota	9.5	Indiana	7.4	Rest	37.0	16239
Cotton	RoTexas	51.8	RoCalifornia	10.1	Georgia	7.7	Mississippi	6.2	Arkansas	5.4	Rest	18.8	3461
DairyCattle	Wisconsin	20.2	RoCalifornia	14.5	NewMexico	9.7	RoNewYork	7.7	RoPnnsylvnia	5.9	Rest	42.0	4800
Grapes	RoCalifornia	66.0	SanFranCtyCA	11.1	Washington	8.0	RoNewYork	5.4	RoMichigan	2.0	Rest	7.5	2124
Nursery	RoCalifornia	24.2	Oregon	7.0	OrangeCA	6.0	RoTexas	4.5	RoFlorida	4.4	Rest	53.8	16833
Hogs	Iowa	33.3	Minnesota	16.1	NorthCarolin	11.9	Nebraska	6.7	Indiana	5.5	Rest	26.4	3653
OthFruit	HillsbrghFL	88.3	RoMissouri	4.0	Wisconsin	2.8	RoMichigan	2.1	Washington	1.8	Rest	1.0	1185
OthLivestock	RoTexas	14.0	Colorado	9.9	Kentucky	7.5	Wyoming	6.0	SouthDakota	5.8	Rest	56.8	75
Citrus	RoFlorida	43.9	RoCalifornia	40.6	RoTexas	6.4	Arizona	3.8	RiversideCA	3.6	Rest	1.8	915
Potatoes	Washington	27.1	Idaho	24.4	Wisconsin	10.2	Colorado	8.5	NorthDakota	5.0	Rest	24.8	3761
Rice	Arkansas	35.2	RoCalifornia	28.4	Louisiana	11.9	Mississippi	8.2	RoTexas	8.2	Rest	8.1	1149
Sorghum	Kansas	48.5	RoTexas	32.2	Nebraska	5.8	NewMexico	2.1	Louisiana	2.0	Rest	9.5	650
Soybean	Iowa	17.2	Minnesota	11.9	RoIllinois	10.8	Nebraska	10.4	Indiana	8.9	Rest	40.8	11964
Strawberries	RoCalifornia	61.2	HillsbrghFL	5.9	Washington	4.6	RoNewYork	3.9	OrangeCA	3.5	Rest	20.9	938

(continued)

Table 2.2 (continued)

Output	Rank 1	%	Rank 2	%	Rank 3	%	Rank 4	%	Rank 5	%		%	National value-added c$m 2010
Sugarbeet	Minnesota	37.8	NorthDakota	15.3	RoMichigan	12.0	Idaho	11.7	Montana	5.2	Rest	18.0	580
Tobacco	NorthCarolin	45.3	Kentucky	25.6	Virginia	6.6	SouthCarolin	5.8	Tennessee	4.6	Rest	12.1	1511
Tomatoes	RoPnnsylvnia	13.7	Hawaii	9.2	RoNewYork	7.7	Vermont	6.3	Washington	5.7	Rest	57.3	2941
Turkeys	Minnesota	22.5	NorthCarolin	17.3	RoMissouri	7.9	Arkansas	6.6	Virginia	6.3	Rest	39.4	658
Wheat	Kansas	17.0	NorthDakota	15.8	Montana	9.8	SouthDakota	8.8	RoTexas	7.0	Rest	41.6	4471

Source Estimates based on http://quickstats.nass.usda.gov/ and http://www.bea.gov/iTable/iTable.cfm?reqid=70&step=1&isuri=1&acrdn=1#reqid=70&step=1&isuri=1 accessed 26 June 2015

value-added activity. For every broadacre livestock farmer relying on rain-fed pasture, the moment comes when handfeeding becomes necessary, as drought is an inevitable part of farming in most parts of the world. In some studies, there may be a case for dividing cattle production into rain-fed and feed-lotting technologies.

Corn production arguably best fits the traditional perceptions of a crop that has overtaken the prairies of the northern states: Iowa, Nebraska, Illinois, Minnesota and Indiana produce around two-thirds of the national crop. The U.S. is the world's largest producer of corn. The commodity has been the subject of debate after the enactment of NAFTA, which led to an increase in the volume of exports to another corn producer, Mexico. Nadal and Wise (2004) argue that an increase in exports from the United States to Mexico is detrimental to the environment, because corn production north of the border relies on production techniques less sustainable than those in Mexico.

Some cropping patterns reflect stark differences in climate. Sugar cane, typically grown only in tropical and sub-tropical regions, is confined to the states of Louisiana, Florida and Texas. Sugar beet, on the other hand, is grown in northern states with a severe winter: Minnesota, North Dakota, Michigan, Idaho and Montana produce more than four-fifths of the nation's crop. Sugarhas been subject to substantial market distortions historically. Since the 1981 Farm Act, U.S. domestic sugar prices have been maintained at above the world price. High levels of protection have persisted since then, despite the Uruguay Round opening up the U. S. market to imports. Separate tariff-rate quotas now apply to raw cane sugar and refined sugar. The quantity of sugar imported at the in-quota tariff rate is determined prior to the start of each fiscal year. No limit applies to the quantity that can be imported at the higher over-quota tariff rate.[3]

Wheat is among the commodities that has been the subject of considerable policy intervention over the past decades. In part, policies were aimed at dealing with the decline in farmers' terms of trade. For example, between 1978 and 2005, the price of farm outputs declined relative to the price of farm inputs at 2% per annum. In the 1960s, wheat export subsidies were provided by the U.S. government and remained in place for several decades. In 1993, these subsidies amounted to $1.3 billion on wheat alone but thereafter, declined to zero. In part, the Uruguay Round Agreement on Agriculture contributed to the end of export subsidies, to be replaced by direct support. The 1996 Farm Act made provision for assistance of $4.8 billion annually, with an expanded commitment under the 2002 Act. In 2004, commodities accounting for 42% of U.S. farm production received significant support (Gardner 2009). Since the global financial crisis, U.S. agriculture has been among the winners in the domestic economy. This is because a substantial depreciation of the U.S. dollar has enhanced agriculture's competitiveness. Moreover, agricultural prices have risen with the growing demands of China and

[3]See http://www.ers.usda.gov/topics/crops/sugar-sweeteners/policy.aspx#.UY9HGaL7CHc accessed 27 January 2017.

India. With an improvement in the international competitiveness of U.S. farm produce, the perceived need for domestic assistance has declined.

The common thread in cotton production between the relatively arid regions of California and the relatively moist humid regions of the southern Mississippi Valley is the need for abundant water. In some cotton-growing regions, particularly in the humid south-east of the nation, cotton is mainly rain-fed. In other regions, cropping is almost totally reliant on irrigation. Texas is the largest producer of cotton, accounting for just over half of national production. USDA statistics indicate that cotton is grown in around 120 Texan counties. The crop is grown across a range of climates. The largest contiguous cotton region is around Lubbock county in the highlands of Texas. Rainfall and snowfall in the region provide less than half the water required for cotton production in the region. Irrigation top-ups from the Ogallala Aquifer are depleting the aquifer. In the Far West region of Texas, between Pecos and El Paso, the arid climate implies that cotton is almost entirely reliant on irrigated water. In the Rolling Plains region east of Lubbock, a slightly higher rainfall average reduces the reliance on irrigation. Similarly, the Blacklands region south of Dallas and the more humid Coastal Bend and Upper Gulf Coast regions are substantially rain-fed (Texas AgriLife Extension Service, 2009). Mississippi production occurs mainly on ancient and existing creek beds within the Mississippi Delta.[4] In California, the relative abundance of land and dry climate contributed to more rapid mechanisation of cotton production than elsewhere historically (Musoke and Olmstead, 1982). Cotton is another example of a crop in which it may be worthwhile to split production into rain-fed and irrigation technologies, with factor mobility between the two. Since both irrigation practices and competition from urban uses are threatening future water availability, building such mobility into the model may enhance policy scenarios. The theoretical modifications required to reflect factor mobility between rain-fed and irrigation technologies are elaborated in Dixon et al. (2011; 2012). A version of this theory applies in Chap. 11 of this volume.

Rice is an even more intensive user of water than cotton. States with high levels of production include the Mississippi Valley states of Arkansas, Louisiana and Mississippi. The Rest of California region is second to Arkansas. Wharton, Colorado and Matagora counties account for around two-thirds of Texan rice production, with USDA data indicating that another nine counties produce some rice. Texas suffered its worst drought on record in 2011. In order to supply water to rice farmers downstream in that year, the Local Colorado River Authority[5] (LCRA) depleted the upstream Highland Lakes. The lakes fell below the trigger point (around 40% of capacity) on 1 March 2012. Consequently, for the first time ever,

---

[4]See http://www.nass.usda.gov/Education_and_Outreach/Reports_Presentations_and_Conferences/Presentations/Gregory_Beltwide10_MS_Statistics.pdf accessed 27 January 2017.

[5]This Colorado River flows in its entirety through Texas and drains into the Gulf of Mexico, unlike its better known namesake to the west which drains into the Gulf of California.

the LCRA stopped the flow of water to rice farmers in southeast Texas in 2012. Again in 2013, upstream dam levels were below the trigger point, so once again, rice farmers missed out on water.[6] The competing needs of irrigators has echoes of what occurred in Australia from 2006 to 2008 (Wittwer and Griffith, 2011). A severe three year drought resulted in rice mills in Australia closing as rice production virtually ceased. A key part of the response of farmers in Australia to the drought crisis was the ability to trade water. Since water rights are now separate from land ownership in Australia's Murray-Darling Basin, rice farmers found it profitable to sell their diminished allocations to farmers of perennial crops. Temporary water prices (i.e., the spot price, not the asset price) rise many-fold during drought. Hence, even with severe cuts to their usual allocations, rice farmers can earn income during drought through water sales.

The rapidly growing urban population of Texas is increasing urban demands for water. Climate change potentially will make water supply more variable. In these circumstances, aspects of Australian legislation dealing with the separation of water and land ownership may be of interest to policy makers in Texas as they explore options for future water management.

While there has been a recovery of seasonal rainfall in Texas, California endured four successive years of drought between 2012 and 2015. Chapter 11 details USAGE-TERM modifications to examine impacts of the Californian drought.

2.5 Agriculture's Share of Regional Economies

In pioneering research, Leontief (1936) devised an input–output table of the U.S. The Bureau of Labor Statistics hired Leontief to estimate the economic impacts of demobilization following the U.S. entry into World War II (Kohli 2008). Leontief's input–output analysis implied a multiplier impact on the economy arising from an initial demand stimulus. A key assumption in this analysis is that supplies are perfectly elastic. In 1938, the unemployment rate in the United States was 19%. Four years later, unemployment had fallen to only 4.7%.[7] With the initial unemployment rate being so high and many factories being idle, the assumption of elastic supply was valid in this unusual circumstance. Unfortunately, input–output has been used repeatedly since the Great Depression, in economic circumstances that bear little resemblance to those of the late 1930s. Input–output analysis is often called on by lobbyists in order to concoct multipliers arising from their industry of interest, which in turn may be used to justify industry subsidies.

To illustrate how such analysis is used to inflate an industry, we use the example of Georgia. USDA data indicate farm output sales in 2007 of $6.8 billion. The USAGE-TERM database has value-added of $2.4 billion in 2010 in Georgia,

[6]Source: http://stateimpact.npr.org/texas/tag/texas-rice-farming/ accessed 27 January 2017.

[7]Source: http://www.infoplease.com/ipa/A0104719.html accessed 27 January 2017.

contributing 1.6% of the state's GDP (Table 2.3). Even after adding all hunting and trapping, fishing, food processing and textile processing to farm output, the share of GDP rises to no more than 3.5%. Yet the Georgia Farm Bureau asserts that the contribution of farming to the state's economy is $74 billion, and that one in 7 Georgians workers is employed in agriculture and related sectors.[8] Such a figure can only arise from a combination of double-counting and the spurious use of multipliers. Curiously, the bureau's website notes that in 2012, Georgia's farms numbered 42,257, with an average size of 228 acres. It seems quite a stretch to go from this number of farms to a statewide employment share of one in seven in a state with almost 10 million citizens.

Despite agriculture contributing little more than 1% to U.S. GDP, it remains large in a number of states. North Dakota (21%) and South Dakota (25%) have the largest agricultural shares in regional income (Table 2.3). North Dakota's production includes oil seeds, wheat, corn, beef cattle and soybeans, sales of which all exceeded $700 million in 2007. The composition of farm production is quite similar in neighboring South Dakota. Other states in which agriculture's share of GDP exceeds 10% include Idaho, Iowa, and Nebraska, with Kansas next. In absolute terms, the Rest of California region has the largest farm output, with an estimated value-added more than double that of the second largest producer, Rest of Texas. The remainder of Texas, represented in the USAGE-TERM master database by the counties of Harris (the Houston-Sugartown-Bayland metropolis) and Tarrant (Fort Worth-Arlington), has almost negligible farm activity.

In developed nations, agriculture's percentage contribution to national income has declined over time. The United States is no exception. Agriculture's share of U.S. GDP in 1980 was closer to 3% than the present 1%.[9] Yet a temporarily favorable exchange rate, growing incomes in China and India, and climate change may all contribute to rising prices that result in agriculture's share of national and regional income rising in the future.

Agricultural shares matter when it comes to interactions between the United States and the rest of the world. In the wake of the global financial crisis, job losses and loan defaults in the U.S. received a great deal of attention. Another side of the story is that with a depreciation of the U.S. dollar against other major currencies following the GFC, sectors with a degree of export orientation such as farming enhanced their global competitiveness. The regional representation in USAGE-TERM with, for example, California split into a number of regions, provides us with the potential to examine winners and losers in considerable detail. For example, predominantly urban regions within California may have suffered substantial losses in the wake of the GFC, while more farm-intensive regions of the

[8]Source: http://www.gfb.org/aboutus/georgia_agriculture.html accessed 2 March 2016. The site records 2014 farm gate value of $14 billion which appears to be a reasonable estimate.

[9]World Bank: http://data.worldbank.org/indicator/NV.AGR.TOTL.ZS?page=6 accessed 2 March 2016.

Table 2.3 Contribution of agriculture to each region

Region	Agri/GDP (%)	Agri value-added $m 2012	Region	Agri/GDP (%)	Agri value-added $m 2012	Region	Agri/GDP (%)	Agr value-added $m 2012	Region	Agri/GDP (%)	Agri value-added $m 2012
Alabama	1.0	1809	PalmBeachFL	1.8	498	RoMissouri	4.9	3067	PhladlphiaPA	0	0
Alaska	0.0	11	Georgia	1.1	4703	StLouisCtyMO	0.0	17	RhodeIsland	0.1	30
Arizona	0.6	1546	Hawaii	0.7	472	Montana	4.4	1847	SouthCarolin	0.6	1054
Arkansas	2.4	2898	Idaho	6.1	3538	Nebraska	7.9	8152	SouthDakota	10.5	4591
SanFranCtyCA	0.2	867	RoIllinois	5.0	5852	Nevada	0.2	312	Tennessee	0.5	1439
RoCalifornia	6.0	21178	ChicagoCtyIL	0.1	582	NewHampshire	0.1	70	RoTexas	2.9	8514
LosAngelesCA	0.1	856	Indiana	1.5	4493	NewJersey	0.1	740	DallasTX	0	6
OrangeCA	1.0	1383	Iowa	7.1	11164	NewMexico	1.9	1672	HarrisTX	0.1	86
RiversideCA	2.3	883	Kansas	3.4	4753	RoNewYork	0.7	2030	TarrantTX	0	6
SacramentoCA	1.1	397	Kentucky	1.3	2324	NewYorkCity	0.1	387	Utah	0.5	608
Colorado	1.0	2697	Louisiana	0.8	2108	NorthCarolin	1.1	4874	Vermont	1.1	306
Connecticut	0.1	285	Maine	0.7	351	NorthDakota	10.6	5253	Virginia	0.3	1544
Delaware	0.6	335	Maryland	0.3	977	RoOhio	2.5	3887	Washington	1.3	5144
DC	0.0	0	Massachusett	0.1	298	CuyahogaOH	0	0	WestVirginia	0.2	173
RoFlorida	0.7	1859	RoMichigan	3.8	3646	ColumbusOH	0.3	62	Wisconsin	1.8	5018
BrowardFL	0.2	70	DetroitCtyMI	0.0	26	Oklahoma	1.6	2731	Wyoming	1.5	620
HillsbrghFL	4.5	1571	Minnesota	3.3	9819	Oregon	1.1	2376	**National**	**1.0**	**166,938**
MiamiDadeFL	0.8	586	Mississippi	2.4	2466	RoPnnsylvnia	0.6	3119			

Source Estimates based on http://quickstats.nass.usda.gov/ and http://www.bea.gov/iTable/iTable.cfm?reqid=70&step=1&isuri=1&acrdn=1#reqid=70&step=1&isuri=1. Accessed 26 June 2015

Table 2.4 Natural gas marketed production by state, 2013 (cubic feet 10^9)

Alabama	196	Louisiana	2407	Oklahoma	2144
Alaska	338	Maryland	<0.1	Oregon	770
Arizona	<0.1	Michigan	124	Pennsylvania	3259
Arkansas	1140	Mississippi	59	South Dakota	16
California	252	Missouri	9	Tennessee	5
Colorado	1605	Montana	63	Texas	7445
Florida	0.3	Nebraska	1	Utah	471
Illinois	3	New Mexico	1195	Virginia	139
Indiana	8	New York	23	West Virginia	718
Kansas	292	North Dakota	236	Wyoming	1858
Kentucky	95	Ohio	186	**National**	**25,691**

Source U.S. Energy Administration, https://www.eia.gov/dnav/ng/ng_prod_sum_a_epg0_vgm_mmcf_a.htm accessed 18 May 2017

state may have benefited from the depreciation of the U.S. dollar—prior to the four year drought starting in 2012.

2.6 Mining in the United States

Three energy mining activities are at the forefront of policy issues in the United States. Coal mining remains important in U.S. energy production, especially in electricity generation, though relatively high labor costs, the rise of coal seam gas and concerns about high carbon emissions are leading to mine closures and output reductions. High oil prices, spurred on China's and India's burgeoning demands since the middle of the first decade of the new millennium, have reinvigorated oil exploration and extraction globally. In the U.S. context, the spread of hydraulic fracturing (fracking) techniques to extract coal seam gas has resulted in rapid growth in gas output Table 2.4.

The most striking changes have been in North Dakota. Between 2010 and 2012, the state's oil output doubled (Table 2.5). According the U.S. Energy Information Administration (2013), North Dakota produced no gas for three years from 1994 to 1996. For more than a decade thereafter, the state's gas production hovered between 50,000 and 60,000 million cubic feet (mcf) per annum. In 2010, output shot up 38% as marketed production totalled almost 82,000 mcf. In 2011, marketed production jumped another 19%, exceeding 97,000 mcf. A telling statistic in this growth phase is that the volume of vented and flared gas doubled in one year to nearly 50,000 mcf in 2011.[10] This has some relevance, if transient, in examining carbon emissions.

[10]See http://www.eia.gov/dnav/ng/ng_prod_sum_dcu_snd_a.htm accessed 27 January 2017.

Table 2.5 Oil production by state/offshore region (thousands of barrels)

	2010	%	2011	%	2012	%
Florida	1777	0.1	2023	0.1	2157	0.1
New York	378	0.0	370	0.0	366	0.0
Pennsylvania	3226	0.2	3388	0.2	4257	0.2
Virginia	12	0.0	11	0.0	11	0.0
West Virginia	1842	0.1	2146	0.1	2193	0.1
Illinois	9067	0.5	9234	0.4	9792	0.4
Indiana	1835	0.1	1987	0.1	2354	0.1
Kansas	40,467	2.0	41,503	2.0	43,563	1.8
Kentucky	2519	0.1	2326	0.1	3198	0.1
Michigan	6790	0.3	6977	0.3	7251	0.3
Missouri	146	0.0	118	0.0	129	0.0
Nebraska	2327	0.1	2542	0.1	2941	0.1
North Dakota	113,064	5.7	152,985	7.4	242,486	10.2
Ohio	4753	0.2	4853	0.2	4866	0.2
Oklahoma	67,730	3.4	76,681	3.7	89,627	3.8
South Dakota	1606	0.1	1615	0.1	1742	0.1
Tennessee	257	0.0	245	0.0	288	0.0
Alabama	7102	0.4	8374	0.4	9569	0.4
Arkansas	5733	0.3	5877	0.3	6536	0.3
Louisiana	67,367	3.4	68,984	3.3	70,768	3.0
Mississippi	24,080	1.2	24,216	1.2	24,153	1.0
New Mexico	65,386	3.3	71,274	3.5	84,179	3.5
Texas	427,386	21.4	531,524	25.8	734,770	30.9
Colorado	32,574	1.6	39,125	1.9	49,007	2.1
Montana	25,333	1.3	24,151	1.2	26,424	1.1
Utah	24,670	1.2	26,272	1.3	30,254	1.3
Wyoming	53,242	2.7	54,710	2.7	58,192	2.4
Alaska	219,536	11.0	204,829	9.9	192,368	8.1
Arizona	40	0.0	37	0.0	52	0.0
California	201,385	10.1	193,691	9.4	195,680	8.2
Nevada	426	0.0	408	0.0	368	0.0
Federal Offshore West Coast	21,702	1.1	19,818	1.0	17,960	0.8
Federal Offshore–Gulf of Mexico	565,974	28.3	480,638	23.3	463,324	19.5
Total	1,999,732	100.0	2,062,932	100.0	2380825	100.0

Source Energy Information Administration, http://www.eia.gov/dnav/pet/pet_crd_crpdn_adc_mbbl_a.htm accessed 17 March 2015

Although carbon emissions per unit of energy output are lower for natural gas than coal, at the observed levels of venting and flaring in North Dakota, much of this advantage is lost. In 2011, for each unit of marketed gas in North Dakota, 0.51 units of gas were vented or flared. As the gas pipeline infrastructure is developed, the ratio of waste gas emitted per unit of marketed gas will decline. North Dakota's state regulations allow producers to be exempt from paying royalties on gas vented or flared for 12 months. After that period, the practice is still permitted but waste gas is taxed at the same rate as if it were marketed. The national ratio of vented or flared to marketed gas for all of the U.S.A. in 2009 was 0.01 so that effectively natural gas remains a less greenhouse gas intensive fuel than coal.[11]

In USAGE-TERM, following USAGE which in turn is based on publicly available input–output tables, oil and gas production is treated as a single sector. In one sense, this adds to the difficulty of preparing a database. We need to combine data of each of oil and gas to calculate regional shares. Why do the compilers of input-output tables put us to this trouble? The short answer is that oil and gas represented as a single sector is an international convention in input–output tables. Oil and gas have often been joint products from oil wells. But this is changing with new extraction technologies. Gas can be extracted from oil wells, gas wells, shale gas wells or coal-bed wells. The present master database of USAGE-TERM retains oil and gas as a single sector, although some studies would be enhanced by a split.

The role of coal in the U.S. economy is changing. Growing concerns about greenhouse emissions and the rise of fracking to extract coal seam gas have diminished the role of coal. At the regional level, the most striking difference is between the labor intensity of open-cut mines in Wyoming and the underground mines in the other large producing states, including Kentucky and West Virginia. Wyoming's workforce in the coal mines was less than one fifth of that in West Virginia in 2010, yet its coal output was three times as large.

Black Thunder mine in Campbell county, Wyoming, opened in 1977. It accounts for more than one tenth of national production. Overall, Campbell county's coal production is over 36% of national production, yet it employs only 3% of the nation's coal miners. Jobs in traditional mining regions are being lost through a combination of cost pressures and environmental considerations, including the health hazards faced by underground workers. Once again, we may have a case for splitting a sector, by dividing coal into underground and open-cut technologies. Given the relatively high labor costs of underground mining, it is likely that this technology will make a decreasing share to national coal production and open-cut mining an increasing share in the future.

Although data are available on the output of various other minerals, including iron ore, copper and nickel, gold and other non-ferrous ores, stone, sand and gravel, and other non-metallic minerals, the primary source of data for the remaining mining products is employment data from the 2010 census. These remaining sectors are small compared with coal, oil and gas (Table 2.6).

[11]See http://www.eia.gov/todayinenergy/detail.cfm?id=4030 accessed 27 January 2017. Methane leaks remain an issue in natural gas extraction (Krauss 2016).

Table 2.6 Coal employment and output, 2010

	Employment	Tons 10^6		Employment	Tons 10^6
Alabama	4341	19.9	Montana	1206	44.7
Alaska	127	2.2	NewMexico	1269	21.0
Arizona	422	7.8	NorthDakota	1114	28.9
Arkansas	29	0.03	RoOhio	2826	26.7
Colorado	2247	25.2	Oklahoma	217	1.0
RoIllinois	3649	33.2	RoPnnsylvnia	7716	54.1
Indiana	3342	34.9	Tennessee	546	1.8
Kansas	36	0.1	RoTexas	2787	41.0
Kentucky	17,966	105.0	Utah	1822	19.4
Louisiana	261	3.9	Virginia	4957	22.4
Maryland	422	2.6	WestVirginia	21,643	139.7
Mississippi	232	4.0	Wyoming	3982	442.5
RoMissouri	23	0.5			

Source U.S. Energy Administration, http://www.eia.gov/coal/data.cfm accessed 17 March 2015

2.7 The Potential for Further Industry Splits in Agriculture and Mining in USAGE-TERM

This chapter started by outlining the advantages of undertaking sectoral splits from the initial national database. In both agriculture and mining, as we examine regional production, doubts set in as to whether the additional splits are sufficient for us to feel comfortable with using the same technology for a given industry in different regions. In livestock production, there may be a case for splitting beef cattle into rain-fed and feed-lotting technologies. The advantage of this would be that with the onset of drought, for example, a collapse in rain-fed productivity would induce a switch to feed-lotting. With a seasonal recovery, production would then revert to a rain-fed technology. In the case of cotton, regional differences in the reliance on rain-fed technologies are apparent.

Oil and gas appears as a single sector in the national USAGE database, yet oil wells are only one of several sources of gas. A split of oil and gas therefore may be a reasonable move, either in the master database or in subsequent data processing for a particular study. That is, we are not stuck with a particular sector once we have devised a multi-regional database. Coal produced in Wyoming uses relatively little labor and has relatively higher intermediate-input costs per ton of output. Underground mining elsewhere is much more labor-intensive and the value-added share of the output value is also higher. If we were undertaking a study examining coal scenarios, there would be a case for splitting coal into open-cut and underground technologies. There are traps. Although employment data suggest that open-cut mining dominates in Wyoming and underground mining dominates elsewhere, surface mining was introduced in the Central Appalachian coalfields in the 1940 and 1950s.[12] That is, there is open-cut mining in more traditional coal mining regions.

An optimal strategy in preparation of a multi-regional database might be to split sectors when the data are readily available and when the advantages of a split are immediately obvious. It may not be worthwhile to consider every possible split in response to concerns about different technologies. The effort that goes into such preparation should reflect the expectations of the modeling benefits that may arise from such splits.

2.8 A Tale of Two Colorado Rivers

In the 2010s, drought has led to unprecedented cuts in water allocations to irrigators by the Local Colorado River Authority (LCRA) in Texas. In addition to supplying water to irrigators, the LCRA caters for the water needs of around one million people.

Drought has also affected the better known Colorado River which drains a watershed across seven U.S. states straddling the Rockies and passes through two Mexican states before reaching the Gulf of California between Baja California and Sonora. This is a larger, economically more important waterway than its eastern namesake.

The southern Californian region relying on Colorado water currently has a population of 19 million, with the expectation that this will grow by several million over the next few decades (Wines 2014). It may be understandable for managers of water and electricity utilities to assume that consumption will grow in proportion to population. In the case of countries such as China in which household incomes are being lifted rapidly, such consumption growth may be more rapid than population growth. This is because households may now make regular use of a shower, washing machines and automatic dishwashers. With rising incomes, demand for recreational facilities that are relatively intensive in water usage, such as golf courses and artificial snowfields, also grows. But in high income nations, there is evidence that in response to worsening urban water scarcity, substantial per capita water savings have occurred. For example, in Sydney, Australia, a government media release noted that the city consumed the same volume of water in 2010 as 40 years earlier, despite the population growing by 50% in that time (Wittwer 2013). New technologies, including household appliances that are more water-efficient, and recycling technologies that are extending available water resources, are contributing to per capita reductions in water usage. Wines (2014)

[12]http://en.wikipedia.org/wiki/Eastern_Kentucky_Coal_Field_region accessed 17 March 2015.

notes that in Los Vegas, virtually all water used indoors is treated and returned to Lake Mead, the nation's largest reservoir, which is fed by the Colorado River. Consumers are modifying their behaviour, either through water restrictions or voluntary actions, with a reduction in water applied to suburban lawns and gardens.

What has urban water usage to do with the present chapter that deals mainly with agriculture? Quite simply, water used in agriculture accounts for 65% of water used for economic purposes in the United States (USGS Water Science School 2010), while agriculture accounts for only 1.1% of GDP (Table 2.3). For this reason, as urban populations grow, the pressure to divert water from agricultural to urban purposes grows.

In the US case, this is nothing new. The California Water Wars led to an aqueduct being completed in 1913 that diverted water from the Owens Valley to Los Angeles. While this made an important water source available to a growing metropolis, it devastated the local irrigation-based economy of the Owens Valley. Sauder (1994, Chap. 11) concludes that this should never happen again. He noted that there was considerable scope for water savings in irrigation production, particularly as in the absence of water markets, there may be high levels of water wastage.

The modeling relevance of the water issues concerning either Colorado River basin is that USAGE-TERM could be adapted to depict different scenarios. Such adaptations would require substantial research projects. In the Texan case, water trading may enhance the ability of irrigators to cope with diminished and variable water allocations: USAGE-TERM could be enhanced to include water accounts and water trading possibilities along the lines of the Dixon et al. (2011) study. A study of the Colorado River that wends through multiple states in the west would be in the spirit of Young et al. (2006) and Qureshi et al. (2012). These studies examined an urban water crisis in Australia that affected all mainland state capital cities after the turn of the millennium. They examined various policy options, including desalination and rural-urban water trading in response to changing urban demands and variable water supply.

2.9 The Prolonged Drought in California

Chap. 11 outlines the theory of USAGE-TERM-H2O, which includes water accounts for irrigation activities within California, concentrating on the Central Valley region. The chapter examines the potential role that water trading may have in alleviating water scarcity. Water trading could also reduce the extent to which new wells are bored in response to drought.

References

Dixon PB, Rimmer MT (2012) Validation in CGE modeling. In: Jorgenson D, Dixon P (eds) Elsevier, Handbook of computable general equilibrium modeling

Dixon PB, Rimmer MT, Wittwer G (2012) The theory of TERM-H_2O. In: Wittwer G (ed) Economic modeling of water, the Australian CGE experience. Springer, Dordrecht

Dixon PB, Rimmer MT, Wittwer G (2011) Saving the southern Murray-Darling basin: the economic effects of a buyback of irrigation water. Econ Rec 87:153–168

Gardner B (2009) Distortions to agricultural incentives in the United States and Canada. In: Anderson K (ed) Distortions to agricultural incentives: a global perspective, 1955-2007. Palgrave Macmillan, World Bank, London, Washington DC

Hertel T (ed) (1997) Global trade analysis: modeling and applications. Cambridge University Press, Cambridge

Horridge M (2012) The TERM model and its database. In: Wittwer G (ed) Economic modeling of water: the Australian CGE experience. Springer, Dordrecht, pp 13–36

Krauss (2016) Future of natural gas hinges on stanching methane gas leaks. http://www.nytimes.com/2016/07/12/business/energy-environment/future-of-natural-gas-hinges-on-stanching-methane-leaks.html. Accessed 18 July 2016

Kohli M (2008) Leontief and Bureau of Labor Statistics, 1941–54: an unfinished chapter in the history of economic measurement. http://www.bls.gov/ore/pdf/st020190.pdf. Accessed 18 July 2016

Leontief W (1936) Input and output relations in the economic systems of the United States. Rev Econ Stat 18(3):105–125

Musoke M, Olmstead A (1982) The rise of the cotton industry in California: a comparative perspective. J Econ Hist 42:385–412

Nadal A, Wise T (2004) The environmental costs of agricultural trade liberalization: Mexico-U.S. Maize trade under NAFTA. Working Group on Development and Environment in the America Discussion Paper No. 4. http://ase.tufts.edu/gdae/pubs/rp/DP04NadalWiseJuly04.pdf. Accessed 18 July 2016

Qureshi E, Proctor W, Young M, Wittwer G (2012) The economic impact of increased water demand in Australia: a computable general equilibrium analysis. Econ Pap 31:87–102

Sauder R (1994) The lost frontier: water diversion in the growth and destruction of Owens Valley agriculture. The University of Arizona Press, Tucson

Texas AgriLife Extension Service (2009) Crop profile for cotton in Texas. http://www.ipmcenters.org/cropprofiles/docs/TXcotton.pdf. Accessed 3 May 2013

USGS Water Science School (2010) Irrigation water use. http://ga.water.usgs.gov/edu/wuir.htm. Accessed 9 Jan 2014

Wines M (2014) Colorado River drought forces a painful reckoning for states. New York Times. January 5

Wittwer G (2013) Urban water management in response to prolonged droughts and urban growth. Econ Pap 32:41–50

Wittwer G, Griffith M (2011) Modelling drought and recovery in the southern Murray-Darling basin. Aust J of Agric Resour Econ 49:342–359

Young M, Proctor W, Qureshi ME, Wittwer G (2006) Without water: the economics of supplying water to 5 million more Australians. Water for a health country flagship report. CSIRO and Centre of Policy Studies, Monash University, Melbourne

Chapter 3
Manufacturing Industries in the United States

Glyn Wittwer

Abstract The ongoing decline in manufactures in the United States over several generations has had marked regional impacts. The nation was far ahead of the rest of the world in economic terms after World War II. Gradually, the forces of globalization, with consequent technology transfers, have altered the manufacturing landscape. The rise of Asian nations in particular, first Japan, later South Korea and now China, has contributed to the whittling away of U.S. comparative advantage in manufactures. This chapter outlines regional data sources and summarizes the regional distribution of U.S. manufactures.

Keywords Structural change · Manufacturing · Globalization

3.1 Introduction

The status of manufacturing in the U.S. economy at any time has considerable bearing on the nation's status in the global economy. The nation came out of World War II with a substantial manufacturing base and, by virtue of the maturity of state-level economies, the largest customs union in the world. The nation utilized the legacy of generations of inventors, innovators, entrepreneurs and visionaries who converted ideas into new goods for the market. The contrast with other nations was stark. As a bruised and battered Western Europe rebuilt after the war, the Iron Curtain descended on Eastern Europe. Japan began its rise from the ashes of a defeated war-based economy to be re-machined slowly as a peace-based economy. Much of Asia remained in a state of under-development. The United States was undisputedly the global leader, the wealthiest nation, the most advanced economy on earth. But from the 1950s onwards, U.S. dominance in manufactures and in the global economy would diminish gradually.

G. Wittwer (✉)
Centre of Policy Studies, Victoria University, Melbourne, VIC, Australia
e-mail: glyn.wittwer@vu.edu.au

G. Wittwer (ed.), *Multi-regional Dynamic General Equilibrium Modeling of the U.S. Economy*, Advances in Applied General Equilibrium Modeling,
DOI 10.1007/978-3-319-58866-7_3

Times have changed. Japan, in an ascendant phase in the 1960s was dismissed by consumers around the globe as the source of "cheap Japanese junk". The success of Japan in moving gradually into high technology, high quality manufactures provided a new source of competition for the global leaders of manufactures in the United States and Western Europe.

Globalization has had a profound impact on manufacturing. Amid reforms, nations liberalized foreign investment rules, financial flows and exchange rates. With reforms, manufacturing investment moved offshore as firms sought cheaper wages to maintain competitiveness in an increasingly global environment. Globalization raised issues of national sovereignty yet it marched on, rapidly changing the structure of economies around the world. The Uruguay round of GATT, spanning 1986 to 1994, brought agricultural reforms to the table for negotiations for the first time, as trade liberalization broadened.

In Western nations, manufacturing's share of GDP and national employment has fallen dramatically, ripping the employment heart out of many industrial cities. Some have reinvented themselves as service centers; others have faded. What is left of manufacturing is more specialized, more integrated with the rest of the world, more export-oriented and more import-dependent than ever before. No longer is manufacturing a sure source of lasting employment that underpins middle-class lifestyles. Jobs are less secure, wages have fallen relative to those in other sectors of the economy and regional economies have frayed under the stresses of structural change.

Now that the industrial revolution has become truly globalized, the economies of relatively poor nations are growing quickly and the economies of relatively wealthy nations are slowing. China's GDP is poised to overtake that of the United States in coming years, a somewhat pyrrhic victory when one considers that China's per capita income will still be little more than one quarter that of the citizens of the union.[1] Nevertheless, even a generation ago, such a possibility appeared to be a dim distant dream.

3.2 Manufacturing in the United States from the 1950s Onwards

The global whirl of change is reflected in what has happened in U.S. regions. The changing structure of the U.S. economy over time provides some hints as to regions that are most vulnerable to decline. During the substantial global ascendancy of the U.S. economy in the 1950s, manufacturing of durables and non-durables together plateaued at around 30% of national GDP. While the U.S. economy was ruffled by

[1]IMF data indicate that in purchasing power parity units, China's GDP overtook that of the U.S. in 2014: http://www.imf.org/external/pubs/ft/weo/2015/02/weodata/weoselgr.aspx accessed 17 November 2015.

the tensions with the Soviet Union in this time, defense-related manufacturing provide a sturdy base for employment in many regions. The slide in manufacturing's share was relatively gradual between 1960 and 1980, starting at 28.5% and falling to 22.5% by the end of that 20 year period. Thereafter, the slide became more dramatic, the rumbles in the regional heartland of U.S. manufactures intensified, and manufactures' share of GDP fell to 18.0% in 1990, 14.9% in 2000 and bottomed out after the global financial crisis at 9.7% in 2009 (Fig. 3.1). Since then, a weaker U.S. dollar has contributed to a recovery, however transient, in this increasingly trade exposed segment of the economy.

Changing comparative advantage is at the heart of the decline of manufactures in virtually all Western economies. In the 1960s and 1970s, the ascension of Japan as a global manufacturing base contributed to the decline in the West, as Japan's relatively lower wages gave it a cost advantage over established manufacturing nations. By the 1980s, other emergent nations such as South Korea were contributing to a relative decline in the manufacturing base in higher wage nations including the United States. Then China's ascendancy as a manufacturing base started to have an impact on an unprecedented scale around the turn of the millennium.

Yet changing comparative advantage is not bad news for consumers around the world, for whom the real prices of manufactures have steadily fallen, and need not be bad news for individual industries in developed economies. Rising incomes in ascendant nations bring additional consumers to the global market. More people than in all of human history have been lifted out of poverty in a relatively short time with the seismic shift in global production. Resource-rich nations such as Australia and Canada have benefited, at least in the medium term, from soaring commodity prices and terms-of-trade gains for almost a decade from around 2004. In the United States, there has been an upward swing in agriculture and mining as China has

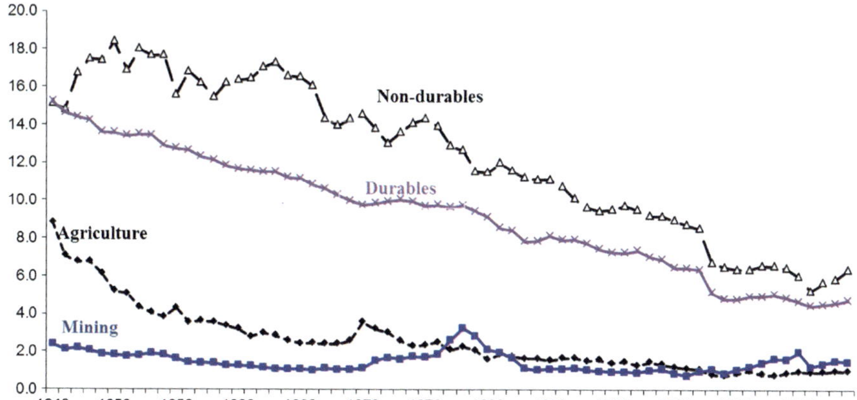

Fig. 3.1 Changing composition of U.S. GDP. *Source* http://www.bea.gov/iTable/iTable.cfm?ReqID=9&step=1#reqid=9&step=1&isuri=1 accessed 14 May 2015

boomed, though the agricultural and mining bases are not large enough to lift the entire economy. Chinese tourists have provided a boost to service exports in nations around the world. Fee-paying Chinese students have provided a lifeline for universities around the globe that are seeking to broaden their funding base. And at a time when the costs of human time have slowed birth rates in Western economies, immigrants from China and elsewhere have slowed the aging profile. This at least is so in nations which have permitted immigration. In fortress Japan, an aging population, a lack of immigration and an eventual loss in comparative advantage in manufacturing were significant contributors to economic stagnation. Japan's nominal GDP was jammed at 1990 levels for the next two decades.

Yet, amid all the forces of globalization, what is indisputable is that U.S. cities and counties that traditionally have relied heavily on manufacturing have suffered over the past several decades. In Detroit city, the population peaked at 1.8 million in 1950.[2] The former heart of the city is now strewn with empty houses and abandoned factories. In the 2010 census, the population was little more than 0.7 million. This statistic is a little misleading in that the population in the suburbs surrounding Detroit has grown substantially in this period. The six-county metropolitan area's population of over 4 million dwarfs that of the city. A similar story is evident in other cities, such as Cleveland, Ohio and Buffalo, New York. As the manufacturing bases of these cities have declined, the inner city residents have moved to the suburbs, and the services component of local economies has grown.

Perhaps less attention is paid to numerous small to medium sized cities across the nation built on manufacturing. Such cities, with populations of between 10,000 and 100,000 have been at risk of becoming industrial wastelands as the factories have closed. Some cities may be reinvented as suburbs of larger cities nearby, particularly if transport links are upgraded, thereby making feasible commuting between the smaller and larger city. As an example of changing circumstances, Billy Joel composed *Allentown* in the middle of a 50 year period in which the population of the city barely changed, amid considerable gloom about its future. Compounding the woes of Allentown in Lehigh County at the time was the closure of the rail link to Philadelphia in 1979.[3] Yet at the 2010 census, the city earned the distinction of being the fastest growing in Pennsylvania. There has been no magic solution in Allentown: commuters to Philadelphia either have to make do on shuttle buses or by driving one third of the way to Philadelphia and catching the train at Lansdale. The commute by car is sufficiently burdensome to have its own web forum (see http://www.city-data.com/forum/pennsylvania/64698-commuting-allentownAllentown-area-philly.html, accessed 22 September 2016).

Manufacturing has not been alone in its declining importance in the United States. The decline in agriculture as a share of GDP was at its most rapid during the 1950s, falling from 8.8% of GDP in 1948 to 3.6% by 1960 (Fig. 3.1). While the

[2]http://www.detroitparcelsurvey.org/ accessed 14 May 2015.

[3]https://en.wikipedia.org/wiki/Allentown,_Pennsylvania accessed 22 September 2016.

decline in agriculture's share is the largest proportionally of any sector, it in part reflects that land is a fixed factor in geographic terms and almost fixed in terms of total availability, whereas labor has grown with the population. In 1948, the U.S. population was 143 million. By 2002, when agriculture's share bottomed out at 0.7% of GDP, the population had doubled to 288 million. The impact of agriculture's decline has been more on smaller towns rather than those with populations exceeding 10,000. Agriculture may now be making a comeback as other segments of the economy struggle. Global demand for food is growing and the temporary fall in the U.S. dollar around 2011 assisted international competitiveness. With worsening global water and land scarcity, agriculture may prosper, at least in farming regions less affected by local water shortages, even with a resurgent dollar.

Structural change in the national economy is magnified at the regional level. Rural communities had their heyday in the 1950s. Unless geographic advantages, such as proximity to large cities or mineral deposits, have enabled substantial diversification into either services or mining, rural communities continue to face decline.

3.3 Census Data as a Starting Point

The objective of the present chapter is to find regional industry outputs for the manufacturing industries in the national USAGE CGE database (Dixon and Rimmer 2012). The regional activities will be used to split the national database as part of the process of devising a multi-regional CGE database for the USAGE-TERM model. Although the main focus of database preparation is to provide a snapshot of regional manufacturing, structural change in the economy over time points to some of the economic stresses that have occurred at a regional level.

The idea of using census data to provide estimates of regional shares has been used by input-output practitioners for decades. Using such data as a starting point for a multi-regional CGE database is more recent (Wittwer and Horridge 2010). Employment data are most useful in sectors that are relatively labor-intensive. This makes census data a convenient source for most services and manufactures, for which alternative sources of data are relatively aggregated. An obvious alternative source of data is in national accounts data, which in U.S. states provide data on about 60 sectors. National accounts data remain useful as control totals, both in the regional and sectoral dimensions.[4]

The U.S. Bureau of Labor Statistics provides NAICS level employment data for industry by small region (i.e., county) and by state. The census employment details are contained in a single text file that includes 2.5 million lines of data. Our task is to use the data to estimate small region activities shares for as many input-output

[4]http://www.bea.gov/iTable/iTable.cfm?reqid=70&step=1&isuri=1&acrdn=1#reqid=70&step=1&isuri=1 accessed 22 September 2016.

sectors in the national database as possible. In this chapter, we concentrate on manufacturing sectors.

We extract three different groups of numbers from the raw census data. First, we extract the annual payroll bill. The coverage of this is far from comprehensive due to confidentialized cells. The census data contains both state level and county level detail. Fewer than 100 of the industries in the CGE database had non-zero entries at the state level. Adding up county-level data to the 70 bottom-up regions that are in the master database provides better coverage, but there are many cells in which data are missing. We denote county level wages bills as $LAB_{i1,c1}$, where i1 is the subset of industries for which such data are available and c1 is the subset of counties c with available data.

At this stage, there are many examples of industry x county combinations without a value for LAB. Our objective is to use known wages bills ($LAB_{i1,known,}$ the non-zero elements of $LAB_{i1,c1}$) to extend estimates to missing cells. First, we calculate a suitable wage (WAGE) that we can use to fill LAB cells without data in which EMP is known:

$$WAGE_{i1,known} = LAB_{i1,known}/EMP_{i1,known} \tag{3.1}$$

Next, we extract the number of employed $EMP_{i2,c2}$, where i2 includes industries and c2 counties for which data are available. These two items of information give us wages per employee WAGE that we can use in inferring wages bills for confidential cells in which EMP is available.

That is, employment numbers provide a better coverage than wages bills (the set i1 is a subset of i2). After this, using median employment numbers inferred by the employment flags (i.e., ranges of employment provided within census data in the absence of a specific number), we extract numbers for cells containing only a flag thereby extending the number of cells in which we have EMP values. In order to obtain regional activity shares, we must infer wages bill for the confidential cells from the census data. We can do this by using wages per employee calculated in Eq. (3.1). In the data processing program, wages may be borrowed from interstate. For example, wage rates for ReadyMix for all regions are based on those estimated at this point for California.

$$LAB_{i1,c2} = EMP*_{i1,c2}.WAGE_{i1,``known"} \quad i1 \in i, c2 \in c \tag{3.2}$$

where $EMP*_{i1,c2}$ is either the given number employed or the median of the range given by a flag.

At this stage, there are still some industries i3 in which no wages data are available. Eventually, to fill in missing cells, we resort to broad sector wages $WAGEN_b$ (i.e., b = primary, manufacturing and services) to provide wages for which there is no more specific estimate. The more specific wage rates are not replaced by broad wage rates when the former are available.

$$\mathrm{LAB}_{\mathrm{i3,c}} = \mathrm{EMP}_{\mathrm{i3,c}}.\mathrm{WAGEN}_{\mathrm{b(i3)}} \quad \mathrm{i3} \in \mathrm{i} \tag{3.3}$$

Wages bills are normalized to align with more aggregated wages data $\mathrm{LABS}_{\mathrm{ns}}$ (n = national accounts sector and s = state) from state accounts:

$$\mathrm{LAB}{*}_{\mathrm{ic}} = \frac{\mathrm{LAB}_{\mathrm{ic}}}{\mathrm{LABS}_{\mathrm{n(i)s(c)}}} \sum_{\mathrm{n}\in\mathrm{i}} \sum_{\mathrm{s}\in\mathrm{c}} \mathrm{LAB}_{\mathrm{ic}} \tag{3.4}$$

This process provides us with county-level share estimates of national activity for over 450 industries. The process is based on estimates of wages bills rather than employment numbers alone, so as to capture any differences in wages between regions in a given industry. In this chapter, we concentrate on the 335 manufacturing industries in the database.

3.3.1 Manufacturing at the Regional Level

Table 3.1 shows the concentration of transport and defense equipment manufactures. For example, automobile manufacturing remains highly concentrated in Detroit, in which more than two-thirds of national production takes place. Those seeking a holiday on the road are catered for by Indiana's production base, as it manufactures most of the national motor home and travel trailer output. In turn, Elkhart County dominates production within Indiana. Other manufactures in this group are less concentrated. It would be difficult to concentrate defense-related manufactures in any particular state, as members of congress jostle for defense jobs amid the struggle for regional votes in their constituencies.

Among food sectors, some food processing follows local upstream agriculture produce and some does not. As an example of the former, rice milling is concentrated heavily in the rice-growing states. Arkansas, California, Texas and Louisiana account for more than three-quarters of national rice processing. Wet corn milling appears to be disproportionally concentrated in Iowa, with 44% of corn milling (Table 3.2) compared with only 18% of national corn production.

There are some limitations with census data. These were particularly evident in the case of South Carolina's food and beverages sector. National accounts data for this broad sector indicate that the state has a much larger share of national food and beverages manufacturing than is implied by census data. Moreover, the national accounts indicate relatively high capital intensities in the state's food processing sectors, making a labor measure a less reliable estimator. In response, as part of the database preparation, we trebled South Carolina's shares of national output for those food sectors in which capital exceeds 40% of total value-added.

Table 3.1 Transport and defense equipment output, 2010 (% of national)

	Rank 1		Rank 2		Rank 3		Rank 4				Value-added 2005 $m
Automobiles	DetroitCtyMI	68.3	Kentucky	15.1	Indiana	6.9	RoMichigan	4.9	Rest	4.9	31,207
HeavyTruck	RoMichigan	25.4	NorthCarolin	15.8	Indiana	9.5	RoOhio	9.4	Rest	39.9	3695
VehicleBody	RoMichigan	25.4	NorthCarolin	15.8	Indiana	9.5	RoOhio	9.4	Rest	39.9	1198
TruckTrailer	Indiana	29.9	Iowa	10.6	Nebraska	6.7	Wisconsin	5.9	Rest	46.9	1619
MotorHome	Indiana	89.5	Tennessee	2.7	RoMichigan	1.6	Iowa	1.3	Rest	4.8	897
TravlTrlr	Indiana	82.3	Iowa	3.3	RoOhio	2.0	RoMichigan	2.0	Rest	10.4	1822
VehiclParts	Indiana	26.0	DetroitCtyMI	16.4	RoMichigan	13.6	RoOhio	9.1	Rest	34.9	55,529
Aircraft	StLouisCtyMO	27.3	TarrantTX	25.3	Georgia	9.7	LosAngelesCA	8.4	Rest	29.3	17,001
AirEngines	RoOhio	34.2	RoMichigan	11.8	DetroitCtyMI	8.7	NorthCarolin	6.7	Rest	38.6	13,567
OthAirParts	DallasTX	16.7	RoOhio	11.8	Indiana	10.3	Tennessee	6.5	Rest	54.7	12,309
Missiles	Alabama	54.2	SanFranCtyCA	20.4	Arizona	5.5	RoTexas	4.9	Rest	15.0	7238
MissilPrts	Kentucky	51.5	RoOhio	9.0	Arkansas	7.7	Utah	7.4	Rest	24.5	4135
RlrdCars	RoPnnsylvnia	18.8	SouthCarolin	16.0	Indiana	7.1	Tennessee	6.1	Rest	52.1	3129
Ships	Mississippi	20.6	Indiana	13.9	Tennessee	10.4	Virginia	10.4	Rest	44.8	8460
Boats	Tennessee	21.8	Indiana	20.4	RoMissouri	8.6	RoMichigan	8.5	Rest	40.7	5910
MotrBikes	Wisconsin	44.3	RoMissouri	11.9	Indiana	11.7	Tennessee	4.7	Rest	27.4	1760
ArmyTanks	RoMichigan	40.8	DetroitCtyMI	30.1	RoPnnsylvnia	6.5	SouthCarolin	5.4	Rest	17.2	399
OthrTransEq	Indiana	16.2	SouthCarolin	11.4	Iowa	9.1	Wisconsin	7.5	Rest	55.8	3943

Source Estimated from U.S. Bureau of Labor Statistics census data and BEA national accounts

Table 3.2 Cereal, dairy and pet food products, 2010 (% of national)

	Rank 1		Rank 2		Rank 3		Rank 4				Value-added 2005 $m
DogCatFood	LosAngelesCA	24.8	RoMissouri	6.0	Iowa	5.6	Kansas	5.5	Rest	58.1	1807
OthAnFood	NorthCarolin	7.9	Iowa	6.3	RoTexas	5.8	Georgia	5.6	Rest	74.4	3200
FlourMill	NorthCarolin	11.2	Virginia	7.4	RoTexas	6.8	RoIllinois	6.2	Rest	68.3	1158
RiceMill	Arkansas	46.7	RoCalifornia	22.8	RoTexas	6.3	Louisiana	5.2	Rest	19.1	307
Malt	NorthCarolin	22.1	Minnesota	19.7	Wisconsin	17.8	Idaho	15.4	Rest	25.1	140
WetCornMill	Iowa	44.4	Indiana	10.0	Tennessee	9.2	RoIllinois	7.7	Rest	28.7	1132
SoyProc	Iowa	19.8	RoIllinois	15.0	RoOhio	9.5	NorthCarolin	7.5	Rest	48.3	468
OthOilseed	Tennessee	25.2	Georgia	12.4	RoTexas	11.5	RoCalifornia	10.8	Rest	40.0	113
FatsOils	RoIllinois	14.0	Georgia	10.7	Virginia	6.4	NorthCarolin	5.3	Rest	63.7	849
BrkCereal	Virginia	21.1	Nebraska	8.4	RoIllinois	8.3	RoCalifornia	8.2	Rest	54.0	1980
SugarManuf	Louisiana	18.0	Minnesota	10.9	RoMichigan	9.7	SanFranCtyCA	7.4	Rest	54.0	1273
ConfCacao	RoPnnsylvnia	17.3	Wisconsin	13.4	SanFranCtyCA	10.4	NewHampshire	8.5	Rest	50.5	519
ConfChoc	Virginia	13.6	ChicagoCtyIL	9.8	RoPnnsylvnia	9.4	RoIllinois	8.3	Rest	59.0	3887
ConfNonchoc	RoNewYork	19.1	Georgia	6.3	RoPnnsylvnia	6.2	Tennessee	6.2	Rest	62.1	2486
FrozFood	LosAngelesCA	12.1	Kentucky	7.5	NorthCarolin	7.3	Virginia	6.0	Rest	67.1	6489
FrtVegCDry	RoCalifornia	21.5	NorthCarolin	15.5	RoFlorida	4.1	Kentucky	4.0	Rest	54.9	8240
Milk	Virginia	8.1	NorthCarolin	5.7	RoNewYork	5.3	RoOhio	5.2	Rest	75.8	3813
Butter	Wisconsin	24.1	RoMichigan	11.4	RoTexas	9.4	RoCalifornia	9.3	Rest	45.7	201
Cheese	Wisconsin	27.8	RoNewYork	8.9	Minnesota	6.5	RoCalifornia	6.4	Rest	50.4	2089
DCEDairy	Virginia	14.7	RoMichigan	13.1	Wisconsin	10.4	Kentucky	6.4	Rest	55.4	2393
IceCream	RoTexas	6.9	RoPnnsylvnia	6.5	RoCalifornia	6.5	RoMissouri	5.5	Rest	74.5	1759
AnSlauXPlt	NorthCarolin	31.5	RoMissouri	11.2	RoTexas	6.3	Kansas	5.8	Rest	45.2	5268

Source Estimated from U.S. Bureau of Labor Statistics census data and BEA national accounts

Will Kellogg's legacy to the world, flaked breakfast cereal, has broken the reins of its origins in Battle Creek, Michigan. Although Kellogg's headquarters remain in Battle Creek to this day, breakfast cereal manufacturing has a diversified base, with no state accounting for much more than one-tenth of national production (Table 3.2).

A food processing product that is diversely spread is likely to be relatively less traded between regions. On this basis, soft drink and ice manufacturing appears as the least traded of the food sectors, with upstate New York leading the way with 4.5% of national output. Bread, which includes various baking products, and prepared dough are also local industries. Not far behind are other perishables, milk and meat. Ice-cream is slightly more concentrated. On the other hand, two states, Wisconsin and Minnesota, produce around two-fifths of national output of butter and cheese (Table 3.3).

California, particularly in the counties surrounding San Francisco, dominates wine production. Within California, Fresno County produces 21% of national grape output but only 1.4% of national wine output. This indicates two features of the local industry. First, a substantial share of Fresno's grape output is of table grapes. Second, some wine grapes appear to be transported to other counties for processing. Napa County, for example, accounts for around one-quarter of national wine production but produces only 4.6% of the national grape harvest (Table 3.3). This is an idiosyncratic if not intoxicating case of comparative advantage: Napa has the wine image and other counties have the grapes.

Census data indicate that no regions dominate the logging industry: Oregon, Georgia, Washington, Alabama and North Carolina all contribute more than 5% to the national industry, but a string of states are not far behind. As expected, there is a high correlation between logging and sawmill regional shares. Thereafter, downstream wood and paper products are spread across a number of states. These contrast with pulp mills, which are more concentrated: Georgia and the Rest of Florida together produce 60% of national output. As products move from paper further downstream to printing, the location of activities moves towards cities. For example, Chicago and Los Angeles have substantial shares of prepress services (Table 3.4).

Given their proximity to off-shore oil extraction sites, two states aligning the Gulf of Mexico, namely Texas and Louisiana, account for almost one-third of petroleum refining (Table 3.5). California's refineries produce a larger share of the industry than is implied by their oil and gas share: their refinery share exceeds 30% of national output, whereas Energy Information Administration data indicate that the state's oil production is no more than 10% of the national total. This appears to indicate inter-regional rather than international imports, as import data by port indicate that Californian ports are relatively modest importers of fuel and oil. The most concentrated of the industries shown in Table 3.5 is petrochemicals: Texas and Louisiana produced 95% of the national total. Most of the industries shown in the table have a much more diverse spread, as is indicated by the relatively high percentages in the "Rest" column.

Table 3.3 Meat, baking and beverages output, 2010 (% of national)

	Rank 1		Rank 2		Rank 3		Rank 4				Value-added 2005 $m
Meat	Kentucky	9.2	NorthCarolin	8.2	Iowa	6.2	ChicagoCtyIL	6.0	Rest	70.4	6171
RendByprod	NorthCarolin	33.9	Virginia	12.7	RoTexas	4.1	Georgia	4.0	Rest	45.4	933
PoultryProc	NorthCarolin	15.8	Virginia	13.0	Georgia	10.4	Arkansas	8.3	Rest	52.6	8950
Seafood	Alaska	19.0	Washington	17.4	Virginia	7.1	Georgia	6.4	Rest	50.2	1742
FrozCake	RoPnnsylvnia	14.1	Georgia	8.7	RoTexas	6.8	NorthCarolin	5.4	Rest	65.0	1019
Bread	NorthCarolin	6.0	Tennessee	5.9	Georgia	5.1	ChicagoCtyIL	4.8	Rest	78.2	15,031
Cookies	Kentucky	15.1	Georgia	13.5	NorthCarolin	8.5	RoOhio	8.2	Rest	54.7	3818
PrepDough	RoMissouri	6.4	SouthCarolin	6.1	Virginia	5.6	Tennessee	5.3	Rest	76.6	1787
Pasta	Virginia	18.0	RoMissouri	9.1	RoCalifornia	9.0	NorthDakota	8.8	Rest	55.1	548
Tortilla	NorthCarolin	16.5	Georgia	12.2	RoCalifornia	10.7	LosAngelesCA	6.3	Rest	54.3	460
NutsPnutBtr	RoCalifornia	24.4	NorthCarolin	16.9	Virginia	11.0	Kentucky	9.1	Rest	38.7	1088
OthSnack	RoPnnsylvnia	13.6	Virginia	12.0	NorthCarolin	9.6	RoOhio	5.9	Rest	58.9	4181
CoffTea	Virginia	19.1	NorthCarolin	11.0	Louisiana	5.3	RoMissouri	4.4	Rest	60.2	1377
FlavorSyrup	RoCalifornia	15.4	RoOhio	9.4	Georgia	6.8	RoPnnsylvnia	6.4	Rest	62.0	2528
MayoDrsng	Kentucky	11.9	NorthCarolin	7.4	Georgia	6.2	RoOhio	6.2	Rest	68.4	1906
Spices	ChicagoCtyIL	8.7	RoIllinois	7.5	Kentucky	5.4	Maryland	5.2	Rest	73.2	1880
OthrFoodMf	RoCalifornia	7.2	NewJersey	6.8	ChicagoCtyIL	6.0	Wisconsin	6.0	Rest	74.0	4193
SoftDrinks	Virginia	15.9	NorthCarolin	8.8	RoFlorida	3.7	RoNewYork	3.6	Rest	68.1	8399
Breweries	Virginia	17.8	Colorado	12.0	RoNewYork	8.9	Georgia	7.9	Rest	53.4	9001
Wineries	SanFranCtyCA	41.5	RoCalifornia	17.2	NorthCarolin	4.3	Virginia	4.1	Rest	33.0	2022
Distilleries	Kentucky	57.4	Arkansas	4.8	Tennessee	4.7	Maryland	3.9	Rest	29.2	1429

Source Estimated from U.S. Bureau of Labor Statistics census data and BEA national accounts

Table 3.4 Wood milling/paper products/printing output, 2010 (% of national)

	Rank 1		Rank 2		Rank 3		Rank 4				Value-added 2005 $m
Sawmills	Oregon	16.3	Washington	14.4	Maine	6.4	Arkansas	5.3	Rest	57.7	5253
WoodPrsrv	SouthCarolin	12.4	Virginia	8.2	Oregon	7.8	Washington	7.7	Rest	64.0	421
RecWoodPrd	Oregon	13.9	Louisiana	9.2	SouthCarolin	6.9	Virginia	6.5	Rest	63.6	1551
VeneerPlwd	Oregon	18.7	Louisiana	13.7	Washington	5.1	Virginia	5.1	Rest	57.4	1635
WoodTruss	Washington	7.4	RoFlorida	6.5	Virginia	5.8	Minnesota	5.1	Rest	75.3	1723
WoodWndoDoor	Iowa	14.3	Oregon	12.3	Washington	6.7	NorthDakota	4.8	Rest	61.9	2433
WoodSawPlane	Oregon	17.3	Arkansas	6.7	Washington	6.2	Minnesota	4.7	Rest	65.1	644
Millwork	Minnesota	9.4	WestVirgini	8.1	Virginia	6.3	NorthCarolin	6.0	Rest	70.2	893
WoodCntnr	RoPnnsylvnia	7.1	Kentucky	6.9	RoOhio	5.9	Louisiana	4.3	Rest	75.9	1271
MfMoblHome	RoTexas	13.6	Oregon	11.1	Tennessee	8.6	Alabama	6.8	Rest	60.0	4980
PrefWdBldgs	RoPnnsylvnia	18.1	Oregon	7.5	Virginia	5.4	Montana	4.0	Rest	65.1	692
MscWoodProd	Maine	10.1	Washington	9.8	Oregon	4.9	RoOhio	4.6	Rest	70.6	1038
PulpMills	Georgia	38.6	RoFlorida	21.7	Mississippi	9.5	SouthCarolin	8.7	Rest	21.4	1983
PaperMills	Wisconsin	13.1	Alabama	9.7	RoPnnsylvnia	7.9	Tennessee	5.9	Rest	63.4	21,334
PprContainer	Georgia	6.4	ChicagoCtyIL	5.9	RoPnnsylvnia	5.3	Louisiana	4.9	Rest	77.4	11,964
FlxPkingFoil	Virginia	16.3	RoTexas	11.8	RoPnnsylvnia	11.5	Kentucky	9.9	Rest	50.5	390
CoatPprbrd	Louisiana	23.1	Virginia	15.0	Arkansas	9.4	RoOhio	8.8	Rest	43.7	199
CoatPprPck	RoPnnsylvnia	10.2	RoOhio	8.8	Tennessee	7.4	Wisconsin	5.6	Rest	67.9	4505
PaperBag	Louisiana	8.6	RoPnnsylvnia	7.2	Arkansas	6.6	RoOhio	6.5	Rest	71.1	1074
DieCutPpr	Louisiana	23.4	Arkansas	15.0	Georgia	6.3	RoMissouri	6.2	Rest	49.0	805
Envelopes	Louisiana	11.9	RoMissouri	11.0	Virginia	9.9	RoOhio	5.2	Rest	62.0	1401
Stationery	RoPnnsylvnia	18.3	Georgia	6.0	ChicagoCtyIL	5.2	DallasTX	5.2	Rest	65.3	724
SanitPpr	RoPnnsylvnia	10.3	Tennessee	5.5	Georgia	5.5	Virginia	4.9	Rest	73.8	2676
OthPprProd	Georgia	11.9	Wisconsin	10.9	Arkansas	10.0	RoTexas	8.7	Rest	58.5	1656

(continued)

Table 3.4 (continued)

	Rank 1		Rank 2		Rank 3		Rank 4				Value-added 2005 $m
BsnsForms	Wisconsin	10.4	NewJersey	8.0	Virginia	7.5	Washington	6.0	Rest	68.1	4866
BookPrntng	Iowa	11.1	Kentucky	9.6	Virginia	8.0	Wisconsin	6.5	Rest	65.0	3483
BlnkBook	RoPnnsylvnia	7.8	ChicagoCtyIL	6.7	Minnesota	6.1	Wisconsin	5.6	Rest	73.8	1336
Printing	RoPnnsylvnia	7.8	ChicagoCtyIL	6.7	Minnesota	6.1	Wisconsin	5.6	Rest	73.8	30,585
Binding	NewJersey	7.3	Wisconsin	6.5	Iowa	5.5	Indiana	4.3	Rest	76.4	1491
PrepressSvc	RoOhio	8.3	LosAngelesCA	7.0	ChicagoCtyIL	6.7	Kentucky	6.0	Rest	71.9	4262

Source Estimated from U.S. Bureau of Labor Statistics census data and BEA national accounts

Table 3.5 Petroleum, plastics, rubber, fertilizer and pesticide output, 2010 (% of national)

	Rank 1		Rank 2		Rank 3		Rank 4				Value-added 2005 $m
PetrolRefine	LosAngelesCA	18.1	Louisiana	16.4	RoTexas	15.3	SanFranCtyCA	12.6	Rest	37.7	35,182
AsphaltPave	RoTexas	18.8	RoOhio	9.1	RoCalifornia	9.0	Louisiana	6.8	Rest	56.4	3375
AsphltShngl	Minnesota	9.1	RoCalifornia	9.0	RoOhio	8.0	LosAngelesCA	7.7	Rest	66.1	6092
PetOilGrease	Louisiana	20.9	RoOhio	11.1	HarrisTX	8.4	ChicagoCtyIL	7.3	Rest	52.4	5523
OthPetCoal	Louisiana	44.8	RoTexas	9.3	Indiana	7.4	Alabama	5.7	Rest	32.8	1103
Petrochem	HarrisTX	42.1	Louisiana	31.8	RoTexas	21.9	Kentucky	1.0	Rest	3.3	9542
IndGas	Louisiana	27.8	Indiana	8.0	RoTexas	5.9	Washington	5.1	Rest	53.3	8330
SynthDye	RoPnnsylvnia	14.0	RoOhio	12.5	Louisiana	8.1	Indiana	6.2	Rest	59.2	3672
OthInorgChem	RoTexas	13.4	HarrisTX	13.3	Louisiana	10.3	Indiana	5.9	Rest	57.2	18,388
OthOrgChem	Louisiana	17.4	HarrisTX	16.1	RoTexas	12.8	Tennessee	7.7	Rest	46.0	20,531
Plastics	RoTexas	14.3	HarrisTX	13.9	RoPnnsylvnia	8.3	RoOhio	6.0	Rest	57.5	15,843
SynthRubber	RoTexas	31.6	Louisiana	15.8	HarrisTX	11.9	RoCalifornia	5.2	Rest	35.6	3297
CelFiber	Virginia	45.8	SouthCarolin	11.4	Alabama	9.6	Massachusett	8.7	Rest	24.6	666
NoncelFiber	NorthCarolin	24.6	RoTexas	19.2	Virginia	14.4	SouthCarolin	12.9	Rest	28.9	5668
NitroFert	Louisiana	15.2	Wyoming	11.0	RoOhio	7.5	RoCalifornia	7.5	Rest	58.8	943
PhosphFert	Louisiana	24.0	HarrisTX	9.6	RoFlorida	9.3	HillsbrghFL	9.3	Rest	47.7	2095
Pesticide	Louisiana	21.4	NorthCarolin	12.3	Iowa	9.7	RoMissouri	9.0	Rest	47.6	5905

Source Estimated from U.S. Bureau of Labor Statistics census data and BEA national accounts

Table 3.6 Pharmaceuticals and other chemicals output, 2010 (% of national)

	Rank 1		Rank 2		Rank 3		Rank 4				Value-added 2005 $m
PharmaMeds	Indiana	14.1	SanFranCtyCA	11.6	NorthCarolin	9.7	NewJersey	8.3	Rest	56.4	50,404
Paint	NorthCarolin	8.6	RoTexas	7.7	RoPnnsylvnia	6.4	Indiana	6.1	Rest	71.1	9430
Adhesives	Indiana	7.3	HarrisTX	6.4	NewJersey	5.9	RoPnnsylvnia	5.0	Rest	75.5	3974
SoapDetrgnt	RoOhio	13.2	NorthCarolin	11.0	Indiana	9.0	StLouisCtyMO	5.9	Rest	60.9	8966
Polish	Wisconsin	11.2	Indiana	8.9	RoOhio	8.8	RoNewYork	5.8	Rest	65.2	6476
SurfAgent	NorthCarolin	25.5	ChicagoCtyIL	11.7	Louisiana	10.6	NewJersey	5.9	Rest	46.4	2384
ToiletPrep	NewJersey	19.0	LosAngelesCA	10.2	ChicagoCtyIL	6.7	RoNewYork	6.6	Rest	57.6	16,632
Ink	NorthCarolin	13.2	RoOhio	7.0	LosAngelesCA	6.4	ChicagoCtyIL	5.2	Rest	68.3	1728
Explosives	Connecticut	15.0	RoTexas	14.1	RoFlorida	7.0	Arizona	6.0	Rest	58.0	951
ResinComp	Indiana	14.2	HarrisTX	9.5	RoNewYork	7.5	RoOhio	6.4	Rest	62.5	2979
PhotoFilm	RoNewYork	46.3	NorthCarolin	8.2	RoPnnsylvnia	5.3	WestVirgini	3.4	Rest	36.8	9250
MscChemProd	RoTexas	14.3	Indiana	8.4	RoPnnsylvnia	6.4	NorthCarolin	5.9	Rest	65.0	6562

Source Estimated from U.S. Bureau of Labor Statistics census data and BEA national accounts

Table 3.7 Metals output, 2010 (% of national)

	Rank 1		Rank 2		Rank 3		Rank 4				Value-added 2005 $m
IronStlMills	Indiana	24.2	RoPnnsylvnia	16.2	RoOhio	10.3	Alabama	6.9	Rest	42.4	22,501
Ferroalloy	RoOhio	47.3	Kentucky	10.8	RoPnnsylvnia	10.5	Alabama	7.8	Rest	23.6	943
SteelWire	RoPnnsylvnia	8.6	Indiana	7.9	Arkansas	7.4	RoMissouri	5.6	Rest	70.5	5214
Alumina	RoTexas	57.8	Louisiana	24.7	RoOhio	3.6	Arkansas	3.1	Rest	10.8	189
Aluminum	Kentucky	28.6	RoOhio	15.0	Indiana	10.3	Washington	8.6	Rest	37.6	2279
AlumSheet	Utah	13.6	RoMichigan	10.4	Indiana	9.9	Georgia	5.1	Rest	61.0	4689
OthAlum	Maryland	9.7	RoTexas	7.3	TarrantTX	6.9	Alabama	6.0	Rest	70.1	175
CopperSmelt	Utah	77.2	RoTexas	12.9	Arizona	7.5	Arkansas	1.0	Rest	1.4	476
NonferrMetl	Utah	47.8	RoMichigan	8.8	RoOhio	7.1	RoPnnsylvnia	6.9	Rest	29.4	911
CoprRollDraw	RoTexas	9.3	RoPnnsylvnia	7.8	RoMichigan	6.5	RoNewYork	6.2	Rest	70.2	1513
NonferrShape	RoPnnsylvnia	11.4	RoOhio	7.7	Utah	7.5	NewJersey	5.5	Rest	67.9	2216
NonFerSecond	RoPnnsylvnia	15.2	RoMichigan	11.5	Alabama	6.3	Utah	5.3	Rest	61.8	242
FerrFoundry	Indiana	10.0	Alabama	9.2	RoOhio	8.4	Wisconsin	8.1	Rest	64.4	8526
AlumFoundry	Utah	22.4	RoOhio	10.8	RoTexas	4.9	Tennessee	4.6	Rest	57.4	4557
IronForging	RoOhio	10.3	HarrisTX	9.1	Wisconsin	9.0	RoTexas	8.1	Rest	63.5	2440
NonForging	Massachusett	16.4	LosAngelesCA	15.1	ChicagoCtyIL	12.4	CuyahogaOH	9.8	Rest	46.3	1308
RollForming	RoOhio	10.3	RoTexas	7.5	HarrisTX	5.6	Indiana	4.7	Rest	71.9	1339
OthForgStmp	RoOhio	8.9	ChicagoCtyIL	7.6	RoPnnsylvnia	7.4	Wisconsin	6.7	Rest	69.4	8079
Cutlery	Massachusett	30.1	Connecticut	15.8	RoNewYork	14.1	RoPnnsylvnia	5.0	Rest	35.0	1373
HandEdgeTool	RoOhio	9.2	RoPnnsylvnia	7.0	Massachusett	6.4	Minnesota	6.3	Rest	71.2	2673
SawBlade	Massachusett	38.0	RoOhio	16.2	Kansas	4.8	SouthCarolin	3.9	Rest	37.1	546
KitchenUtn	Wisconsin	22.4	RoOhio	12.3	Tennessee	8.1	RoIllinois	6.6	Rest	50.7	525
PrefMtlBldg	HarrisTX	9.0	RoTexas	9.0	Tennessee	6.1	Nebraska	4.6	Rest	71.3	1416
FabStrctMtl	RoTexas	9.2	RoPnnsylvnia	5.7	Indiana	4.4	Louisiana	4.1	Rest	76.7	7643

Source Estimated from U.S. Bureau of Labor Statistics census data and BEA national accounts

Table 3.6, covering pharmaceuticals and other chemical products, reveals little in the way of regional concentration. In Table 3.7, covering mainly basic metals, a handful of industries are highly concentrated. These industries are alumina, copper smelting and (other) non-ferrous metals, reflecting that there are only a small number of significant commercially exploited deposits of bauxite, copper ores and other non-ferrous ores in the U.S. Alumina is freighted to other states, so that aluminum production has a more diverse base than alumina. The feature of the remaining industries shown in Table 3.7 is their diverse geographic spread. A similar pattern is evident in other metal products (Table 3.8).

Machinery manufactures are also geographically dispersed (Tables 3.9, 3.10). There are three exceptions. Oil and gas machinery and equipment manufacturing ("OilGasMach") is most important in regions in which oil and gas drilling is relatively dominant. Texas and Louisiana account for over four-fifths of production. Semiconductor manufacturing is centered on Silicon Valley, so that the San Francisco region is the leading producer (Table 3.9). Measuring and Dispensing Pump Manufacturing ("MeasDspPump"), which primarily produces fuel pumps to dispense petroleum, is concentrated in Texas (Table 3.10).

Among the group of electrical, electronic and information technology manufactures, there are few signs of geographic concentration (Tables 3.11, 3.12). The nearest is in household appliances. Laundry appliance manufacturing is concentrated in Kentucky, Iowa and Michigan. South Carolina, Wisconsin and Indiana produce three-quarters of refrigerators (Table 3.12).

3.4 Conclusion

A careful inspection of regional manufacturing points to long-standing strengths and weaknesses in the U.S. economy. Among the strengths is the extent to which substantial development of a diverse array of manufactures has occurred across the nation. A weakness is that rising globalization has threatened the competitiveness of developed nations in manufactures, in which labor costs comprise a substantial share of total production costs. As a nation that has prided itself on inventiveness and innovation, available data indicate that the United States has not yet waved the white flag on whitegoods or other manufactures. Innovation still plays a part. Silicon Valley led the IT revolution and remains a global leader, even as computing hardware and software spread around the world.

Table 3.8 Other metal products, 2010 (% of national)

	Rank 1		Rank 2		Rank 3		Rank 4				Value-added 2005 $m
PlateWork	RoPnnsylvnia	9.0	Wisconsin	8.1	RoTexas	6.9	RoOhio	5.6	Rest	70.5	1905
MtlWndoDoor	RoPnnsylvnia	12.9	RoOhio	8.4	Tennessee	6.3	Wisconsin	4.6	Rest	67.8	4914
SheetMtl	RoOhio	4.2	RoPnnsylvnia	4.1	Indiana	4.0	SanFranCtyCA	3.8	Rest	83.8	10,146
OrnArchMtl	RoOhio	5.6	RoPnnsylvnia	4.7	Arkansas	4.2	Alabama	4.1	Rest	81.6	2416
Boiler	Oklahoma	13.4	RoTexas	10.8	RoNewYork	8.7	Wisconsin	7.0	Rest	60.2	2360
MetalTank	RoTexas	9.7	Oklahoma	7.7	Indiana	6.3	Wisconsin	5.8	Rest	70.6	3002
MetalCntnr	RoOhio	10.4	ChicagoCtyIL	7.1	RoIllinois	6.7	RoPnnsylvnia	6.1	Rest	69.7	3030
Hardware	RoPnnsylvnia	9.4	Wisconsin	7.4	RoIllinois	5.6	Minnesota	5.3	Rest	72.3	4097
SprnWirePrd	RoPnnsylvnia	7.2	ChicagoCtyIL	6.6	RoOhio	6.0	Indiana	5.6	Rest	74.6	2129
MachShops	RoOhio	6.4	RoPnnsylvnia	4.9	RoTexas	4.7	Wisconsin	4.7	Rest	79.3	15,875
ScrewNut	RoOhio	8.0	ChicagoCtyIL	6.2	Indiana	5.9	LosAngelesCA	5.3	Rest	74.6	9050
MtlHeatTrt	HarrisTX	9.8	Indiana	8.4	RoOhio	8.0	DetroitCtyMI	7.3	Rest	66.6	2041
MtlCoatEngrv	RoOhio	6.3	Wisconsin	6.2	Massachusett	5.9	Indiana	5.9	Rest	75.8	4556
ElcPlatAnod	ChicagoCtyIL	7.6	RoOhio	6.9	Massachusett	6.2	LosAngelesCA	5.8	Rest	73.6	4402
MtlValve	RoOhio	6.5	RoTexas	5.7	RoPnnsylvnia	5.4	RoMichigan	5.2	Rest	77.2	10,770
BallBearng	SouthCarolin	16.5	RoOhio	13.3	NewHampshire	10.1	NorthCarolin	7.0	Rest	53.1	2692
SmallArms	NewHampshire	13.1	Connecticut	12.9	RoNewYork	11.3	Arizona	7.5	Rest	55.2	933
OthOrdnance	RoPnnsylvnia	24.2		10.9	Kentucky	8.4	Tennessee	6.4	Rest	50.1	1299
FabPipeFtng	HarrisTX	18.8	RoTexas	8.5	Arkansas	6.9	DetroitCtyMI	5.8	Rest	60.0	2174
IndPattern	RoOhio	18.3	Wisconsin	10.0	Indiana	8.2	RoPnnsylvnia	6.9	Rest	56.6	474
EnamIronMtl	NorthCarolin	19.4	ChicagoCtyIL	14.0	Wisconsin	12.2	LosAngelesCA	11.5	Rest	42.8	695
MsFabMtlMfg	ChicagoCtyIL	6.5	Indiana	4.8	Minnesota	4.6	Wisconsin	4.5	Rest	79.7	4231
Ammunition	Massachusett	20.4	Tennessee	14.4	Minnesota	13.3	Iowa	7.6	Rest	44.4	1340

Source Estimated from U.S. Bureau of Labor Statistics census data and BEA national accounts

Table 3.9 Machinery manufactures output, 2010 (% of national)

	Rank 1		Rank 2		Rank 3		Rank 4				Value-added 2005 $m
FarmMach	Iowa	22.7	RoIllinois	12.2	RoTexas	7.0	Nebraska	6.9	Rest	51.3	5717
LawnEquip	RoIllinois	22.0	Tennessee	18.3	Georgia	7.2	Wisconsin	5.8	Rest	46.7	2398
ConstMach	Wisconsin	16.5	Iowa	11.9	RoIllinois	10.3	NorthCarolin	7.5	Rest	53.9	8280
MiningMach	Virginia	20.4	RoPnnsylvnia	13.3	Iowa	6.9	RoIllinois	6.5	Rest	52.9	1344
OilGasMach	HarrisTX	50.5	RoTexas	22.9	Louisiana	11.2	Oklahoma	5.4	Rest	10.1	3296
SawmillMach	Indiana	13.0	NorthCarolin	9.7	Washington	8.8	RoIllinois	8.4	Rest	60.1	596
PlstRbrMach	ChicagoCtyIL	17.0	RoOhio	9.6	Virginia	6.9	RoMichigan	6.7	Rest	59.8	1858
PaperMach	Wisconsin	40.5	Washington	6.4	RoPnnsylvnia	6.3	RoIllinois	4.8	Rest	42.0	850
TxtlMach	NorthCarolin	16.3	ChicagoCtyIL	13.9	Connecticut	10.4	SouthCarolin	10.2	Rest	49.2	635
PrintingMach	ChicagoCtyIL	13.9	NewHampshire	8.0	RoIllinois	8.0	Connecticut	6.9	Rest	63.2	943
FoodMach	RoIllinois	13.0	ChicagoCtyIL	11.7	Wisconsin	7.0	Washington	6.4	Rest	62.0	1058
SemicondMach	SanFranCtyCA	30.8	Massachusett	11.5	RoCalifornia	9.3	Oregon	8.9	Rest	39.5	4065
OthIndMach	ChicagoCtyIL	9.6	Oklahoma	7.7	RoPnnsylvnia	6.5	RoNewYork	6.1	Rest	70.1	3241
OfficeMach	TarrantTX	18.3	ChicagoCtyIL	16.5	NewJersey	11.7	DallasTX	8.5	Rest	45.0	868
OptInstLens	SanFranCtyCA	11.3	NewJersey	9.9	Massachusett	9.2	RoNewYork	7.2	Rest	62.4	2921
PhotoEquip	Indiana	23.0	LosAngelesCA	12.2	NewYorkCity	9.4	OrangeCA	6.6	Rest	48.9	1978
OSvcIndMach	RoIllinois	11.1	ChicagoCtyIL	7.9	RoTexas	5.5	Louisiana	4.5	Rest	70.9	2052
VendingMach	SouthCarolin	25.3	DallasTX	22.8	ChicagoCtyIL	7.5	Iowa	7.1	Rest	37.4	469
AirPurMach	NorthCarolin	12.4	ChicagoCtyIL	11.3	RoIllinois	6.2	RoTexas	4.8	Rest	65.3	1119
FanBlower	ChicagoCtyIL	22.6	RoOhio	9.6	RoMissouri	7.1	Indiana	6.4	Rest	54.3	1190
HeatingEq	SanFranCtyCA	11.5	RoCalifornia	6.3	RoIllinois	6.1	RoPnnsylvnia	6.0	Rest	70.2	1931
ACRefrig	RoTexas	12.3	Georgia	6.1	Tennessee	5.6	RoIllinois	5.4	Rest	70.6	6975
MoldMfg	ChicagoCtyIL	10.1	RoMichigan	8.6	RoOhio	6.9	Wisconsin	6.7	Rest	67.8	3064

Source Estimated from U.S. Bureau of Labor Statistics census data and BEA national accounts

Table 3.10 Tools, pumps and other machinery output, 2010 (% of national)

	Rank 1		Rank 2		Rank 3		Rank 4				Value-added 2005 $m
CuttingMach	RoIllinois	7.7	RoOhio	7.7	Washington	5.9	ChicagoCtyIL	5.5	Rest	73.2	2560
FormingMach	RoOhio	24.2	RoIllinois	8.2	RoMichigan	6.9	ChicagoCtyIL	5.1	Rest	55.6	944
ToolDieJig	DetroitCtyMI	13.7	RoMichigan	11.1	ChicagoCtyIL	9.1	RoOhio	6.8	Rest	59.3	3879
ToolAccessry	RoIllinois	12.3	ChicagoCtyIL	9.8	RoMichigan	7.2	RoPnnsylvnia	6.3	Rest	64.5	1422
RollMillMach	RoOhio	23.8	SouthCarolin	18.7	RoPnnsylvnia	10.7	Indiana	9.4	Rest	37.4	1586
Turbine	HarrisTX	18.4	Iowa	10.0	NorthCarolin	7.5	RoPnnsylvnia	6.7	Rest	57.4	4579
OthEngEquip	RoIllinois	13.2	Wisconsin	9.3	SouthCarolin	6.4	Iowa	5.8	Rest	65.4	7871
SpeedChng	RoIllinois	13.2	Wisconsin	9.3	SouthCarolin	6.4	Iowa	5.8	Rest	65.4	2727
Pumps	Oklahoma	11.8	RoTexas	8.7	ChicagoCtyIL	8.2	HarrisTX	6.0	Rest	65.4	3819
AirGasCmprs	HarrisTX	18.8	RoTexas	11.6	ChicagoCtyIL	8.7	RoNewYork	8.3	Rest	52.6	2551
MeasDspPump	RoTexas	48.2	RoOhio	8.6	StLouisCtyMO	7.9	Wisconsin	7.7	Rest	27.7	632
Elevators	RoIllinois	13.1	Tennessee	9.6	ChicagoCtyIL	9.6	NewYorkCity	7.9	Rest	59.8	551
Conveyors	ChicagoCtyIL	7.7	RoIllinois	7.6	RoMichigan	7.6	Virginia	7.3	Rest	69.8	3105
Hoists	RoTexas	11.5	NorthCarolin	8.9	ChicagoCtyIL	8.0	Louisiana	6.0	Rest	65.6	1549
IndTrukTrac	DallasTX	9.4	HarrisTX	9.2	RoTexas	9.0	Indiana	6.8	Rest	65.6	1650
PdrivnHandTl	Virginia	10.3	RoIllinois	8.1	RoPnnsylvnia	6.7	ChicagoCtyIL	6.4	Rest	68.5	1297
WeldEquip	RoTexas	21.2	RoOhio	9.3	Indiana	8.0	RoPnnsylvnia	6.1	Rest	55.4	1690
PackngMach	ChicagoCtyIL	13.5	Wisconsin	8.8	SouthCarolin	5.0	RoOhio	4.0	Rest	68.7	1934
IndFurnace	RoPnnsylvnia	9.4	RoOhio	7.6	Wisconsin	7.0	ChicagoCtyIL	6.8	Rest	69.2	1534
FluidCylindr	RoTexas	8.6	RoIllinois	7.3	Washington	7.0	Iowa	6.3	Rest	70.8	1635
FluidPump	RoIllinois	23.8	Iowa	13.6	SouthCarolin	9.1	RoTexas	5.1	Rest	48.4	1043

Source Estimated from U.S. Bureau of Labor Statistics census data and BEA national accounts

Table 3.11 Electronic and IT manufactures, 2010 (% of national)

	Rank 1		Rank 2		Rank 3		Rank 4				Value-added 2005 $m
Scales	Wisconsin	9.7	Minnesota	8.5	ColumbusOH	7.9	RoMissouri	7.8	Rest	66.1	4663
Computers	HarrisTX	30.7	Oregon	26.4	NorthCarolin	6.4	Wisconsin	2.8	Rest	33.7	14,081
CmptrStorage	NorthCarolin	18.8	RoCalifornia	15.1	Colorado	13.4	Oregon	9.2	Rest	43.5	2716
ComptrTermnl	RoNewYork	33.4	Oregon	28.8	Georgia	13.2	RoCalifornia	5.5	Rest	19.1	633
OCptrPeriph	Minnesota	11.8	Oregon	9.6	Massachusett	8.3	OrangeCA	7.5	Rest	62.9	7523
Telephone	Massachusett	21.2	SanFranCtyCA	15.4	RoTexas	10.7	NorthCarolin	8.5	Rest	44.3	6268
BroadcastEq	LosAngelesCA	25.7	OrangeCA	13.2	SanFranCtyCA	12.4	RoFlorida	8.5	Rest	40.3	9056
CommunEquip	Oregon	19.9	ChicagoCtyIL	11.2	Idaho	9.0	RoNewYork	5.0	Rest	54.9	826
AudVidEquip	Oregon	35.1	NewMexico	11.8	LosAngelesCA	6.0	Tennessee	5.0	Rest	42.0	2650
ElectTube	SanFranCtyCA	22.3	LosAngelesCA	14.1	Arizona	13.1	Massachusett	7.4	Rest	43.2	1194
Semicondctr	Oregon	31.4	SanFranCtyCA	23.6	DallasTX	5.6	Massachusett	5.3	Rest	34.1	23,875
OtElectrnic	Oregon	9.5	NorthCarolin	7.4	RoCalifornia	5.9	Massachusett	5.3	Rest	72.0	15,441
ElectroMedic	Oregon	20.9	SanFranCtyCA	14.9	Massachusett	14.2	RoPnnsylvnia	7.0	Rest	43.0	4694
SearchNavig	LosAngelesCA	14.8	Arizona	10.8	RoFlorida	8.9	Oregon	8.4	Rest	57.2	16,638
EnviroContrl	RoIllinois	12.6	Minnesota	11.5	Indiana	9.4	Idaho	6.2	Rest	60.2	993
ProcVblInsts	Massachusett	9.3	RoPnnsylvnia	7.2	HarrisTX	5.6	Connecticut	4.6	Rest	73.4	3987
FluidMeters	NorthCarolin	20.6	Oregon	15.1	Tennessee	9.9	RoPnnsylvnia	5.6	Rest	48.8	1422
ElecTestInst	SanFranCtyCA	27.1	Oregon	9.1	Colorado	7.4	NorthCarolin	6.5	Rest	49.9	5163
LabInsts	SanFranCtyCA	32.8	Massachusett	10.0	Minnesota	5.6	NorthCarolin	4.4	Rest	47.2	3412
RadiationIns	SanFranCtyCA	23.1	ChicagoCtyIL	13.7	Utah	13.1	Tennessee	12.6	Rest	37.5	1309
WatchClock	NorthCarolin	18.1	Oregon	9.2	Massachusett	8.3	LosAngelesCA	6.4	Rest	58.0	2890
SoftwareRep	OrangeCA	13.3	Minnesota	9.9	SanFranCtyCA	9.1	Oregon	7.0	Rest	60.7	686
AudVidReprod	NorthCarolin	31.2	Idaho	8.0	LosAngelesCA	6.1	NewYorkCity	4.8	Rest	49.9	1472

Source Estimated from U.S. Bureau of Labor Statistics census data and BEA national accounts

Table 3.12 Electrical manufactures, 2010 (% of national)

	Rank 1		Rank 2		Rank 3		Rank 4				Value-added 2005 $m
MagOptMedia	LosAngelesCA	12.1	NorthCarolin	10.1	Massachusett	9.8	Alabama	8.6	Rest	59.3	1285
Lightbulbs	RoOhio	22.6	RoIllinois	15.1	RoPnnsylvnia	10.6	Kentucky	9.0	Rest	42.7	1724
LightFxtr	ChicagoCtyIL	6.3	Georgia	6.3	Wisconsin	6.0	LosAngelesCA	5.2	Rest	76.3	4342
EleHswrFans	NorthCarolin	12.7	Massachusett	9.5	NewJersey	7.8	Kansas	5.4	Rest	64.7	766
HshldVacuum	RoPnnsylvnia	20.6	CuyahogaOH	17.9	Tennessee	16.9	RoMichigan	11.8	Rest	32.8	1026
HshldStove	Tennessee	21.2	ChicagoCtyIL	19.6	Georgia	12.8	Mississippi	10.4	Rest	36.0	1449
HshldFridge	SouthCarolin	29.5	Wisconsin	26.1	Indiana	16.8	Tennessee	6.9	Rest	20.7	2322
HshldLaundry	Kentucky	46.1	Iowa	29.5	RoMichigan	20.5	Indiana	1.9	Rest	2.0	1451
OthHshldApp	NorthCarolin	32.1	Tennessee	26.4	RoMichigan	14.7	Wisconsin	8.7	Rest	18.2	1419
PwrTrnsfrmr	RoMissouri	11.8	Virginia	10.8	NorthCarolin	7.7	Georgia	5.6	Rest	64.1	1634
MotorGenratr	RoTexas	18.0	RoOhio	13.8	Wisconsin	8.0	NorthCarolin	6.3	Rest	53.9	4497
Switchboard	ChicagoCtyIL	10.3	NorthCarolin	7.9	SouthCarolin	7.0	Tennessee	7.0	Rest	67.9	4023
Relays	Wisconsin	15.1	NorthCarolin	8.3	RoOhio	7.7	Virginia	5.8	Rest	63.2	3984
StorBattery	RoPnnsylvnia	30.7	RoMissouri	16.3	RoOhio	5.3	Tennessee	4.6	Rest	43.2	1536
PrimBatter	NorthCarolin	23.3	RoMissouri	13.3	Connecticut	11.7	Georgia	9.8	Rest	41.9	1332
FibOptCable	NorthCarolin	20.4	SouthCarolin	13.0	Georgia	12.4	NewHampshire	9.0	Rest	45.2	1400
OtherWire	NorthCarolin	12.9	RoPnnsylvnia	7.7	Connecticut	6.2	RoFlorida	5.5	Rest	67.9	3658
WireDevice	RoOhio	7.5	ChicagoCtyIL	6.9	Connecticut	6.7	Tennessee	6.3	Rest	72.6	4666
CarbonProds	RoPnnsylvnia	17.9	Utah	10.5	RoMichigan	8.1	RoOhio	7.6	Rest	55.9	1090
MsElEquip	SanFranCtyCA	9.9	Massachusett	8.6	NorthCarolin	6.8	Connecticut	6.4	Rest	68.3	2963

Source Estimated from U.S. Bureau of Labor Statistics census data and BEA national accounts

As wages rise in coastal China, there is some relief for manufactures in Western nations. At the same time, the manufacturing base is being ferried to the second tier cities of inland China, or to poorer nations in South-East Asia. For the United States, innovation will enable some manufacturers to preserve competitiveness in the global market. Moreover, China's rapid manufacturing expansion has brought with it two major issues. One is the quality of merchandise: be it steel products, glass products, some electrical goods, motor vehicles or solar panels, a perception pervades home owners, builders, motorists and other users that domestically sourced manufactured products may cost more but are of superior quality to imports. A second issue concerns the dumping of imports at below the costs of production. Under international trading rules, countervailing duties may be imposed on such goods, providing some respite for domestic manufacturers.

From the perspective of U.S. cities that have relied heavily on manufacturing for several generations, the relative decline of manufactures in the United States is a threat to communities and living standards. Jobs in manufacturing that formerly provided a relatively high standard of living no longer provide that guarantee. The average manufacturing employment wage rose from around $10.50 per hour in 1990 to $20.73 per hour in December 2016.[5] After adjusting for inflation, this indicates little gain at all in quarter of a century. Hidden within the data there has also been a decline in job security and a widening of wages disparity.

Obama's bailout of the car industry in 2009 halted the decline in the industry. Due to cheaper fuel prices since then, sales of domestically produced SUVs and pickups have soared: the nation's comparative advantage appears to remain in this market segment (Kiley 2016).

The ongoing structural change in the U.S. economy, indicated by the declining share of manufactures in national income over several generations, highlights the potential relevance of a CGE model that can capture changes in industry activities over time. Dixon et al. (2000) devised a method of historical simulation that they have subsequently applied to the U.S. economy (Dixon and Rimmer 2004, 2010, 2012). This method links changes in industry structure to changing industry technologies, household consumption, household preferences, exchange rates and other international conditions. Such compositional changes may be even more pronounced at the regional level than the national level. Historical simulations provide an important empirical foundation for dynamic CGE modeling. Estimates from these simulations are used as inputs in updating models from that of an available input-output year to a more recent year. Beyond that, technological changes in particular, or in the context of the U.S. economy since the global financial crisis shifts in household consumption, investment and the trade balance as a share of GDP, are used to project a CGE model into the future to provide a forecast baseline for dynamic analysis. Section 9.2.3 outlines the methodology by which

[5]http://www.tradingeconomics.com/united-states/wages-in-manufacturing accessed 27 January 2017.

USAGE-TERM is aggregated and updated for a particular policy application. Through the use of available observed variables and economic theory, this method of updating reduces the reliance of the practitioner on timely provision of input-output data.

References

Dixon PB, Menon J, Rimmer MT (2000) Changes in technology and preferences: a general equilibrium explanation of rapid growth in trade. Aust Econ Pap 39:33–55

Dixon PB, Rimmer MT (2012) Validation in CGE modelling, In Dixon PB, Jorgenson DW (eds) Handbook of computable general equilibrium modeling. Elsevier

Dixon PB, Rimmer MT (2004) The US economy from 1992 to 1998: results from a detailed CGE model. Econ Rec 80:S13–S23

Dixon PB, Rimmer MT (2010) Validating a detailed, dynamic CGE model of the U.S. Econ Rec 86:S22–S34

Kiley D (2016) As Obama takes victory lap over auto industry rescue, here are the lessons of the bailout. http://www.forbes.com/sites/davidkiley5/2016/01/20/obamas-takes-victory-lap-over-auto-industry-rescue/#65ad45085497. Accessed 22 Sept 2016

Wittwer G, Horridge M (2010) Bringing regional detail to a CGE model using census data. Spat Econ Anal 5:229–255

Chapter 4
Regional Electricity Supply in the United States

Glyn Wittwer

Abstract Electricity and economic development moved together in much of the twentieth century. The development of electricity grids raised standards of living in regional U.S. Energy Security and greenhouse gas emissions are among the competing tensions in government policy. Electricity projects historically have been among major infrastructure projects sponsored by government. A significant step forwards in policy modeling with a versatile multi-regional CGE model is to represent electricity by different types of generation, with a separate transmission/distribution sector.

Keywords Electricity generation · Electricity transmission and distribution · Substitution in fuel types

4.1 The Beginning of Electrification

The construction of electricity networks, alongside transport and communications infrastructure, has contributed much to bringing the modern world into being. In turn, the spread of electricity networks has had much to do with regional development. Without electricity, many manufacturing processes would be difficult or unthinkable. Even the provision of electric lighting was a significant advance, enabling factories to work beyond daylight hours. In the United States, the spread of electricity enabled a more extensive and rapid development of the manufacturing base than otherwise, raised living standards in rural communities and illuminated regional settlements.

Electricity networks had the most humble of beginnings. Small coal-fired generators distributed electricity over strictly local networks. A network was confined to a factory or a neighborhood with a range limited to a street or two. Direct current (DC) distribution systems dotted local areas in the 1870s and 1880s, missing most

G. Wittwer (✉)
Centre of Policy Studies, Victoria University, Melbourne, VIC, Australia
e-mail: glyn.wittwer@vu.edu.au

G. Wittwer (ed.), *Multi-regional Dynamic General Equilibrium Modeling of the U.S. Economy*, Advances in Applied General Equilibrium Modeling,
DOI 10.1007/978-3-319-58866-7_4

residents and most regions. In 1882, portending greater penetration of electricity in households and industries, a high voltage DC transmission line was constructed from Miesback to Munich in Germany, a distance of 57 km (Edison Tech Center 2013).

In 1886 in Great Barrington, Massachusetts, the first alternating current (AC) distribution system using transformers was built, over a distance of less than half a kilometre. The war of the currents had begun. Thomas Edison, anxious to preserve patent royalties, backed DC distribution.[1] He invented a meter that allowed customers to be billed, but the meter only worked with direct current. Other advantages of DC were that it could be used with storage batteries that provided load levelling and power backup. When Edison's system was introduced, practical AC motors were not available. George Westinghouse, on the other hand, believed in AC distribution systems. But early AC systems used series connected distribution systems. When a single electrical appliance (usually a lamp) was turned off, the voltage of all appliances on the circuit was affected. In 1886, Westinghouse hired William Stanley Jr. to develop AC distribution systems with a series of step-up and step-down transformers. Stanley was succeeded by Oliver Shallenberger.[2]

The breakthrough on the western side of the Atlantic came on May 16 1888, when Nikola Tesla (1888) addressed the American Institute of Electrical Engineers. He acknowledged the failure of AC distribution up to that point. His innovation was to make a polyphase induction motor. Westinghouse paid for a license to use Tesla's patent. In 1890, his company established two phase AC generators at Oregon City Falls, allowing the transmission over 14 miles to Portland (Edison Tech Center 2013). Edison embarked on a campaign to discredit AC electricity by directing his technicians to demonstrate that AC shocks were lethal when applied to live animals, and to show that DC shocks were not (McNichol 2006).

While the battle between AC and DC was conducted in the United States, a similar battle proceeded in Europe. August Haselwander developed three-phase AC power in Germany in 1887. In 1891, the first long distance three-phase AC transmission was demonstrated on the 110 mile link at the World Electrotechnical Exhibition in Frankfurt, Germany, the brainchild of Michael Dolivo-Dobrovolsky.[3] Meanwhile, Charles Steinmetz who emigrated from Europe to the United States in 1889, enhanced the understanding of three-phase AC power by explaining the mathematics of it and by his elaboration of magnetic hysteresis.[4]

In the 1890s, power stations started dotting the U.S. landscape more prominently, with relatively short transmission lines tentatively linking generators to potential users. A hydroelectric plant was built near Telluride in San Miguel

---

[1]See http://en.wikipedia.org/wiki/War_of_Currents, accessed 27 August 2016.

[2]Ibid.

[3]See http://to-name.ru/english/biography/michael-osipovich-dolivo-dobrovolsky.htm, accessed 27 August 2016.

[4]See http://en.wikipedia.org/wiki/Charles_Proteus_Steinmetz, accessed 27 August 2016.

County, Colorado to power mining operations 2.5 miles away. Helped by Steinmetz's discoveries, the first commercial three-phase AC power plant was built at Redlands in San Bernardino County, California, with a transmission line length of 7 miles. In Pelzer, in Anderson County of South Carolina, a hydroelectric plant came into operation in 1895 to light up the textile mills. In the same year, hydroelectric plants were built at Folsom in California, Willamette Falls in Oregon and the most trumpeted of all, Niagara Falls. The Niagara plant was not the first, but it was the biggest at the time. A year later, 25 miles of transmission lines originating at the plant were constructed (Edison Tech Center 2013).

A patchwork of AC and DC grids was built across the country in the following decades. Some were in direct competition. Other had local monopolies that enabled the extortion of the highest possible prices from consumers for electricity, which remained a luxury item. But some sought wealth through grand visions rather than extortion. Samuel Insull became president of the Chicago Edison Company in 1892. His vision was to provide power to light up the entire city. Unlike his company's founder, he embraced the use of both AC and DC power, using AC power to transmit electricity to sub-stations, from where DC power supplied consumers. Insull introduced a tool of monopoly power to the market, price discrimination. Heavy consumers of electricity paid less for each unit than small consumers. Insull built his fortune with control of 60 utility corporations, but then came the stock market crash of 1929. He lost his wealth; his empire's stocks and bonds held by the public were rendered worthless. Insull was acquitted of fraud charges in 1934, but with his reputation ruined, he crossed the Atlantic, never to return (Schmidt 2011).

There were rumblings among consumers that too many of them were paying too much for electricity, and that suppliers were restricting supply in order to keep prices high. Trust in the supply of electricity by private companies waned. The Great Depression provided the platform for government intervention in many areas of the economy, not least electricity provision. Before Congress on 10th April 1933, President Roosevelt revealed his plan:

> I, therefore, suggest to the Congress legislation to create a Tennessee Valley Authority , a corporation clothed with the power of Government but possessed of the flexibility and initiative of a private enterprise.[5]

Congress passed the Tennessee Valley Authority (TVA) Act on May 18 1933. Ideological disputes over the role of the TVA, its costs and its benefits have been generated ever since. Yet the difference it made to the inhabitants of Tennessee River Valley, who suffered severe poverty and high unemployment during the depression, meant that for decades that followed, support within the valley for the TVA from the left and the right did not falter.

[5]From http://www.presidency.ucsb.edu/ws/?pid=14614, accessed 27 August 2016.

The Centers for Disease Control and Prevention (2010) note that 30% of the population of Tennessee River Valley was affected by malaria prior to eradication efforts by the Tennessee River Valley Authority. The TVA not only had jurisdiction over countering malaria. It had to manage navigation, flood control, electricity generation and transmission, economic development and fertilizer manufacturing. This was big government at a time when the Great Depression had in the eyes of many been a working demonstration of the failure of *laissez faire* economics. Building up the valley's electricity generating capacity brought jobs into the region. But dam construction also displaced 15,000 families from their farms.[6] However, for the farmers that remained, the TVA contributed to increased yields and steadily increased the proportion of families with access to electricity. In 1935, little more than 10% of rural households in the United States had access to electricity. By 1949, over 75% of such households had access (Day and Gibbons 2010).

At the time, not everyone regarded the Tennessee Valley Authority as an overwhelming success. Russell (1949) questioned both the costs and the measured benefits of the TVA. He was concerned that electricity generation and flood mitigation were two objectives, sometimes conflicting, that should not be handled by the same organization. He also regarded the costs of all of the authority's programs as excessive, and he thought of TVA's reach as seemingly unlimited, almost totalitarian. He estimated that the authority made substantial losses over the first 14 years of its existence once interest rates were included in financial calculations. Yet, he appeared to be unaware of the extent of penetration of electricity into the homes of rural United States between when the authority was formed and when he penned his criticisms. By not acknowledging the impact that the TVA had on the quality of life of people in regional U.S., Russell may have given readers of his work a reason to discount it.

Massive publicly-funded works were changing the face of regions away from the cities. The Hoover Dam, shared between Clark County, Nevada, and Mohave County, Arizona, was dedicated on 30th September 1935 by Roosevelt. This was among many works that helped bring the intent of the 1935 Rural Electrification Act to reality. Government development grants and loans were taken up by co-ops; utility companies had fallen out of favor with many politicians. Indeed, the Public Utility Holding Company Act was also passed in 1935, regulating electricity generation and transmission.[7] The act limited the operations of electric utilities to a single state or region, and prevented regulated utility companies from being involved in unregulated businesses. The act facilitated the spread of the electricity grid through regulated local distribution networks.

With the U.S. war effort came the need for aircraft, which in turn required aluminum, produced in energy-hungry smelting plants. The construction of the

[6]From http://en.wikipedia.org/wiki/Tennessee_Valley_Authority, accessed 27 August 2016.

[7]The act was not repealed until 8th August 2005, when the Energy Policy Act passed both houses of Congress (source: see footnote 6).

electricity grid provided a decentralized base from which the manufacturing for war could take place. The impact of the war effort on the economy was spectacular, as the unemployment rate dropped from 19% in 1938 to less than 5% four years later.[8] Without the construction of major generation plants and extending of electricity grids, an upsurge in manufacturing output would have been much more difficult.

4.2 The Electricity Grid Today

Today, there are three main power grids within the nation, the Western grid, the Eastern grid and the Texan grid. The Western grid includes New Mexico, Colorado, Wyoming and Montana, plus all the mainland states to the west of these. It stretches into British Columbia and Alberta to the north of the national border, and into Baja California to the south. The Eastern grid includes a number of electric reliability councils under the North American Electric Reliability Corporation, formed in response to the northeast blackout of 1965. The Northeast Power Coordinating Council covers Maine, Vermont, New Hampshire, Massachusetts, New York, Connecticut and Rhode Island, and also the Canadian provinces of Ontario, Quebec, New Brunswick, Nova Scotia and Prince Edward Island. The Florida Reliability Coordinating Council, the South East Reliability Corporation and the Southwest Power Pool are among the other councils, which also have Canadian representation. Given their isolation, Alaska and Hawaii alone are without grids that share loads across states.[9]

The default version of USAGE-TERM includes a split of electricity generation by type and distribution. But to do regional CGE modeling of electricity will require more; an important task in electricity scenarios will be to devise electricity trading regions, as outlined in Adams and Parmenter (2013). Historically, Texas has been reluctant to join other grids, facing a collective fear that trading may allow the utilities to raise their price. On the other hand, not being part of an interstate grid means that when Texan electricity output falls, interstate imports cannot make up the shortfall.

Another strand of CGE modeling of electricity scenarios may be to link the model with an existing energy model based on linear programming, such as the International Energy Agency's MARKAL. Adams and Parmenter (2013, Sect. 9.3.2) explain that in practice, a CGE and energy model can be linked by iterating towards a stable solution rather than via complete two-way integration. The iterative process in practice will be less time-consuming than complete integration, particularly if practitioners of both models cooperate willingly.

[8]Source http://www.infoplease.com/ipa/A0104719.html, accessed 27 August 2016.

[9]http://www.eia.gov/cneaf/electricity/chg_str_fuel/html/fig.02.html, accessed 27 August 2016.

4.2.1 Gathering County Details on Electricity Generation for a CGE Database

From a modeling perspective, there are a number of reasons for putting effort into obtaining estimates of regional electricity generation. As discussed in Chap. 2, a commodity split that aligns better with available detailed data on agricultural output has improved the regional representation in the CGE database. Potentially, even greater returns might arise from a more elaborate representation of electricity, for which there is only a single sector to cover all forms of generation plus transmission and distribution in the available national input–output table. There are several issues. Some states have a relatively high dependence on coal or, in the case of West Virginia, rely almost exclusively on it for electricity generation. Other states have easier access to renewables, most notably hydro-electricity in the case of western states straddled by the Rocky Mountains. The type of generation, generating capacity and the age of a power plant influence the volume of greenhouse gas emissions from a given plant. If we are to use the CGE model to examine greenhouse gas scenarios, an important first step is to disaggregate the single electricity sector in the national USAGE CGE database into various types of electricity generation and electricity distribution. This implies that scenarios involving taxes on carbon emissions would increase the costs of carbon-intensive coal-fired electricity generation relative to renewables and nuclear energy.

Nuclear power generation had been coming into favor as concerns about greenhouse gas emissions grew, given the absence of carbon emissions from nuclear generation. However, the Fukushima Daiichi nuclear disaster in Japan in March 2011 discouraged nuclear expansion around the globe. In the U.S., a gradual upward trend in nuclear power generation between 2003 and 2010 was reversed thereafter in the wake of the disaster (Table 4.1).

Another issue is that the composition of electricity generation has changed relatively quickly. One notable development in greenhouse gas accounting in the U.S. in the past few years has been the rise of hydraulic fracturing (fracking). The increased extraction of coal seam gas has reduced the reliance on coal in electricity generation across the nation. To illustrate, in 2003 coal-fired generation had a 51% share of total generation, but had fallen to 37% by 2012. At the same time, the share of gas-fired electricity rose from 17% to 30%. The output shares in the USAGE-TERM master database(Table 4.3) align with those of 2010.

4.2.2 National Overview

The Carbon Monitoring for Action (CARMA) website contains details on 8690 electricity plants in the United States, which enables us to prepare a county level representation of electricity generation. This website includes generation capacity,

Table 4.1 National electricity generation by source, United States (10^6 GW-h)

Year	Coal	Petroleum products	Gas	Nuclear	Hydroelectric	Other renewables	Other	Total
2003	1973.7	119.4	649.9	763.7	267.3	79.5	14	3883.2
2004	1978.3	121.1	710.1	788.5	259.9	83.1	14.2	3970.6
2005	2012.9	122.2	761.0	782.0	263.8	87.3	12.8	4055.4
2006	1990.5	64.2	816.4	787.2	282.7	96.5	13	4064.7
2007	2016.5	65.7	896.6	806.4	240.6	105.2	12.2	4156.7
2008	1985.8	46.2	883	806.2	248.5	126.1	11.8	4119.4
2009	1755.9	38.9	921	798.9	268.8	144.3	11.9	3950.3
2010	1847.3	37.1	987.7	807.0	254.7	167.2	12.9	4125.1
2011	1733.4	30.2	1013.7	790.2	313.5	194.0	14.2	4100.7
2012	1517.2	22.9	1230.7	769.3	271.9	218.8	12.5	4054.5
2013	1581.1	27.1	1137.6	789.0	263.9	253.5	13.6	4066.0
2014	1581.7	30.2	1138.6	797.2	259.4	279.2	13.5	4093.6

Source U.S. Energy Information Administration (2016)
http://www.eia.gov/electricity/annual/html/epa_03_01_a.html accessed 22 September 2016.

an estimate of carbon emissions and the latitude and longitude coordinates of each plant. Processing of these data includes a combination of automatic and manual techniques. For example, a series of dummy variables ascribed to the data in a spreadsheet enable us to distinguish between coal, gas and renewable sources based on emissions. At the same time, electricity stations producing energy in 2004 but not 2009 are treated as decommissioned. Other stations are designated as future sources, and usually omitted from the database.

Table 4.2 is a sample of the electricity plants for which CARMA provides data. For each of the plants shown, there is a substantial non-zero energy output combined with zero carbon emissions. This indicates that either each plant uses a renewable source such as hydro-electric or wind generation, or it is a nuclear plant.

On the modified spreadsheet containing the data, each of these plants is assigned to a zero-carbon emissions group using a dummy variable. The dummy variable approach based on a conditional formula within the database does some but not all of the hard work for us. From there, we can look for clues in the name of the plant. For example, Wheeler Dam and Diablo Canyon are hydro-electric plants. Browns Ferry, despite containing an aquatic allusion in its name, is a nuclear plant, as are the rest of the plants in Table 4.2.

We require ancillary information to separate nuclear plants from renewables. The United States Nuclear Regulatory Commission provides details of operating nuclear plants.[10] Beyond that, separating hydro-electric plants from other renewable

[10]See http://www.nrc.gov/info-finder/reactor/#listAlpha, accessed 25 January 2017.

Table 4.2 Sample of CARMA data

State	plant_id	Company	Name	carbon_2004	carbon_2009	carbon_Future	energy_2004	energy_2009	energy_Future	Latitude	Longitude
Alabama	5952	Tennessee Valley Authority	Browns Ferry	0	0	0	1,848,8000	2,574,3000	25,743,000	34.704	−87.119
Alabama	13162	Southern Co	Joseph M. Farley	0	0	0	1,314,8000	1,397,4000	13,974,000	31.223	−85.112
Alabama	49531	Tennessee Valley Authority	Wheeler Dam	0	0	0	1,473,700	1,555,000	1,555,000	34.807	−87.382
Arizona	33472	Pinnacle West Capital Corp	Palo Verde	0	0	0	2,811,3000	30662000	30662000	33.389	−112.87
Arkansas	2036	Entergy Corp	Arkansas Nuclear One	0	0	0	15,450,000	15,170,000	15,170,000	35.31	−93.231
California	10752	PG&E Corp	Diablo Canyon	0	0	0	15,230,000	16,265,000	16,265,000	35.211	−120.86

Source http://www.carma.org

Table 4.3 Total number of US power plants by type operating in 2009

Biomass/gas recovery	391
Coal	784
Gas	1310
Geothermal	19
Hydroelectric	690
Nuclear	74
Oil/diesel	561
Renewables (solar/wind)	1619
All sources	5448

Source www.carma.org

sources requires further information. Overall, 690 hydroelectric stations were identified and assigned to an individual county. This relied on a state-by-state check using Wikipedia.[11]

Table 4.3 shows the number of U.S. power plants by type of generation operating in 2009. Since the CARMA data included details of 8690 plants, we can infer that more than 3000 plants were either decommissioned prior to 2009 or yet to commence operations in 2009, given that Table 4.3 sums to only 5448 plants.

4.2.3 Assigning Power Plants to a County

CARMA provide both county and the latitude and longitude coordinates of most of the power plants in its database. It turns out to be easier to use the latitude and longitude coordinates given in the database, and match them to the county's coordinates using a program, than to match the county name in the CARMA list to the name in the USAGE-TERM county set.[12] An initial problem with this method is that CARMA does not assign coordinates to all power plants. Missing coordinates are found manually with online searches.

Table 4.4 shows the percentage of each region's contribution to the national total for each particular type of generation. As is evident in the section below detailing California's generation and electricity usage, electricity trading between regions is an important component in satisfying electricity demands.

[11]California Energy Commission now provides a table of all power plants: http://www.energy.ca.gov/almanac/electricity_data/web_qfer/Annual_Generation-Plant_Unit_base.php?noTable=Yes, accessed 25 January 2017.

[12]The following contains an example of a coordinate matching program: http://www.copsmodels.com/archivep.htm TPMH0121.

Table 4.4 Electricity generation by type by region (% of National)

	Biomass	Coal	Gas	Hydro	Nuclear	Renewables[a]
Alabama	5.2	3.0	3.3	5.0	3.3	0.5
Alaska	0.3	0.0	0.5	0.4	0.0	0.3
Arizona	0.4	0.6	4.1	0.9	3.9	0.1
Arkansas	1.2	1.9	1.3	1.8	1.9	0.2
San Francisco city CA	2.1	0.1	2.1	0.0	0.0	1.0
Ro CA	9.8	0.1	5.7	19.0	0.2	11.3
LosAngeles CA	4.8	0.0	1.0	0.2	0.0	0.2
Orange CA	0.8	0.0	0.5	0.1	2.0	0.0
Riverside CA	0.0	0.0	0.1	0.0	0.0	0.9
Sacramento CA	0.6	0.0	0.6	0.3	0.0	0.1
Colorado	0.7	1.3	1.5	0.3	0.0	1.5
Connecticut	0.6	0.2	1.5	0.2	2.1	0.1
Delaware	0.0	0.2	0.2	0.0	0.0	0.0
DC	0.0	0.0	0.0	0.0	0.0	0.0
Ro Florida	3.2	2.1	9.6	0.0	3.8	2.2
Broward FL	0.1	0.0	0.8	0.0	0.0	0.5
Hillsburgh FL	0.0	0.0	1.0	0.0	0.0	0.2
Miami-Dade FL	0.0	0.0	2.1	0.0	0.0	0.2
Palm Beach FL	0.0	0.0	0.4	0.0	0.0	0.2
Georgia	0.5	4.2	3.8	1.2	5.8	2.8
Hawaii	1.4	0.2	0.5	0.0	0.0	0.5
Idaho	0.1	0.0	0.2	5.6	0.1	1.7
Ro Illinois	0.3	6.4	0.3	0.0	6.1	1.8
Chicago city IL	0.8	1.0	0.3	0.0	4.3	0.2
Indiana	0.1	6.6	0.6	0.3	0.0	1.5
Iowa	0.0	1.3	0.2	0.4	2.5	4.4
Kansas	0.0	1.9	0.4	0.0	1.1	1.7
Kentucky	0.3	4.5	0.3	1.5	0.0	0.1
Louisiana	9.4	1.3	3.7	0.6	3.3	0.6
Maine	0.8	0.0	0.8	0.6	0.0	3.5
Maryland	1.4	1.3	0.1	0.9	4.2	0.0
Massachusetts	1.4	0.2	2.0	0.3	1.4	0.6
Ro Michigan	3.3	3.5	0.5	0.3	1.9	1.4
Detroit city MI	0.0	0.5	0.2	0.0	0.0	0.2
Minnesota	0.7	2.1	0.3	0.1	0.5	3.0
Mississippi	1.1	0.5	3.1	0.0	1.4	0.9
Ro Missouri	0.0	2.8	0.2	0.1	1.3	1.7
St. Louis city MO	0.0	0.0	0.0	0.0	0.0	0.0

(continued)

Table 4.4 (continued)

	Biomass	Coal	Gas	Hydro	Nuclear	Renewables[a]
Montana	0.1	1.0	0.0	1.9	0.0	2.7
Nebraska	0.0	2.3	0.0	0.1	1.2	1.5
Nevada	1.6	0.5	2.7	1.7	0.0	1.1
New Hampshire	0.1	0.2	0.7	0.2	1.1	0.7
New Jersey	5.2	0.4	3.9	0.0	1.9	0.6
New Mexico	0.4	2.6	0.9	0.1	0.0	0.9
Ro New York	1.9	0.7	1.8	11.1	5.6	4.0
New York city	2.5	0.0	3.4	0.0	0.0	0.4
North Carolina	1.5	3.6	0.6	1.2	5.2	2.4
North Dakota	0.0	1.8	0.0	0.7	0.0	1.7
Ro Ohio	0.1	3.4	0.3	0.0	1.9	0.1
Cuyahoga OH	0.0	0.0	0.0	0.0	0.0	0.0
Columbus OH	0.0	0.0	0.0	0.0	0.0	0.0
Oklahoma	0.3	2.1	3.5	0.8	0.0	2.9
Oregon	2.7	0.2	1.8	4.5	0.8	5.7
Ro Pennsylvania	2.2	6.0	2.4	0.6	7.6	1.8
Phladlphia PA	0.3	0.0	0.1	0.0	0.0	0.0
Rhode Island	0.2	0.4	1.3	0.0	0.0	0.1
South Carolina	1.8	2.2	0.7	0.4	6.8	0.7
South Dakota	0.0	0.0	0.0	0.3	0.4	0.9
Tennessee	0.0	1.7	0.2	4.0	2.3	0.8
Ro Texas	14.6	7.4	17.1	0.2	5.3	12.3
Dallas TX	0.0	0.0	0.1	0.0	0.0	0.0
Harris TX	6.8	0.1	1.5	0.0	0.0	0.0
Tarrant TX	0.0	0.0	0.1	0.0	0.0	0.0
Utah	0.5	2.9	0.7	1.7	0.0	0.7
Vermont	0.2	0.0	0.0	0.3	0.0	1.2
Virginia	2.4	1.9	1.1	0.2	3.6	1.4
Washington	2.4	0.5	0.7	29.6	2.5	4.9
West Virginia	0.0	6.2	0.1	0.1	0.0	1.5
Wisconsin	1.1	2.1	0.8	0.2	2.7	1.4
Wyoming	0.0	2.5	0.1	0.1	0.0	1.8
National	100	100	100	100	100	100

[a]Renewables includes solar, wind and geothermal generation, the latter accounting for only 3% of the "renewables" total

Table 4.5 Electricity sources in California, 2014

	Generation (GWh)					Total supply	
	2001	2005	2010	2015	% in 2015	2014 GW h	%
Coal	4041	4283	3406	538	0.27	18888	6.40%
Biomass	5762	6078	5981	6356	3.25	7507	2.50%
Geothermal	13525	13292	12740	11994	6.12	13030	4.40%
Nuclear	33294	36155	32214	18525	9.46	25220	8.50%
Natural gas	116341	97161	109886	117482	59.99	132087	44.50%
Large hydro	20144	33334	28483	11569	5.91	16350	5.50%
Small hydro	4844	6928	5706	2423	1.24	2787	0.90%
Solar PV	3	2	82	12571	6.42	{12566	4.20%
Solar thermal	834	658	879	2446	1.25	{	
Wind	3242	4084	6172	11856	6.05	23913	8.10%
Oil	379	148	52	54	0.03	46	0.00%
Other/unspecified	38	24	12	14	0.01	44449	15.00%
Total	202446	202150	205612	195829	100.00	296843	6.40%

Source http://energyalmanac.ca.gov/electricity/total_system_power.html; http://www.energy.ca.gov/almanac/electricity_data/ accessed 25 January 2017.

4.2.4 California's Electricity Generation and Supply

In California, temperature inversions over Los Angeles make the locals more sensitive to pollution than elsewhere. In addition, the city has a highly car-dependent transport system. The Californian Air Resources Board has legislated stricter emissions levels than those that apply nationally.[13]

California California's within-state electricity generation and total supply are shown in Table 4.5. Coal-fired electricity generation within the state accounts for only 0.5% of total generation. On this statistic, California would appear to be at the low end among states for reliance on coal. But coal-generated electricity imported from elsewhere raises coal-generated electricity's share of total supply to 6.4%. The shares of all sources other than coal in total supply are smaller than the corresponding shares of within-state generation, with the exception of wind-generation.

The composition of in-state generation and state supply indicates a typical motivation for trade. Some states or regions have an excess supply of electricity and many have less stringent environment regulations than California. Therefore, such

[13]By 2009, New Jersey, Massachusetts, Maine, Connecticut, Rhode Island, Pennsylvania, Vermont, New Mexico, Oregon, Washington, Maryland and Florida were in the process of adopting Californian standards (from http://auto.howstuffworks.com/fuel-efficiency/fuel-economy/carb4.htm, accessed 20 August 2016).

states are in a position to export electricity to California. This implies that more stringent regulations in California result in cleaner electricity generation in the state than elsewhere in the United States, but also in the importation of relatively "dirty" electricity from interstate.

4.2.5 The Future

Electricity generation is set to become increasingly decentralized as the costs of renewable generation fall. Advances in battery storage technology will increase the role of renewables and promote decentralization. At the same time, a truly national transmission grid is being planned in the form of the Tres Amigas SuperStation. Announced in October 2009, this project aims to connect the Eastern, Western and Texas Interconnections. The major innovation involved in this project is the use of superconductive high voltage DC transmission lines. Among their advantages, they do not leak power when transmitting over long distances. Tres Amigas is being constructed on a 57 square km site at Clovis, New Mexico.[14] The main impact of Tres Amigas will be to enhance the tradability of electricity between regions. This has the potential to lower capacity requirements for a given national load. The trading impacts of Tres Amigas may make an interesting policy scenario for regional CGE modeling, although the time period of spikes which create the most stress on electricity networks tend to occur over hours rather than months or years, the latter being the usual time interval of dynamic CGE applications.

The truly national grid will reduce the vulnerability of regions with some reliance on renewables. For example, when the wind drops in Texas, wind generation which is relatively important in the state falls, and with it, the amount of power generated. Since Texas does not at this stage have significant interstate electricity trading, calm conditions can cause a power crisis. This usually takes the form of low security users, who pay less per kilowatt-hour than users with more secure supply, having their power cut until the winds return. However, there have been delays in getting the Tres Amigas project off the ground and doubts concerning the willingness of Texas to join the grid (Klump 2014). The Texas Senate Natural Resources and Economic Development Committee is concerned that Tres Amigas will threaten the state's independence from the Federal Energy Regulatory Commission (Argus Media 2015). In the middle of 2015, an inter-connection agreement between Tres Amigas and a key grid partner was terminated (St John 2015). Despite delays, the Tres Amigas has moved forwards, with the expectation that wind-generated electricity will be exported to California in 2017 (Cardillo 2016).

[14]See http://en.wikipedia.org/wiki/Tres_Amigas_SuperStation, accessed 24 March 2015.

4.3 Preparation of the Database and Modifications to the Theory of USAGE-TERM

4.3.1 Database

Given the importance of the electricity grids in the United States to regional development, and the continuing scientific and growing political pressure for a transition to a low carbon economy, a useful step in the preparation of USAGE-TERM is to split the single electricity sector in the model into different generation types, with a separate distribution sector, as outlined in Sect. 4.2.1. Engineers prefer a split into generation, transmission and distribution sectors. This may have some advantage, in so far as the greater the distance electricity is transmitted with existing technologies (i.e., not super-conductive high voltage DC lines), the greater the power leakages. In practice, the engineering preference is probably more relevant to short-time intervals in responding to peak demands. In most economic modeling circumstances, bundling transmission and distribution into a single sector may be sufficient. Modeling scenarios may focus on the impact of carbon taxes or on an emissions trading scheme. Other scenarios might include the regional consequences of a switch from coal to gas in generation or the consequences of policy aimed at increasing the contribution of renewables to total electricity generation. Economic modeling concentrates on industry and regional economic outcomes. Long-term investment plans, structural change in regional economies and national welfare are the main interests of regional economic modelers. On the other hand, engineers may be concerned with managing electricity loads, maintaining networks and generating capacity to cater to peak demands. There is some intersection between the interests of engineers and economists, particularly when it comes to the additional expenses that will be involved in raising the security of an electricity network.

The data provided in Table 4.1 provide a starting point for splitting the national electricity sector in the input–output table into different types of generation. Most of the intermediate splits are relatively straightforward. Coal-generation, gas-generation and petroleum products generation will each use the appropriate fuel input. Renewable and nuclear generation may use little fuel but are designated as more capital-intensive per unit of output than fossil fuel generation. Table 4.4 provides the regional shares of national activity for each sector.

4.3.2 Theory

In specifying the theory of demand for intermediate inputs in USAGE-TERM, there is a variant to the core theory of the ORANI school of models (Dixon et al. 1982). Each industry determines its quantity of intermediate inputs by choosing

$XINI_{c,i,d}$ to minimise

$$\sum_{c} XINI_{c,i,d} * PINI_{c,i,d} \tag{4.1}$$

subject to

$$XINI\_C_{i,d} = CRESH_k\left(XINI_{i,d,k}\right). \tag{4.2}$$

$XINI_{c,i,d}$ is the input to industry i in region d of commodity c;
$PINI_{c,i,d}$ is the cost to industry i in region d of using a unit of input c;
$XINI\_C_{i,d}$ is the total composite intermediate input requirement of industry i in region d

In the percentage-change form, the equations derived from (4.1) and (4.2) that are part of USAGE-TERM are:

$$xini_{c,i,d} = xini\_c_{i,d} - CRESH_{c,i,d} . [pini_{c,i,d} - \sum_k S^{**}{}_{k,i,d} . pini_{k,i,d}] \quad k \in \{COM\} \tag{4.3}$$

where

$xini_{c,i,d}$, $pini_{c,i,d}$ and $xini\_c_{i,d}$ are percentage changes in the variables defined by the corresponding uppercase symbols;

$CRESH_{c,i,d}$ is the CRESH parameter for input c; and

$S^{**}{}_{k,i,d}$ is the CRESH-modified cost share of k in the composite intermediate costs of industry i in region d calculated as:

$$S^{**}{}_{k,i,d} = \frac{PINI_{k,i,d} * XINI_{k,i,d} * CRESH_{k,i,d}}{\sum_j PINI_{j,i,d} * XINI_{j,i,d} * CRESH_{j,i,d}}, \quad j, k \in COM \tag{4.4}$$

Why do we specify CRESH instead of CES substitution possibilities? The reason is that for each industry, the CES form allows only one parameter. We assume that in all industries other than electricity distribution, intermediate inputs are only weakly substitutable. In electricity distribution, we wish different types of electricity generation to be highly substitutable, and are content to assume that all other intermediate inputs to distribution are weakly substitutable.[15]

The three CRESH parameters are:

electricity generation inputs into electricity distribution = 5.0;
all other intermediate inputs into electricity distribution = 0.02; and
all intermediate inputs into all industries other than electricity distribution = 0.1.

[15] In the current version of USAGE-TERM, all generated electricity is sold to electricity distribution. This differs from the convention adopted by the Australian Bureau of Statistics (ABS), which splits generation and distribution in the published input-output table. The ABS convention is that generated electricity is sold to intermediate and final users, accompanied by an electricity distribution margin.

An alternative method would be to split (4.3) into three CES equations corresponding with each of the three CES parameters. However, USAGE-TERM has been devised as a variable aggregation model. Some aggregations might include considerable detail on electricity generation and distribution. Other aggregations might include a single industry "Utilities", which masks specific detail on electricity generation and distribution. In such an aggregation, specific equations covering electricity would be redundant. The path chosen in aggregating USAGE-TERM for policy analysis is to impose appropriate CRESH parameters to cover all aggregations. In the case of a single Utilities sector, the CRESH parameter is set to 0.02.

Some implementations of multi-regional CGE models such as MMRF-Green (Adams and Parmenter 2013) include a separate CES (constant elasticity of substitution) nest for sales of different types of electricity generation to electricity distribution that operate within a given grid. The advantage of the CES form over the CRESH form as in (4.3) is that it is easier to explain intermediate demands in terms of output (proxied by xini_c) and substitution (implied by a specific input price relative to the average price of inputs) effects, due to the relative simplicity of the linearized CES form. The disadvantage of the nested CES approach is that the nested structure may not be ideal if the sectoral aggregation of the model changes. USAGE-TERM has been designed for variable aggregation, whereas the aggregations of MMRF-Green are relatively rigid.

References

Adams P, Parmenter B (2013) Computable general equilibrium modeling of environmental issues in Australia: economic impacts of an emissions trading scheme. In: Dixon P, Jorgenson D (eds) Handbook of computable general equilibrium modeling. North-Holland, Amsterdam, pp 553–657

Argus Media (2015) Texas legislative panel advances grid bill. https://www.argusmedia.com/pages/NewsBody.aspx?id=1013771&menu=yes. Accessed 20 Aug 2016

Cardillo J (2016) Remember that $1.6B energy transmission line? It's quietly moving forward. http://www.bizjournals.com/albuquerque/news/2016/08/03/tres-amigas-transmission-line-quietly-move-forward.html. Accessed 22 Sept 2016

Centers for Disease Control and prevention (2010) The history of malaria, an ancient disease. http://www.cdc.gov/malaria/about/history/#tva. Accessed 20 Aug 2016

Dixon P, Parmenter B, Sutton J, Vincent D (1982) ORANI: a multisectoral model of the Australian economy. Contributions to economic analysis, vol 142. North-Holland, Amsterdam

Edison Tech Center (2013) The history of electrification: the birth of our power grid. http://www.edisontechcenter.org/HistElectPowTrans.html. Accessed 27 May 2013

Klump E (2014) Bid to connect grids needs buy-in from independent Texas. February 21. http://www.eenews.net/stories/1059994882. Accessed 20 Aug 2016

McNichol T (2006) AC/DC: the savage tale of the first standards war. Jossey-Bass, San Francisco
Russell D (1949) The TVA idea. The Foundation for Economic Education, New York
Schmidt J (2011) Guilty or innocent? The saga of Samuel Insull. http://www.wbez.org/blog/john-r-schmidt/2011-10-26/guilty-or-innocent-saga-samuel-insull-93392. Accessed 20 Aug 2016
St John J (2015) Tres Amigas loses key partner for project that would connect regional US grids http://www.greentechmedia.com/articles/read/tres-amigas-loses-key-interconnect-for-grid-connecting-project. Accessed 4 Dec 2015
Tesla N (1888) A new system of alternating current motors and transformers. http://www.pbs.org/tesla/res/res_art02.html. Accessed 20 Aug 2016

Chapter 5
Regional Health Care, Education, International Trade, Other Services and Household Consumption

Glyn Wittwer

Abstract Services account for most economic activity in a developed economy. Health and education are two of the largest expenditure items in private and public consumption. This chapter discusses data sources and data issues concerning these sectors. Regional household consumption data are not available from state-level national accounts data, thereby requiring an indirect approach to estimation.

Keywords Health services · Obamacare · Education · Education exports · Other services · Household consumption

5.1 Introduction

Both health care and education are an important part of a CGE database as they are large expenditure items for households and governments. Since health care and education are at the forefront of policy decisions made in Washington DC and in state governments, some of the policy issues are outlined in this chapter. Policy issues provide some resonance in the preparation of the regional database. As is discussed in Sect. 5.2, health services provision in the United States is more expensive than in other OECD nations. Reforms to the health system may also have equity consequences. Section 5.3 details sources used to estimate regional shares of national health activity.

In education, elementary schooling is usually local, with students attending a school near their family's residence. Secondary schooling may be less local but is usually undertaken in the state of the student's family. College and university education is often undertaken interstate, with the sector becoming increasingly reliant on foreign students. Section 5.4 details regional estimates of national education activity.

G. Wittwer (✉)
Centre of Policy Studies, Victoria University, Melbourne, VIC, Australia
e-mail: glyn.wittwer@vu.edu.au

G. Wittwer (ed.), *Multi-regional Dynamic General Equilibrium Modeling of the U.S. Economy*, Advances in Applied General Equilibrium Modeling,
DOI 10.1007/978-3-319-58866-7_5

International trade is divided into merchandise trade, for which data are readily available by region, and trade in services. Section 5.5 outlines the estimators used to obtain regional shares of national services exports, including education exports.

Aggregate consumption makes up a substantial share of expenditure-side GDP. At present, national accounts data detailing state-level consumption by broad commodity are not available. Section 5.6 outlines the method used to estimate regional shares of national household consumption.

5.2 Health care

The history of health care in the United States is replete with episodes of failure to broaden health care coverage. On occasions when momentum has gathered for reform, concerns that such momentum is tainted with socialism or other impositions on freedom, combined with opposition from groups such as trade unions usually in favor in universal health care, have obstructed the process. Under the New Deal of Franklin Roosevelt's presidency, when the Great Depression might have provided the political conditions for introducing universal health care, other forms of welfare, notably unemployment insurance and old age benefits took precedence (Palmer 1999).

There have been a few victories in public health provision. Congressman Aime Foran proposed to use social security to cover hospital costs for the aged in 1958. Despite the efforts of the American Medical Association (AMA), which up to that point had opposed every effort at reform, widely based support for reforms gathered momentum due to Foran's proposal being centered on the aged. Medicare and Medicaid finally came into being in 1965 under President Johnson, after a series of compromises and concessions (Palmer 1999).

The Consolidated Omnibus Budget Reconciliation Act (COBRA) enacted in 1986 gives workers the right to continue group health insurance when faced with job loss, a reduction in the hours worked or certain other circumstances.[1] Eligible employers are permitted a tax deduction for health insurance costs only if the health insurance plan allows employees and their families to maintain coverage, should a qualifying event such as a job loss arise. The opportunity for a temporary extension of health coverage applies to plans both in the private sector and state and local governments. The act enables employees and their dependents to continue coverage at their own expense following a qualifying event. There are gaps in the coverage. For example, if an employer has gone out of business, COBRA does not apply. Some states have enacted "mini-COBRA" laws to deal with gaps in federal coverage. COBRA did not have direct fiscal implications until the American Recovery and Reinvestment Act of 2009. This included a 65% subsidy to employees for up to

[1] http://www.dol.gov/ebsa/newsroom/fscobra.html accessed 10 October 2016.

nine months (subsequently extended to 15 months) for COBRA-enabled insurance in cases of involuntary termination.[2]

The State Children's Health Insurance Program (known as CHIP), legislated in 1997, covers uninsured families with children earning incomes that are up to a small multiple of the poverty level but too high to qualify for Medicaid.[3] CHIP resulted in a substantial increase in public funding of health insurance coverage. The United States Department of Health and Human Services under the program provides matching funds to states. Gruber and Simon (2008) are concerned that for some families, public provision of health care through Medicaid and CHIP with little or no co-payment is more generous than private insurance. This has the impact of crowding out private health care with a potential efficiency loss. Yet Rimsza et al. (2007) conclude that disenrollment from Medicare/CHIP programs may worsen social outcomes. This is because changes in insurance status result in a shift from health care in relatively inexpensive ambulatory settings to more expensive emergency departments. Gruber and Simon (2008) caution against increasing the percentage of the population with ready access to public health care via limited co-payments. Conversely, Rimsza et al. (2007) believe that reduced public provision would result in false savings, as it may lead to children receiving medical attention at a later stage than otherwise with consequent higher costs.

The economic reason public expenditure on health in developed nations is high is because market failures are rife in health care provision. Diffusion of health technology has the potential to benefit all. Vaccinations provide positive externalities by limiting the spread of disease. The overuse of antibiotics, on the other hand, is a negative externality as it reduces the resistance of bacteria, to the detriment of society. Pandemics provide an extreme version of a negative externality: the 1918 influenza outbreak may have killed as many as 100 million people globally, with war conditions contributing to the spread and hindering development of effective vaccines (Barry 2004). Poor health has an adverse impact on productivity. Not the least of negative externalities is the prevailing negligent attitude of males towards their own health.[4] The problem of adverse selection is widely recognized, with younger, healthier individuals tending not to take up health insurance, thereby raising insurance premiums for those with coverage.

An OECD (2011)briefing compares US health care with that of other nations. Public spending per capita on health is moderately higher than in most other OECD nations. The major difference is in private spending, which is many-fold higher in the United States than elsewhere. Total US expenditure per capita on health in 2011 was $8508, nearly $3000 higher than the next nation, Norway, after adjusting for purchasing power parities. The OECD average was $3339 (OECD 2014).

[2]http://www.irs.gov/uac/COBRA-Health-Insurance-Continuation-Premium-Subsidy accessed 10 October 2016.

[3]https://www.medicaid.gov/chip/eligibility-standards/chip-eligibility-standards.html accessed 10 October 2016.

[4]Northwestern Memorial Hospital (2010) provides an example of a media release on men's health.

The OECD (2011) finds that the United States has fewer physicians, fewer doctor consultations, fewer hospital beds and fewer hospital discharges per capita than the OECD average. The average duration of hospital stays is shorter than elsewhere. Each of these comparisons indicates that health spending in the United States should be lower than elsewhere. It is in interventions that the US health system is more active than elsewhere. There are more MRI units and examinations, and more CT scanners and examinations per capita than in other counties. Elective surgery rates are relatively high. But overall, higher prices rather than higher volumes of medical services are the major cause of relatively high expenditures on health care provision in the United States.

On some health indicators, the United States is worse than the OECD average. For example, in the past 50 years, life expectancy has increased by less than the average OECD increase, moving from being 1.5 years above the OECD average in 1960 to 1.5 years below by 2011 (OECD 2014). The OECD concludes that in terms of health care quality, the US cancer care system is doing well. And the quality of acute care in US hospitals is high. But there is room for improvement in the primary care sector, with hospital admission for asthmas and chronic obstructive pulmonary disease being much higher than in other OECD nations.

Boldrin and Levine (2008, Chapter 9) examine the impact of patents on the global pharmaceutical industry. They report that top pharmaceutical companies spend about twice as much on promotion and advertising as on R&D, and also devote considerable resources to rent-seeking. The authors cite a case of one U.S. based company that has set aside $0.5 billion to cover legal problems arising from fraudulent billing of the government or overcharging Medicaid for drugs. Stiglitz (2006) has suggested that a move away from patents towards prizes could enhance global welfare. George W. Bush succeeded in having prescription drugs included in Medicare in November 2003. Democrats opposed the bill because they wanted Medicare administrators to negotiate prices with pharmaceutical companies (Smith 2016, Chap. 16, footnote iv).

In both the provision of health care and the supply of medical drugs, prices are higher in the United States than elsewhere. Stiglitz (2013) argues that GDP per capita in the U.S. relative to other nations is misleadingly high, because it is inflated by health care prices. According to this argument, when health is re-valued at prices in other countries, the United States falls down the rankings of income per capita. This finding would depend on how GDP per capita is calculated. Inflated rankings on global tables need not occur if the U.S. health expenditure share is appropriately weighted.

On 23rd March 2010, the Patient Protection and Affordable Care Act, known as ObamaCare, became law. The objective of ObamaCare was to broaden health insurance coverage among the U.S. population. As has been the case in other countries such as Australia since the 1990s or earlier, those who choose not to take out health insurance who can afford it pay a penalty tax. Indeed, most Western developed nations other than the United States have had universal health coverage for a number of decades. In addition, ObamaCare aimed to make health insurance more affordable by giving refundable tax credits when household incomes are between 100 and 400%

of the federal poverty line. [5] ObamaCare required health insurers not to bar access to insurance for individuals with pre-existing medical conditions. The list of pre-existing conditions that preclude coverage was whittled away, with the aim of complete removal by 2017. The ObamaCare legislation was drafted on the basis that health services in the nation have operated like a monopolist, restricting supply and keeping prices high to the detriment of many consumers.[6] Significantly, the AMA supported ObamaCare though it opposed some of the details of the act such as the formation of an Independent Payment Advisory Board.[7] (Table 5.1)

The Supreme Court judgment in National Federation of Independent Business v. Sebelius examined the constitutionality of the Medicaid expansion under ObamaCare. Stiglitz (2013, p. xiv) believed that the ruling was likely to leave a significant proportion of the population uncovered by medical insurance, as it gives states the right to opt out of Medicaid expansion without losing funding. The Henry J. Kaiser Family Foundation (2013) maintained a more optimistic interpretation. Thirteen states, including the District of Columbia, have established state-based marketplaces for health insurance, and four states have federally-supported state-based marketplaces. Seven states now have a state-federal partnership marketplace. For the remaining states, the Department of Health and Human Services (HHS) will be responsible for operating a marketplace in that state. Under this arrangement, the department coordinates with state agencies on multiple aspects of the insurance marketplace.

A potential threat in the 27 states with a federally-facilitated marketplace concerned the King v. Burwell case before the Supreme Court in 2015. The plaintiff challenged the legality of health insurance subsidies in these states in which the state does not operate the marketplace under the Affordable Care Act. Had the court ruled that subsidies under the act were invalid, an estimated 12.5 million people would have ceased to be eligible for these subsidies. Many of such people would no longer have been able to afford health insurance. In the event, the court ruled that the relevant act allows for tax credits purchased on any exchange created under the act.[8]

---

[5]Combining a tax penalty/incentive with barring of the practice of denying coverage to persons on health grounds prevents adverse selection, in which individuals are more likely take out insurance as their health deteriorates. With adverse selection comes rising insurance premiums and a decreasing number of participants.

[6]From http://obamacarefacts.com/obamacare-facts, accessed 21 September 2016.

[7]See http://www.ama-assn.org/ama/pub/advocacy/topics/affordable-care-act.page, accessed 21 September 2016.

[8]See http://kff.org/health-reform/issue-brief/are-premium-subsidies-available-in-states-with-a-federally-run-marketplace-a-guide-to-the-supreme-court-argument-in-king-v-burwell/ accessed 11 July 2016. The court ruling is downloadable at http://www.supremecourt.gov/opinions/14pdf/14-114_qol1.pdf, accessed 11 July 2016.

Table 5.1 Health insurance marketplace type by state

Fed-facilitated	Fed-facilitated	State-partnership	State-based	Fed-supported
Alabama	North Carolina	Arkansas	California	Hawaii
Alaska	North Dakota	Delaware	Colorado	Nevada
Arizona	Ohio	Illinois	Connecticut	New Mexico
Florida	Oklahoma	Iowa	DC	Oregon
Georgia	Pennsylvania	Michigan	Idaho	
Indiana	South Carolina	New Hampshire	Kentucky	
Kansas	South Dakota	West Virginia	Maryland	
Louisiana	Tennessee		Massachusetts	
Maine	Texas		Minnesota	
Mississippi	Utah		New York	
Missouri	Virginia		Rhode Island	
Montana	Wisconsin		Vermont	
Nebraska	Wyoming		Washington	
New Jersey				

Fed-facilitated federally-facilitated marketplace in which HHS performs all marketplace functions, *State-partnership* states administer in-person consumer assistance functions and HHS will perform the remaining Marketplace functions, *State-based* state-based Marketplace, in which states are responsible for performing all market place functions, *Fed-supported* In federally-supported state-based marketplaces, states are responsible for performing all marketplace functions, but rely on the federally-facilitated marketplace IT platform
Source http://kff.org/health-reform/state-indicator/state-health-insurance-marketplace-types/. Accessed 10 July 2016

It remains to be seen whether the Affordable Care Act is dismantled substantially under Trump. If so, it may point to ideology being preferred to provision of essential services, and potentially contribute to a worsening of health indicators in the United States relative to other developed economies.

5.2.1 Regional Health Data

Census data on employment are available for health-related sectors. A major challenge is calculating how to apportion each of private and public spending on health within a CGE database. A first step is to work out how public spending enters the input–output table that is the foundation of the CGE database. As is mentioned in Sect. 5.4, Dixon and Rimmer (2002, 2003) used BEA government spending data to create 35 new industries in USAGE. These included two health-related sectors, one concerning expenditure, the other investment. Medicare expenditure in 2009 in the United States was \$502 billion, and Medicaid spending \$373 billion in all categories. The categories as shown in Table 5.2 are Dental Services, Durable Medical Products, Home Health Care, Hospital Care, Nursing Home Care, Other Health, Residential, and Personal Care, Other Professional

Table 5.2 State shares of total Medicare plus Medicaid expenditure

	Dental	Durable medical products	Home health care	Hospital care	Nursing home care	Other health, residental and personal care	Other professional services	Physician and clinical services	Prescription drugs, other non-durables	Total
Alabama	1.5	1.6	1.5	1.3	1.7	1.0	1.4	1.9	1.8	1.5
Alaska	0.6	0.2	0.1	0.2	0.1	0.4	0.2	0.2	0.1	0.2
Arizona	0.6	1.6	1.2	2.6	0.5	0.2	3.2	2.6	1.3	2.0
Arkansas	0.9	1.4	0.6	1.0	1.0	1.0	0.7	1.2	1.1	1.0
California	12.7	10.4	16.4	10.4	9.1	8.6	10.0	12.5	10.7	11.0
Colorado	1.6	2.0	1.0	1.0	1.1	1.0	1.0	1.2	1.0	1.1
Connecticut	1.5	0.8	1.4	1.2	2.5	2.6	1.8	1.2	1.3	1.4
Delaware	0.4	0.2	0.3	0.3	0.4	0.4	0.3	0.3	0.3	0.3
DC	0.4	0.3	0.5	0.3	0.3	0.2	0.1	0.3	0.2	0.3
Florida	2.2	6.8	8.1	6.0	6.7	3.7	7.6	8.6	6.7	6.5
Georgia	1.2	2.5	2.1	2.4	2.0	1.6	1.9	2.5	2.3	2.3
Hawaii	1.6	0.2	0.1	0.3	0.3	0.2	0.4	0.5	0.4	0.3
Idaho	0.2	0.5	0.3	0.3	0.3	0.6	0.6	0.4	0.4	0.4
Illinois	1.9	4.1	2.7	4.7	4.1	3.6	3.0	3.4	4.0	4.0
Indiana	3.7	2.3	1.3	1.9	2.5	1.6	1.2	1.9	1.9	1.9
Iowa	0.9	0.9	0.5	0.9	0.6	1.3	1.7	0.7	1.0	0.9
Kansas	0.8	0.7	0.5	0.8	0.6	1.1	0.7	0.7	0.9	0.8
Kentucky	1.4	2.0	0.9	1.6	1.5	1.4	1.2	1.5	1.7	1.5
Louisiana	1.6	2.0	2.0	1.8	1.3	1.7	1.0	1.6	2.2	1.7
Maine	0.4	0.5	0.3	0.6	0.5	1.3	0.6	0.4	0.5	0.6
Maryland	0.5	1.6	0.9	2.0	2.2	1.7	1.2	1.9	1.5	1.8
Massachusetts	5.7	2.3	3.5	2.8	3.5	3.5	2.2	2.1	2.1	2.8

(continued)

Table 5.2 (continued)

	Dental	Durable medical products	Home health care	Hospital care	Nursing home care	Other health, residental and personal care	Other professional services	Physician and clinical services	Prescription drugs, other non-durables	Total
Michigan	4.4	2.8	4.2	3.7	3.4	1.1	2.9	3.6	2.7	3.3
Minnesota	1.0	1.8	2.1	1.5	1.5	2.8	3.6	1.2	1.7	1.7
Mississippi	0.1	1.0	1.0	1.2	1.0	1.1	0.6	1.0	1.2	1.1
Missouri	0.4	2.3	1.7	2.4	1.8	1.7	1.5	1.7	2.3	2.1
Montana	0.2	0.5	0.2	0.3	0.1	0.3	0.3	0.2	0.3	0.3
Nebraska	0.5	0.7	0.2	0.5	0.5	0.6	0.5	0.5	0.6	0.5
Nevada	0.4	1.0	0.6	0.6	0.5	0.3	0.9	0.7	0.6	0.6
New Hampshire	0.3	0.4	0.2	0.4	0.6	0.5	0.4	0.3	0.3	0.4
New Jersey	0.6	1.9	2.2	2.9	4.4	2.8	2.9	3.2	3.1	3.0
New Mexico	0.6	0.7	0.5	0.8	0.2	0.6	1.1	0.6	0.5	0.7
New York	6.5	5.9	11.8	9.5	11.5	16.0	8.2	7.4	10.6	10.0
North Carolina	4.9	4.5	2.5	2.8	2.6	4.1	2.2	3.1	3.5	3.0
North Dakota	0.1	0.1	0.0	0.2	0.1	0.3	0.2	0.1	0.2	0.2
Ohio	1.7	4.0	3.4	4.0	5.4	4.1	5.0	3.6	3.6	4.0
Oklahoma	1.9	1.6	1.3	1.2	0.9	1.2	0.8	1.3	1.3	1.2
Oregon	0.1	1.1	0.6	1.0	0.7	1.9	1.4	1.2	1.0	1.0
Pennsylvania	5.4	3.9	3.1	4.7	6.6	4.8	4.5	4.7	5.5	4.8
Rhode Island	0.5	0.3	0.3	0.4	0.6	0.8	0.3	0.3	0.4	0.4
South Carolina	2.2	1.9	1.0	1.6	1.2	1.2	1.2	1.7	1.4	1.5
South Dakota	0.2	0.3	0.1	0.2	0.2	0.3	0.2	0.2	0.2	0.2

(continued)

Table 5.2 (continued)

	Dental	Durable medical products	Home health care	Hospital care	Nursing home care	Other health, residental and personal care	Other professional services	Physician and clinical services	Prescription drugs, other non-durables	Total
Tennessee	2.4	2.4	1.5	2.0	2.0	2.0	1.8	2.3	2.5	2.1
Texas	14.8	8.1	10.1	6.7	5.2	5.7	10.8	6.6	6.3	6.8
Utah	0.6	0.7	0.5	0.4	0.4	0.4	0.4	0.6	0.5	0.5
Vermont	0.8	0.2	0.2	0.3	0.2	0.1	0.4	0.3	0.2	0.2
Virginia	1.6	2.8	1.1	1.8	1.8	2.7	1.5	1.9	1.9	1.9
Washington	2.8	2.0	1.5	1.7	1.4	1.9	1.6	1.8	1.7	1.7
West Virginia	0.8	0.8	0.5	0.7	0.7	0.8	0.6	0.7	1.0	0.7
Wisconsin	1.8	1.3	1.8	1.8	2.0	1.6	2.3	1.7	1.7	1.8
Wyoming	0.2	0.2	0.0	0.2	0.1	0.2	0.1	0.1	0.1	0.1
Total public $bn 2009	7436	11760	54126	356.5	72.9	69.0	18.2	149.3	77.6	816.9
Total all sources $bn 2009	102.2	34.9	68.2	759.1	137.0	122.6	66.8	505.8	293.1	2089.8[a]
Public as % of total	7.3	33.7	79.3	47.0	53.3	56.3	27.2	29.5	26.5	39.1

[a] Additional costs include Govt Administration and Net Cost of Health Insurance $163.0 bn, Public Health Activities $77.2 bn and Investment $156.2 bn

Source Centers for Medicare & Medicaid Services (2012)

Services, Personal Health Care, Physician and Clinical Services, and Prescription Drugs and Other Non-durable Medical Products.

Aggregate health spending, both public and private, totaled $2487 billion in 2009. The following sectors are the best candidates as health-related in the CGE database:

- PharmaMeds;
- HomeHlthSvc;
- MedOffices;
- AmbHlthSvce;
- Hospitals;
- NursingFcil;
- InsCarriers; and
- OthSLGEnt.

The entire supply of these sectors within the input–output table, from domestic and imported sources, aligns with the total health expenditure recorded in Centers for Medicare & Medicaid Services (2011) data. The GDP attributed to the health-related sectors in 2009 in the national accounts is around $1550 billion inclusive of insurance carriers (which also includes non-health forms of insurance) but excluding state and local government health expenditures.[9] We could surmise that some employer-provided group health coverage appears in the intermediate input costs of other industries within the input–output table, although this should appear in the value-added of the various health-related sectors.

Medicare caters for people of 65 years or more of age, plus those under 65 with certain disabilities. People of all ages suffering permanent kidney failure requiring dialysis or a transplant are also covered.[10] Medicaid under the Affordable Care Act was expanded to include a larger proportion of low income citizens.[11] Differences between the coverage of Medicare and Medicaid would matter if the database included a disaggregation of households into income or age groups. The two sources of medical funding can be aggregated for the task of compiling regional shares.

Table 5.2 shows public health spending shares for each category. At the national level, public funding is smallest as a proportion of the total for dental services, covering little more than 7% of the total. Public spending is largest in dollar terms on the Personal Health Care and largest in proportional terms for Home Health Care. Total health spending by state varies much less than public health spending. After examining the CGE database, the best use that we can make of state-level data on Medicare and Medicaid is to use the sum of aggregate expenditures of both to

---

[9]Source http://www.bea.gov/industry/gdpbyind_data.htm accessed 11 July 2016.

[10]http://www.cms.gov/Medicare/Medicare-General-Information/MedicareGenInfo/index.html, accessed 9 September 2016.

[11]http://www.medicaid.gov/AffordableCareAct/Affordable-Care-Act.html, accessed 9 September 2016.

apportion regional shares to the industries "*SLGOther*" (Other State and Local Government) and "*NonDefG*" (Non-Defense Government). These two sectors added together align reasonably with combined Medicare and Medicaid expenditures. In the bottom-up master database, population shares are used to allocate state shares to sub-state regions where applicable.

To undertake CGE modelling of health scenarios would require a close look at the CGE database. A first step might be to use the occupational detail available from the Bureau of Labor Statistics to split health into various occupation types (see http://www.bls.gov/oes/current/oes_nat.htm). Given that ObamaCare involved a combination of income tax breaks for households and some additional commitments to public spending, a modelling exercise may be enhanced further by the addition of some fiscal detail to the model. This would improve the representation of households in each region, and bring into focus disparities between regions. An alternative approach would be to divide households into different income levels in each region. This would enable us to examine disparities between income groups. The poor in the United States have less access to health care than the poor in other OECD nations. This raises the potential value of developing multiple households as a feature in USAGE-TERM.

An improved representation of health services within USAGE-TERM would require a substantial research effort. The best chance of such model development will arise from a funded project. While a multi-regional CGE model is much more than a blank canvas, embodying data from many sources, there is always scope for further model developments. Service sectors provide particular challenges for CGE modelers, as they entail much more than accounting for physical quantities, as may be sufficient in the case of primary agricultural or mineral products. The issue of value-for-money in US health services delivery, relative to that of other OECD nations, could provide a motivation for scenario development.

5.3 Education

Downloadable data of regional expenditures on public elementary and secondary education align well with total output of the industry "*SLGEduc*" (State and Local Government Education) in the national CGE database.[12] This alignment gives us confidence to use these data as the basis for regional shares. They supplement census data, used to estimate regional shares of national employment for *EleSecSchool* (Elementary and secondary schools), *Colleges* and *OtherEducSv* (Other Education Services). These three sectors are NAICS industries, used in the development of an earlier national USAGE database (Dixon and Rimmer 2003; Dixon et al. 2007).

[12]https://nces.ed.gov/pubs2013/expenditures/tables/table_01.asp accessed 21 September 2016.

In using census employment data to estimate regional shares of state employment or activity, one must deal with missing data. In the case of *EleSecSchool*, a sensible assumption in the absence of data is that the county share of state activity is equal to the population share. This assumption recognizes that elementary schooling is a local activity which will be non-zero in virtually all counties.

Major changes have occurred in the university segment of education over the past decade or so. In the past, most Americans seeking tertiary education have attended publicly-financed state universities with modest fees. In the wake of financial pressures including the GFC, state governments have slashed spending on universities. This segment of education is regarded as more able to cope with expenditure cuts than elementary and secondary schooling, due to its tuition revenue stream. A growing number of state universities now receive less than 7% of their funding from state governments. In response to financial pressures, courses in state universities have been cut. Tuition fees have soared, while out-of-state enrolments and foreign student enrolments have grown (Mincer 2012).

From the perspective of students, class sizes have increased. Student debts upon graduation have risen. From the perspective of academic staff, full-time positions have shrunk, salaries have shriveled and concerns among academics about the quality of education being provided have grown. Some state universities, such as the University of Michigan, receive almost as much revenue from earnings on endowments as from state government support. In the space of two decades, state funding of the University of New Hampshire fell from 32% of total revenue to 7% (Mincer 2012). The depreciation of the US dollar after the GFC enhanced the competitiveness of the U.S. university sector against other countries. Following the recovery of the U.S. dollar, universities, having become increasing reliant on foreign students, will hope that growing incomes in countries such as China, India and Indonesia will more than outweigh the negative impact of an appreciating dollar on foreign demand in the sector. Concerning domestic enrollees, Dynarksi (2015) raises concerns about the risk of default on student debt.

5.3.1 Education Exports

The industry *ExpEdu* concerns mainly tertiary education exports. The existing shares are based on estimates of *CollegeUni* and *SLCEPubHiEd* activities (two industries covered by *Colleges* and *OtherEducSv* in the NAICS classification) compiled for the top-down module in an earlier version of the national USAGE model (Dixon and Rimmer 2003; Dixon et al. 2007). In USAGE-TERM, the industry *SLGEduc* covers all levels of education as discussed in Sect. 5.3. The correlation coefficient for regional shares of *SLGEduc* and *ExpEdu* is 0.82, indicating similarity between the estimates despite being gathered at different times from different sources. The *CollegeUni* and *SLCEPubHiEd* activities in USAGE were based on IMPLAN data from around a decade earlier than the NCES data (see footnote 12) used to estimate *SLGEduc* shares.

5.4 Attribution of Public Spending in U.S. Input–output Data

The government spending column in BEA U.S. input–output tables confines such spending to four commodities, namely education (*SLGEduc*), other (*SLGOther*), national defense (*NatlDefG*) and non-defense government spending (*NonDefG*).[13] This means that there is no information in the tables on direct government spending on civil and social order, hospitals, ambulatory health services or medical offices, each of which is assigned a sector in the master database.

Digging deeper into the national CGE database does little to unravel the linkages. For example, general government industries (*GenGovInd*) sell entirely to *SLGEduc* and *SLGOther*. Sales of *NonDefG* are mainly to *GenGovInd* (62% of total sales), with *Colleges* (6.4% of total sales) a distant second.

There are two paths by which we could enhance government spending detail in the database. One is to modify the vector of government spending by moving, for example, *GenGovInd* spending to less abstract activities, such as health. Dixon and Rimmer (2002) and Dixon et al. (2013) worked through 35 columns of government expenditures in BEA tables and thereby added 35 government industries and commodities to the USAGE database. This method was not repeated in the USAGE database from which the present version of USAGE-TERM was generated.

Another possible path is to devise a fiscal extension that deals with transfers between agents without altering the core input–output database. Chapters 7 and 8 expand on this.

5.5 International Trade

The theory of USAGE-TERM is that international merchandise exports originating from a state/county or international merchandise imports used in a state/county go through a port, be it in the county/state of origin/use or otherwise. Imports to Nevada, for example, pass through interstate ports first. An international import used in Nevada appears in the USAGE-TERM TRADE matrix as an international import to a port, which is sold from the port to Nevada.

The website www.usatradeonline.gov contains details of international merchandise trade by port website in recent months mean that more detailed data are freely downloadable. The data are mapped to provide estimates of commodity trade shares by county for merchandise input–output sectors within USAGE-TERM.

[13]See https://www.bea.gov/industry/io_annual.htm (accessed 25 January 2017).

5.5.1 Services Exports

Exports of services are a weak point in national input–output databases. Unlike for merchandise exports, comprehensive data collections are not readily available. As the services component of national economic activity grows, so too does the share of service exports in total exports. The following describes essentially makeshift estimates of regional contributions to national service exports. Better estimates may emerge with our growing familiarity of available data sources.

OthNonRes covers the purchases by foreigners working in the United States for embassies and international organizations, plus purchases by nationals from Mexico and the Caribbean islands in the U.S. The relative smallness of *OthNonRes* has meant that as yet, little effort has gone into improving regional estimates for the sector. At present, these estimates are based on regional shares of national disposable income. This calculation does not allow, for example, for the overrepresentation of foreigners in embassies in the District of Columbia.

5.6 Regional Household Expenditure Shares

The detailed national accounts data at the state level provided by the Bureau of Economic Analysis do not provide expenditure-side data. Consequently, another estimator is required. Here the census employment data and national accounts data on the income side might be helpful, in the form of the retail trade sector. We might choose to use retail trade shares as a proxy for household consumption shares. But this is far from a perfect estimator as the commodity composition of consumption will vary widely between states, driven by differences in climate, taxes and tastes. Retail trade shares are also an imperfect estimator of aggregate consumption. This is because the retail margins share of total spending on a given commodity will vary between commodities. Some items, such as alcohol and tobacco, may incur high indirect taxes that lower the retail margin share of total spending. In the case of services, the retail margin share of total spending may be negligible or zero. In summary, the retail margin share may not be the best estimator of regional household spending shares.

The consumption function in USAGE-TERM links household consumption to labor earnings. It follows that a better estimator of regional household consumption shares might be regional labor earnings shares. All master databases of USAGE-TERM have been revised to reflect household shares inferred from labor earnings. Congressional district data provide per capita incomes.[14] These data may be useful if further model development leads to devising multiple households in each district based on income levels. Congressional district data also provide information on various benefits and other social indicators such as unemployment levels.

[14]See http://www2.census.gov/acs2011_1yr/CD113/ accessed 27 January 2017.

References

Boldrin J, Levine K (2008) Against intellectual monopoly. Cambridge University Press, New York

Barry J (2004) The great influenza: the epic story of the deadliest plague in history. Penguin Books, New York

Centers for Medicare & Medicaid Services (2011) Health expenditures by state of residence. http://www.cms.gov/NationalHealthExpendData/downloads/resident-state-estimates.zip. Accessed 15 July 2016

Dixon P, Rimmer M, Tsigas M (2007) Regionalizing results from a detailed CGE model: macro, industry and state effects in the U.S. of removing major tariffs and quotas. Pap Reg Sci 86:31–55

Dixon P, Rimmer M (2002) USAGE-ITC: creating a 1992 benchmark input–output database, further developments. Centre of Policy Studies Mimeo. http://www.copsmodels.com/archivep.htm TPGW0157. Accessed 15 July 2016

Dixon P, Rimmer M (2003) Regional database for USAGE. Centre of Policy Studies Mimeo. http://www.copsmodels.com/archivep.htm TPGW0157. Accessed 15 July 2016

Dixon P, Koopman R, Rimmer M (2013) The MONASH style of computable general equilibrium modeling: a farmework for practical policy analysis. In: Dixon P, Jorgenson D (eds) Handbook of computable general equilibrium modeling. North-Holland, Amsterdam, pp 23–103

Dynarksi, S (2015) We're frighteningly in the dark about student debt. New York Times, March 20. http://www.nytimes.com/2015/03/22/upshot/were-frighteningly-in-the-dark-about-student-debt.html?_r=0&abt=0002&abg=0. Accessed 25 Nov 2016

Gruber J, Simon K (2008) Crowd-out 10 years later: have recent public insurance expansions crowded out private health insurance? J Health Econ 27:201–217

Henry J, Kaiser Family Foundation (2013) Establishing health insurance marketplaces: an overview of state effort. http://kff.org/health-reform/issue-brief/establishing-health-insurance-exchanges-an-overview-of/. Accessed 8 Dec 2016

Mincer J (2012) U.S. recession's other victim: public universities. July 19. http://www.reuters.com/article/us-funding-state-idUSBRE86I04V20120719. Accessed 8 Dec 2016

Northwestern Memorial Hospital (2010) Men's dismissive attitude toward own health can prove dangerous. http://www.nmh.org/nm/malehealth. Accessed 5 July 2013

OECD (2011) Why is health spending in the US so high? http://www.oecd.org/unitedstates/49084355.pdf. Accessed 8 Dec 2016

OECD (2014) How does the United States compare. http://www.oecd.org/unitedstates/Briefing-Note-USA-2014.pdf. Accessed 8 Dec 2016

Palmer K (1999) A brief history: universal health care efforts in the US. http://www.pnhp.org/facts/a-brief-history-universal-health-care-efforts-in-the-us. Accessed 8 Dec 2016

Rimsza M, Butler R, Johnson W (2007) Impact of medicaid disenrollment on health care use and cost. Pediatrics 119(5):e1026–e1032

Smith JE (2016) Bush. Simon & Schuster, New York

Stiglitz J (2006) Scrooge and intellectual property rights. BMJ 333:1279

Stiglitz J (2013) The price of inequality. Allen Lane, London

Chapter 6
Tourism and Transport in a CGE Model and an Illustrative Application

Glyn Wittwer

Abstract Tourism is a relatively labor-intensive sector. Official input-output tables rarely depict tourism in detail. The national USAGE model includes new industries to depict domestic tourism, tourism exports and foreign holidays. In addition, both air transport and water transport are split into two so as to improve representation of these activities in the economy. These modifications have been carried over to USAGE-TERM.

Keywords Tourism · Air transport · Water transport · Margins

6.1 Introduction

Fluctuations in economic activity are often felt acutely in tourism sectors. Regional centers heavily reliant on tourism are sensitive to civil disruptions that raise fear among travelers or economic downturns that discourage consumer spending. From a national accounts perspective, tourism activity is embedded with non-tourism activity in intermediate and final usage columns of available tables. Dixon and Rimmer (2002, 2003) used ancillary data based on BEA tourism satellite accounts (see http://www.bea.gov/industry/tourism_data.htm) to modify the USAGE CGE database in order to enhance the depiction of tourism. Recent BEA satellite accounts provide more detail on the split between tourism and non-tourism activities than earlier accounts.

Air transport is a substantial expenditure share in tourism activity. Modifications to air transport enable the modeler to distinguish between domestic travelers and foreign travelers within the US, and citizens traveling abroad. In addition, water

The original version of this chapter was revised: In Section 6.2.3, the incorrect explanatory text of the equations has been corrected by the author. An erratum to this chapter can be found at https://doi.org/10.1007/978-3-319-58866-7_13

G. Wittwer (✉)
Centre of Policy Studies, Victoria University, Melbourne, VIC, Australia
e-mail: glyn.wittwer@vu.edu.au

G. Wittwer (ed.), *Multi-regional Dynamic General Equilibrium Modeling of the U.S. Economy*, Advances in Applied General Equilibrium Modeling, DOI 10.1007/978-3-319-58866-7_6

transport has been split into two, so as to separate margins and non-margins activities within U.S. borders and beyond, thereby following four decades of tradition in the ORANI school of CGE modeling in which margins activities are separated from non-margins activity.

6.2 Tourism at Home and Abroad

6.2.1 Distinguishing (Domestic) Holiday, Foreign Holiday and Export Tourism

In order to represent tourism adequately within a CGE model, we need to modify available input–output data. Dixon and Rimmer (2002) devised a method to distinguish between different forms of tourism in the USAGE database. Some forms of tourism are relatively labor-intensive, and may provide a substantial stimulus to local economies. A similar employment impact on the US economy will not arise from holidays taken by Americans abroad. This is because US citizens taking holidays in other nations have an expenditure pattern that differs markedly from that of domestic tourists. Domestic air carriers account for the only domestic input into foreign holidays. Expenditure on non-competing imports accounts for almost 70% of total expenditure on foreign holidays. Foreign air carriers and other transport modes account for just over one-fifth of total expenditure on foreign holidays.

The BEA input–output table embeds spending on tourism by domestic residents in household consumption and spending by foreigners in exports, so that direct shocks to tourism activity are not possible without substantial modifications. The objective of database modifications is to capture the commodity composition of different forms of tourism, thereby enabling direct demand shocks to be ascribed to different forms of tourism. The expenditure patterns of domestic and foreign tourists within USA differ. For example, foreign tourists spend a larger proportion of total holiday expenditure on arts and recreation than domestic tourists. They also use foreign air carriers more for transport than domestic tourists.

Moreover, turning to the regional dimension, US citizens follow a different regional pattern for holidays within USA than foreigners. Los Vegas is a popular tourism destination for US citizens, much less so for foreigners. Hawaii is a popular tourism destination for foreigners, but less so for Americans.[1] This difference in the regional pattern of tourism between home citizens and foreigners provides one motivation for distinguishing between Holidays and Tourism Exports. More recent data indicate an increase in international tourism into Nevada (NTTO 2015).

Table 6.1 outlines the industry composition of Holiday, Foreign Holiday and Tourism Exports, as devised by Dixon and Rimmer (2002). International airfares in

[1]According to map.google.com, the flight time from Tokyo to Honolulu is 2 h less than that from New York to Honolulu.

Table 6.1 Tourism industries devised in USAGE model

		Holiday (1)	Foreign Holidays (2)	Exports of Tourism (3)
1	International airfares: US sourced		C	F
2	International airfares: imported		D	G
3	Domestic airfares	A		H
4	Other purchases within US	B		I
5	Other purchases in other countries		E	
6	Total industry output	H (q) = A + B	FH (q) = C + D + E	XT (q) = F + G + H + I
7	Tourism expenditure of US households	H(q) + FH(q)		
8	Tourism expenditure in US by non-residents			=XT(q) − G

Source Dixon and Rimmer, Table 14.1 (2002)

column (3), row 1 are the US exports of air transport from BEA's input–output table. Household consumption of Holiday plus Foreign Holiday of Air Transport is A + D. This must be smaller than total domestic plus imported consumption of air transport in the input–output table, with the difference being non-tourism household expenditure on air transport. Item E for Foreign Holiday is expenditure during travel by US residents abroad. It is assigned to non-competing imports in the USAGE and USAGE-TERM databases.

6.2.2 *The Holiday Industry*

The Holiday sector's output in 2005 was \$230 billion, a large enough sector to warrant serious attention. Dixon and Rimmer (2003) devised an estimator for regional Holiday shares by starting with the Hotels sector. They used the assumption that regional shares of Holiday industry activity are the same as the Hotel input to the Holiday industry. To estimate the state distribution of Hotels input to Holiday, they started with:

$$\begin{aligned} X0(''\text{Hotels}'', r) = {} & D1(''\text{Hotels}'', r) + D2(''\text{Hotels}'', r) + D3(''\text{Hotels}'', r) + D4(''\text{Hotels}'', r) \\ & + D5(''\text{Hotels}'', r) + D(''\text{Hotels},'' \text{Holiday}'', r) \end{aligned} \tag{6.1}$$

where

X0("Hotels",r)	is Hotels output in state r;
D1("Hotels",r)	is business (intermediate) demand for hotel services from state r (excluding hotel inputs to Holiday and ExpTour);
D2("Hotels",r)	is investment demand for hotels services from state r (= 0);
D3("Hotels",r)	is household demand for hotels services from state r;
D4("Hotels",r)	is foreign tourism demand for hotels services from state r;
D5("Hotels",r)	is government demand for hotels services from state r (= 0, as government demands are intermediate inputs into government industries); and
D("Hotels","Holiday",r)	is demand for hotel services from state r by the Holiday industry

Since D2 and D5 have zero demands, D3 is estimated from regional/state incomes and D4 uses the estimates for ExpTour, the only unknowns on the RHS of (8.1) are D1 and D. We now refer to this residual as Bus&Hol("Hotels",r) where

$$\text{Bus\&Hol}(\text{``Hotels''},\text{r}) = \text{D1}(\text{``Hotels''},\text{r}) + \text{D}(\text{``Hotels''},\text{``Holiday''},\text{r}). \quad (6.2)$$

Dixon and Rimmer calculated the holiday part of Bus&Hol("Hotels",r) as:

$$\begin{aligned}\text{D}(\text{``Hotels''},\text{``Holiday''},\text{r}) = {} & \text{Bus\&Hol}(\text{``Hotels''},\text{r}) * \text{Est\_D}(\text{``Hotels''},\text{``Holiday''},\text{r}) \\ & /[\text{Est\_D1}(\text{``Hotels''},\text{r}) + \text{Est\_D}(\text{``Hotels''},\text{``Holiday''},\text{r})]\end{aligned} \quad (6.3)$$

In practice, residuals provide unsatisfactory estimates as they may imply negative values that are not permissible. In (8.3), Est_D("Hotels","Holiday",r) is an estimate of D("Hotels","Holiday",r), calculated as:

$$\begin{aligned}\text{Est\_D}(\text{``Hotels''},\text{``Holiday''},\text{r}) = {} & \text{BAS1}(\text{``Hotels''},\text{``dom''},\text{``Holiday''}) \\ & * \text{SH\_R}(\text{r},\text{``ExpTour''})\end{aligned} \quad (6.4)$$

and Est_D1("Hotels",r) is an estimate of D1("Hotels",r) computed as:

$$\text{Est\_D1}(\text{``Hotels''},\text{r}) = \sum_{\text{s}} \alpha(\text{r,s}) * \sum_{\substack{\text{j}\neq\text{Holiday} \\ \text{j}\neq\text{ExpTour}}} \text{BAS1}(\text{``Hotel''},\text{``dom''},\text{j}) * \text{SH\_R}(\text{s,j}) \quad (6.5)$$

In (6.4) and (6.5), SH_R(s,j) is the state/regional share in the output of industry j, calculated for most industries from various sources (see Table 6.1). In (6.5), α(r,s) is the share of business demand for hotels in region s met by hotels in region r. These shares are set as

$$\alpha\,(\mathrm{r},\mathrm{s}) = 0.5 \quad \text{if } \mathrm{r} = \mathrm{s}$$

$$\alpha(\mathrm{r},\mathrm{s}) = \mathrm{SH\_R}(\mathrm{r}, \text{``Hotels''}) * \beta(\mathrm{s}) \quad \text{if } \mathrm{r} \neq \mathrm{s}$$

where $\beta(s)$ normalizes $\alpha(r,s)$ so that $\sum_r \alpha(r,s) = 1$.

Equation (6.4) imposes the same state/regional profile on domestic tourism demand for hotels as applies to foreign tourism demand for hotels. Under (6.5), Dixon and Rimmer (2003) assumed that 50% of business demand for hotels in state/region s is satisfied by hotels in state/region s, with the remainder of business demand in each state/region being satisfied by other states/regions in proportion to their output of hotels.

The regional distribution of *FgnHol* (foreign holidays) follows the distribution of disposable income.

6.2.3 Tourism Exports and Regional Demand Shifts

In preparing the national CGE database, Dixon and Rimmer (2002) used BEA's Tourism Satellite Accounts to reallocate foreign tourist expenditures from the household expenditure to Export Tourism. OTTI (2000) produced a table of expenditures by foreign tourists across each state, used to provide regional estimates for *ExpTour* (Export Tourism). More recent data are available from NTTO (2015).

Regional scenarios concerning tourism may involve examining export demand shifts in two different ways. The first is an increase in regional demand for tourism exports that occurs at the expense of other tourist destinations, with no net increase in national export demand. The second is an increase in demand for tourism exports in a region that results in an increase in export demand at the national level. To examine how to ascribe shocks, we look at each of the national and regional export demand equations. The national equation in percentage change terms is:

$$x_{e,c} - f_{e,c} = \gamma_c \cdot (p_{e,c} - \phi), \tag{6.6}$$

where $x_{e,c}$ is the export quantity of commodity c demanded, $f_{e,c}$ is an export demand shifter, γ_c is the export demand elasticity (a negative number) and ϕ the nominal exchange rate.

The regional demands for international exports form a CES nest:

$$x_{e,cd} - a_{e,cd} = x_{e,c} - \sigma_c \cdot (p_{e,cd} + a_{e,cd} - p_{e,c}), \tag{6.7}$$

where $x_{e,cd}$ is the export quantity of commodity c demanded in region d, σ_c a CES parameter and $a_{e,cd}$ a foreign demand regional taste change shifter. The national price is an add-up of effective regional prices:

$$p_{e,c} = \sum_d S_{e,cd} \cdot (p_{e,cd} + a_{e,cd}), \tag{6.8}$$

where $S_{e,cd}$ is the value share of national exports of commodity c in region d.

The next problem concerns regional export demand shifts. An increase in export demand in region d of 20% cannot be imposed by a shock of 20% to $a_{e,cd}$ due to substitutability. That is, the regional taste shifter is part of the CES component of Eq. (8.7). We can ascribe targeted demand shifts by adding another equation:

$$t_{e,cd} = a_{e,cd} - \sigma_c \cdot (a_{e,cd} - a_{e,c}), \tag{6.9}$$

where $t_{e,cd}$ is the regional demand shifter, and $a_{e,c}$ is calculated as

$$a_{e,c} = \sum_d S_{e,cd} \cdot a_{e,cd}. \tag{6.10}$$

In the case of a demand twist towards one region at the expense of others, we may wish to ensure no change in international tourism demand overall:

$$\sum_d S_{e,cd} \cdot t_{e,cd} = 0. \tag{6.11}$$

To enforce (6.11), we add:

$$a_{e,cd} = f_{e,cd} + f_{e,c} \tag{6.12}$$

Next, we detail the closure swaps. In order to ascribe a demand shock to commodity c (tourism exports in the present context) in region d, its element of $t_{e,cd}$, must be exogenous. The taste shift $a_{e,cd}$ is made endogenous for all d. In the regions not shocked directly, this is achieved by making $f_{e,cd}$ exogenous. By making $f_{e,c}$ endogenous and $a_{e,c}$ exogenous, we ensure that (6.11) holds.

If we wish to impose a regional tourism export demand shock in region d of the first type above, that is, at the expense of export demands to other regions, we can do so by shocking $t_{e,cd}$ in region d and making the closure swaps described.

The second type of shock concerns an increase in international tourism demand in a particular region that is not at the expense of other regions. We can implement the shocks using the closure described above. In addition to a shock to $f_{e,cd}$ as before, from (6.6), we can ascribe an export demand shift at the national level using $f_{e,c}$. Consider an example of region-specific export demand shift of 10%. If the share of national exports in that region is 15%, an appropriate shift at the national level to $f_{e,c}$ is 1.5%.

6.2.4 The Splits of Air Transport and Water Transport

One of the early tasks in the IMPACT project which started in the 1975 in Australia was to separate margins activity from the good being transacted. This ensures that the supplies of the good are distinguished from the margins supplies (Parmenter 1976, pp 20–29). Consider a halving of the export price of wheat due to a glut in the global market. Without margins, we might assume that producer price also halves. But if margins comprise 30% of the *fob* price of wheat, as may be the case in a relatively remote farming region, then the producer price is 70% of the *fob* price. If the price of margins is fixed, the producer price will fall to 20% of the original *fob* price, or a fall of 71.4% in the producer (farm gate) price.

Campaigning by researchers within the IMPACT project, which later morphed into the Centre of Policy Studies, has resulted in the Australian Bureau of Statistics (ABS) producing separate matrices of margins transactions ever since. Other downloadable tables include commodity outputs by industry (the *MAKE* matrix), inputs to users at basic prices, plus tables of various indirect taxes, subsidies, import usage and import duties.[2] The ABS tables are close to a CGE-ready format.

Input–output tables produced by the statistical agencies of other countries do not present as much detail on the separation of basic values and different types of margins and indirect taxes. In the US case, the BEA provides input–output details for around 400 industries, and presents data using both producer prices and purchasers' prices. In response to tables presented in this form, a CGE practitioner who wishes to follow the ORANI style of separating margins activity from direct activity needs to move at least some of the input–output usage of a margin commodity into a margin activity.

[2]The ABS input–output tables and accompanying data are downloadable from http://www.abs.gov.au/AUSSTATS/abs@.nsf/DetailsPage/5209.0.55.0012013-14?OpenDocument. Accessed 19 August 2016. Tables 23–34 from this site link separate margins activities to direct transactions.

In dealing with the existing BEA tables and in order to improve the depiction of economic activity in the national USAGE model, Dixon and Rimmer (2002) split both air transport and water transport into two. *AirTrans* produces air transport services within USA, whereas *AirInt* refers to such services produced outside of the nation. Similarly, *WaterTrans* produces services within USA and *WaterInt* refers to shipping elsewhere. The intent in this chapter is not to recount the laborious task undertaken by Dixon and Rimmer as they interacted with BEA staff in the early years of USAGE model development. Rather, it is to summarize salient features of the split, starting with Table 6.2, which presents values in the updated USAGE-TERM database.

The Dixon–Rimmer split removes import competition from *AirTrans*, thereby reallocating air transport usage for foreign holidays entirely to *AirInt*. The split also assigns all air transport usage in domestic holidays to *AirTrans*. Air transport usage by foreign students in exports of education is assigned to *AirInt*.

The initial BEA database assigns intermediate inputs of air transport across industries. A substantial share is reallocated from direct industry inputs to margins usage for both domestic and imported inputs. Non-competing imported inputs are allocated almost entirely to *AirInt*.

A key point concerning water transport is that it is a very important margin activity for the transportation of goods, most notably in the Mississippi Basin. Therefore, a substantial share of direct inputs of water transport, as presented in BEA tables, is reallocated as a margin on domestic and imported merchandise inputs (Table 6.3).

US ships move cargo around the globe, some consisting of US exports and some US imports. All shipping outside USA supplied by the domestic *WaterInt* industry is treated as a margins activity. Finally, all non-competing imports to water transport are assigned to *WaterInt*.

Table 6.2 Allocation of air transport sales, 2013 ($ bn)

	AirTrans		*AirInt*	
	Domestic	Imported	Domestic	imported
Inputs to users				
Foreign holidays	0	0	8.3	19.2
Domestic holidays	23.6	0	0	0
Exports of tourism	7.2	0	25.8	32.7
Exports of education	0	0	0.9	0.9
Other	46.9	0	5.3	4.7
Total	77.7	0	40.3	57.5
Margins usage	19.9	12.8	9.7	1.6
Inputs of non-competing imports	0	0.03	0	11.1

Table 6.3 Allocation of water transport sales, 2013 ($ bn)

	WaterTrans		*WaterInt*	
	Domestic	Imported	Domestic	Imported
Inputs to users				
Households	0.3	1.5	0	0
Exports of tourism	3.1	0	0	0
National defense	1.1	0	0	0
Holidays	2.6	0	0	0
Other	1.3	0	0	0
Total	8.4	1.5	0	0
Margins usage	8.8	1.9	24.0	4.1
Inputs of non-competing imports	0	0	0	5.5

6.3 Illustrative Application: Tourism Impacts by National Origin and US Region

We undertake seven separate simulations of the long-run effects of a $10 billion increase in international tourism exports (a boost of about 5.8%). The first simulation refers to a $10 billion boost spread proportionally across visitors from all origins. In subsequent simulations, the $10 billion boost refers to visitors from specific regions: Brazil, China, Mexico, Russia, Taiwan and Other.

Although in each case, the boost is $10 billion, potentially the effects can differ, reflecting differences in the regional distribution of expenditures within the US. For example, as shown in Table 6.4, Brazilian visitors spend heavily in New York relative to visitors in general, whereas for Chinese visitors, expenditure is relatively intense in California and Nevada.

Table 6.4 Expenditure shares (%) by visitors to US

	1 ALL	2 Brazil	3 China	4 Mexico	5 Russia	6 Taiwan	7 Other
1 NewYork	30	49	23	22	48	7	30
2 California	19	8	36	11	21	48	18
3 Florida	17	25	1	16	7	0	17
4 Hawaii	9	0	9	0	0	8	10
5 Nevada	4	4	9	14	3	5	4
6 Texas	2	1	1	20	0	2	2
7 Massachusett	2	1	3	1	1	3	2
8 DC	2	5	3	1	8	1	2
9 RoUSA	15	7	15	15	12	26	15
10 Total	100	100	100	100	100	100	100

Source: US Dept of Commerce, based on NTTO (2015)

Table 6.5 Impact on macro variables of tourism boost (% relative to base case)

	1 ALL	2 Brazil	3 China	4 Mexico	5 Russia	6 Taiwan	7 Other
1 Real consumption	0.026	0.025	0.027	0.025	0.025	0.027	0.027
2 RealInv	0.006	0.006	0.005	−0.001	0.004	0.005	0.006
3 RealGov	0	0	0	0	0	0	0
4 ExpVol	0.145	0.148	0.146	0.154	0.151	0.147	0.145
5 Impvol	0.233	0.231	0.234	0.229	0.231	0.234	0.233
6 RealGDP	0.003	0.002	0.003	0.002	0.003	0.003	0.003
7 AggEmploy	0	0	0	0	0	0	0
8 averealwage	0.052	0.05	0.052	0.051	0.05	0.053	0.053
9 AggCapStock	0	0	0	0	0	0	0
10 CPI	0.145	0.145	0.143	0.139	0.143	0.142	0.145
11 Terms of trade	0.142	0.14	0.142	0.137	0.139	0.141	0.142

Table 6.5 shows long-run percentage effects on national macroeconomic variables. The most striking feature of these results is their similarity across columns. While there is potential for differences in the results from the seven simulations, this potential is not realised at the national macro level. At that level, the origin of the extra $10 billion of tourist expenditure doesn't matter.

In the long-run closure, we assume no effect on aggregate employment or capital stock. Under this assumption, the results in row 1 of Table 6.5 for real consumption are a legitimate indicator of welfare. In each column of Table 6.5, US welfare is stimulated by about 0.026%, or $3.0 billion. The welfare effect is less than $10 billion because resources (capital and labor) are diverted from other activities towards providing services to tourists. The fact that the welfare effect is positive arises from improvement in the terms of trade (Table 6.5, row 11). Boosting tourism exports generates a real appreciation. This increases US supply prices for all exports, forcing foreign buyers up their demand curves with a resulting increase in foreign currency export prices. Under the assumption of no change in foreign currency import prices, the increase in export prices translates into an increase in the terms of trade. An increase in the terms of trade allows the US to expand its consumption because a given volume of US products can be exchanged for an increased volume of imports.

Results at the national level for industry outputs are shown in Table 6.6. As in Table 6.5, we find no significant variation across simulations in these national results. Regardless of tourist origin, the $10 billion boost in expenditures (5.8 or 5.9%, Table 6.6, row 25) generates significant increases in the outputs of Air Transport (0.5%, row 9), Accommodation (1.0%, row 19) and Eating and Drinking Places (0.2%, row 20). There is also an increase in US tourism abroad (Foreign Holiday, 0.4%, row 24). This is associated with real appreciation. The effects of real appreciation can be seen in the results for export education (−0.3%, row 26) and other durables (−0.2%, row 6). These two industries are trade exposed and contract with real appreciation. Air International output increases (2.8%, row 28) due to its

Table 6.6 National industry output due to tourism boost (% relative to base case)

	1 ALL	2 Brazil	3 China	4 Mexico	5 Russia	6 Taiwan	7 Other
1 Primary	−0.1	−0.1	−0.1	−0.1	−0.1	−0.1	−0.1
2 Utilities	0.0	0.0	0.0	0.0	0.0	0.0	0.0
3 Construction	0.0	0.0	0.0	0.0	0.0	0.0	0.0
4 FoodBevTob	0.0	0.0	0.0	0.0	0.0	0.0	0.0
5 NonDurables	0.0	0.0	0.0	0.0	0.0	0.0	0.0
6 OthDurables	−0.2	−0.2	−0.2	−0.2	−0.2	−0.2	−0.2
7 TransportEqp	−0.1	−0.1	−0.1	−0.1	−0.1	−0.1	−0.1
8 Trade	0.0	0.0	0.0	0.0	0.0	0.0	0.0
9 AirTrans	0.5	0.5	0.5	0.5	0.5	0.5	0.5
10 RailTrans	0.0	0.0	0.0	0.0	0.0	0.0	0.0
11 OthTransport	0.0	0.0	0.0	0.0	0.0	0.0	0.0
12 PubMediaInfo	0.1	0.1	0.1	0.1	0.1	0.1	0.1
13 BankFinIns	0.0	0.0	0.0	0.0	0.0	0.0	0.0
14 HireLeasRent	0.0	0.0	0.0	0.0	0.0	0.0	0.0
15 ProfServ	0.0	0.0	0.0	0.0	0.0	0.0	0.0
16 OthService	0.1	0.1	0.1	0.1	0.1	0.1	0.1
17 Education	0.0	0.0	0.0	0.0	0.0	0.0	0.0
18 Health	0.0	0.0	0.0	0.0	0.0	0.0	0.0
19 Accomodation	1.0	1.0	1.0	1.0	1.0	1.0	1.0
20 EatDrinkPlce	0.2	0.2	0.2	0.2	0.2	0.2	0.2
21 GovAdminDef	0.0	0.0	0.0	0.0	0.0	0.0	0.0
22 Own OccDwell	0.0	0.0	0.0	0.0	0.0	0.0	0.0
23 Vacation	−0.1	−0.1	−0.1	−0.1	−0.1	−0.1	−0.1
24 FgnHoliday	0.4	0.4	0.4	0.4	0.4	0.4	0.4
25 ExpTour	5.8	5.8	5.8	5.9	5.9	5.8	5.8
26 ExpEdu	−0.3	−0.3	−0.3	−0.3	−0.3	−0.3	−0.3
27 OthNonRes	−0.3	−0.3	−0.3	−0.3	−0.3	−0.3	−0.3
28 AirInt	2.8	2.8	2.8	2.8	2.8	2.8	2.8
29 WaterInt	−0.1	−0.1	−0.1	−0.1	−0.1	−0.1	−0.1

substantial inputs to Export Tourism. Water International, mainly associated with US merchandise trade, contracts due to a real appreciation.

Tables 6.7, 6.8, 6.9, 6.10, 6.11, 6.12, 6.13 give regional macro results for the seven simulations. The results in Table 6.7 for a general stimulation of export tourism reflect the importance of export tourism for the regional economies. Hawaii has the strongest percentage effects, even though Table 6.3 shows that this destination accounts for only 9% of total export tourism expenditure. Similarly, Nevada which accounts for only 4% of tourism expenditure, shows a strong result in Table 6.7. Hawaii and Nevada are small economies with relatively large tourism sectors.

Table 6.7 Impacts on state macro variables, all tourists (%)

	1 NY	2 CA	3 FL	4 HI	5 NV	6 TX	7 MA	8 DC	9 Rest
1 Real consumption	0.137	0.052	0.258	1.337	0.481	−0.032	0.013	0.052	−0.020
2 RealInv	0.133	0.010	0.210	1.180	0.243	−0.037	0.022	0.076	−0.022
3 RealGov	0	0	0	0	0	0	0	0	0
4 RealGDP	0.074	0.015	0.139	0.834	0.241	−0.031	−0.002	0.028	−0.025
5 AggEmploy	0.055	0.013	0.116	0.654	0.227	−0.029	−0.007	0.013	−0.023
6 averealwage	0.108	0.065	0.168	0.707	0.280	0.023	0.046	0.065	0.029
7 AggCapStock	0.081	0.010	0.149	0.985	0.226	−0.035	−0.001	0.071	−0.029

Table 6.8 Impacts on state macro variables, Brazilian tourists (%)

	1 NY	2 CA	3 FL	4 HI	5 NV	6 TX	7 MA	8 DC	9 Rest
1 Real consumption	0.235	0.003	0.383	0.092	0.416	−0.038	0.004	0.107	−0.024
2 RealInv	0.224	−0.012	0.311	0.080	0.207	−0.037	0.012	0.179	−0.026
3 RealGov	0	0	0	0	0	0	0	0	0
4 RealGDP	0.135	−0.010	0.212	0.045	0.208	−0.034	−0.008	0.073	−0.028
5 AggEmploy	0.105	−0.011	0.179	0.033	0.195	−0.032	−0.011	0.041	−0.025
6 averealwage	0.155	0.039	0.229	0.083	0.245	0.019	0.039	0.091	0.025
7 AggCapStock	0.145	−0.012	0.226	0.055	0.194	−0.038	−0.008	0.166	−0.032

Table 6.9 Impacts on state macro variables, Chinese tourists (%)

	1 NY	2 CA	3 FL	4 HI	5 NV	6 TX	7 MA	8 DC	9 Rest
1 Real consumption	0.102	0.125	0.011	1.343	0.915	−0.033	0.027	0.070	−0.017
2 RealInv	0.100	0.044	0.010	1.185	0.460	−0.029	0.037	0.107	−0.018
3 RealGov	0	0	0	0	0	0	0	0	0
4 RealGDP	0.053	0.053	−0.006	0.838	0.472	−0.031	0.007	0.042	−0.023
5 AggEmploy	0.038	0.049	−0.008	0.657	0.444	−0.030	0.000	0.021	−0.022
6 averealwage	0.090	0.102	0.044	0.710	0.496	0.023	0.052	0.074	0.030
7 AggCapStock	0.059	0.044	−0.006	0.989	0.446	−0.033	0.010	0.102	−0.026

Tables 6.7, 6.8, 6.9, 6.10, 6.11, 6.12 show the implications for the regional economies of the source of the $10 billion increase in tourism exports. For example, Table 6.8 shows that a boost in Brazilian visitors is particularly beneficial for New York (increasing the consumption effect from 0.137% in Table 6.7 to 0.235% in Table 6.8). Table 6.9 shows that a boost in tourists from China is particularly

Table 6.10 Impacts on state macro variables, Mexican tourists (%)

	1 NY	2 CA	3 FL	4 HI	5 NV	6 TX	7 MA	8 DC	9 Rest
1 Real consumption	0.095	0.021	0.242	0.099	1.164	0.054	−0.004	0.032	−0.019
2 RealInv	0.095	−0.001	0.198	0.087	0.574	−0.061	0.006	0.040	−0.015
3 RealGov	0	0	0	0	0	0	0	0	0
4 RealGDP	0.050	0.000	0.130	0.050	0.611	0.006	−0.012	0.013	−0.022
5 AggEmploy	0.036	−0.002	0.109	0.037	0.569	0.015	−0.014	0.004	−0.022
6 averealwage	0.086	0.049	0.159	0.088	0.620	0.066	0.036	0.054	0.029
7 AggCapStock	0.056	−0.003	0.140	0.060	0.581	−0.009	−0.010	0.039	−0.025

Table 6.11 Impacts on state macro variables, Russian tourists (%)

	1 NY	2 CA	3 FL	4 HI	5 NV	6 TX	7 MA	8 DC	9 Rest
1 Real consumption	0.234	0.060	0.111	0.100	0.430	−0.037	0.006	0.163	−0.015
2 RealInv	0.222	0.015	0.089	0.087	0.221	−0.033	0.014	0.281	−0.020
3 RealGov	0	0	0	0	0	0	0	0	0
4 RealGDP	0.134	0.019	0.052	0.050	0.212	−0.033	−0.007	0.117	−0.023
5 AggEmploy	0.104	0.017	0.042	0.036	0.201	−0.032	−0.010	0.068	−0.021
6 averealwage	0.154	0.067	0.092	0.087	0.252	0.018	0.040	0.118	0.029
7 AggCapStock	0.145	0.014	0.056	0.061	0.199	−0.036	−0.006	0.262	−0.027

Table 6.12 Impacts on state macro variables, Taiwanese tourists (%)

	1 NY	2 CA	3 FL	4 HI	5 NV	6 TX	7 MA	8 DC	9 Rest
1 Real consumption	0.020	0.173	−0.009	1.209	0.709	−0.027	0.023	0.032	−0.011
2 RealInv	0.023	0.068	−0.006	1.067	0.368	−0.029	0.034	0.038	−0.013
3 RealGov	0	0	0	0	0	0	0	0	0
4 RealGDP	0.003	0.078	−0.017	0.753	0.359	−0.027	0.005	0.012	−0.018
5 AggEmploy	−0.003	0.073	−0.018	0.590	0.341	−0.027	−0.002	0.003	−0.018
6 averealwage	0.049	0.126	0.035	0.643	0.394	0.026	0.051	0.056	0.034
7 AggCapStock	0.006	0.068	−0.017	0.888	0.339	−0.030	0.008	0.038	−0.021

favorable for Nevada (increasing the consumption effect from 0.481% in Table 6.7 to 0.915% in Table 6.9). The consumption (welfare) result for Texas in all of the Tables 6.7, 6.8, 6.9, 6.10, 6.11, 6.12, with one exception, is negative. Texas has little reliance on export tourism and its export and import-competing industries are negatively impacted by the real appreciation associated with the tourism stimulus in other parts of the US. The exception is Table 6.10, which shows that expenditure

Table 6.13 Impacts on state macro variables, other tourists (%)

	1 NY	2 CA	3 FL	4 HI	5 NV	6 TX	7 MA	8 DC	9 Rest
1 Real consumption	0.137	0.048	0.259	1.474	0.477	−0.032	0.013	0.052	−0.020
2 RealInv	0.133	0.008	0.211	1.301	0.240	−0.037	0.022	0.076	−0.022
3 RealGov	0	0	0	0	0	0	0	0	0
4 RealGDP	0.074	0.013	0.139	0.921	0.238	−0.032	−0.002	0.028	−0.025
5 AggEmploy	0.055	0.011	0.116	0.722	0.225	−0.029	−0.007	0.013	−0.023
6 averealwage	0.108	0.063	0.169	0.775	0.278	0.023	0.046	0.065	0.029
7 AggCapStock	0.081	0.008	0.149	1.087	0.223	−0.036	−0.001	0.071	−0.029

by Mexican visitors has a positive effect for Texas. As can be seen in Table 6.3, Mexicans spend a disproportionate share of their tourist dollars in Texas (20% compared with 2% for all international tourists).

References

Dixon P, Rimmer M (2003) Regional database for USAGE. Centre of Policy Studies Mimeo. http://www.copsmodels.com/archivep.htm. Accessed 15 July 2016

Dixon P, Rimmer M (2002) USAGE-ITC: Creating a 1992 Benchmark input–output database, further developments. Centre of Policy Studies Mimeo. http://www.copsmodels.com/archivep.htm. Accessed 15 July 2016

NTTO (National Travel and Tourism Office) (2015) Overseas visitation estimates for U.S. states, cities, and census regions: 2014. http://tinet.ita.doc.gov/outreachpages/download_data_table/2014_States_and_Cities.pdf. Accessed 11 July 2016

OTTI (Office of Travel and Tourism Industries) (2000) Similarly for "Impact of International Visitor Spending on State Economies" 97/96

Parmenter B (1976) Input–output accounting and the ORANI module. http://www.copsmodels.com/ftp/workpapr/op-05.pdf. Accessed 19 Aug 2016

Part II
Potential Household and Fiscal Extensions

Chapter 7
Enhancing the Links Between Income Sources, User Expenditures and Taxes in a CGE Database

Janine Dixon

Abstract A Computable General Equilibrium (CGE) model that is relevant to policy makers requires a highly detailed, multi-dimensional database. Even a single-region model with many industries—100 is typical in policy-focused research—will require a database with several hundred thousand elements. The data is subject to many constraints: commodity and factor markets must clear and income, savings and expenditure must balance for every agent. It is therefore advisable that the data is arranged in a framework that clearly illustrates these requirements. A popular framework that meets these needs is the social accounting matrix (SAM). This chapter describes an alternative framework, which readily fits in with the existing format of the standard input–output table.

Keywords Input–output · Absorption · Income · CGE database · Social accounting matrix

7.1 Introduction

CGE modelling relies on a comprehensive and detailed database which captures the transactions made between economic agents at a sufficient level of detail. Most but not all of this information is available from a country or region's input–output tables produced by an official statistical agency such as the Australian Bureau of Statistics (ABS) in Australia or the Bureau of Economic Analysis (BEA) in the United States. Input–output tables are essentially a set of expenditure accounts, arranged in such a way that each column represents the expenditures of an economic agent, while each row represents the sales of a commodity. However, input–output tables are silent on income accrual: in all but the simplest of models, a framework is also required to keep track of income as it accrues to domestic households and governments and non-residents.

J. Dixon (✉)
Centre of Policy Studies, Victoria University, Melbourne, VIC, Australia
e-mail: janine.dixon@vu.edu.au

G. Wittwer (ed.), *Multi-regional Dynamic General Equilibrium Modeling of the U.S. Economy*, Advances in Applied General Equilibrium Modeling,
DOI 10.1007/978-3-319-58866-7_7

The primary purpose of this chapter, addressed in Sects. 7.2 and 7.3, is to describe two tables that provide a comprehensive framework in which to organize the required expenditure and income data and ensure that necessary balancing conditions are met. The first table closely resembles the well-known input–output table or absorption matrix, while the second resembles the input–output table in structure, but records income rather than expenditure. Together, the tables are known as the absorption-income matrices. The absorption-income matrices provide and alternative presentation to data presented in a social accounting matrix (SAM). A brief comparison of the two approaches is given in Sect. 7.4.

The chapter then moves on to a discussion of some data conventions in CGE modelling in Sect. 7.5. Complexities around subsidies, government owned resources and government revenue mean that it is often possible to find several ways in which to account for the same flow of funds while still satisfying the database balancing conditions. As the primary purpose of the database is to provide coefficients for the CGE model, the most suitable accounting method will be that which leads to the appropriate cost shares, GDP and welfare calculations, or other relevant indicators.

For completeness, data items required for a CGE model but not recorded in the absorption-income matrix are listed in Sect. 7.6.

The extension of this framework to multi-regional modelling is described in Sect. 7.7. A full multi-regional representation of an economy under this framework is extremely data-intensive because it requires data for flows all of commodities from source region to using agent also disaggregated by region. Under the TERM methodology, the data requirements on the absorption side are much less onerous, as described in Horridge (2012). Regional disaggregation of fiscal accounts is slightly more complex. A single government sector disaggregated into regional government sectors is not equivalent to a federal system in which there are two or more tiers of government. The VURM model (Adams et al. 2015) includes a fiscal system in which two levels of government collect taxes and undertake expenditure at the regional level.

7.2 The Absorption Matrix

Table 7.1 shows the familiar input–output structure for a single-region open economy. This structure is also referred to as an absorption matrix or a use matrix. Readers familiar with ORANI-G (Horridge 2014) will recognize the naming conventions: the letter V stands for "value", and the digits 1–6 represent the economic agents industries, investors, households, rest of the world, government and inventories respectively. The remaining three letters indicate the commodity flow: "BAS" for commodities valued at basic prices, "MAR" for margins, "TAX" for indirect taxes and so forth. The following paragraphs give a brief description of the data items in Table 7.1, beginning with a description of the agents. For alternative descriptions refer to Dixon and Rimmer (2002) or Horridge (2014).

Table 7.1 Absorption matrix

	(1) Industries [i]	(2) Investors [i]	(3) Households [1]	(4) Exports [1]	(5) Government [1]	(6) Change in inventories [1]	(7) Total sales (sum columns 1 to 6)
Goods and services							
(1) Domestic [c]	V1BAS(c,*dom*,i)	V2BAS(c,*dom*,i)	V3BAS(c,*dom*)	V4BAS(c)	V5BAS(c,*dom*)	V6BAS(c,*dom*)	V0BAS(c,*dom*)
(2) Imported [c]	V1BAS(c,*imp*,i)	V2BAS(c,*imp*,i)	V3BAS(c,*imp*)		V5BAS(c,*imp*)	V6BAS(c,*imp*)	V0BAS(c,*imp*)
(3) Margins [c*s*m]	V1MAR(c,s,i,m)	V2MAR(c,s,i,m)	V3MAR(c,s,m)	V4MAR(c,m)	V5MAR(c,s,m)		V0MAR(c,s,m)
(4) Indirect taxes [c*s]	V1TAX(c,s,i)	V2TAX(c,s,i)	V3TAX(c,s)	V4TAX(c) *s = dom only*	V5TAX(c,s)		V0TAX(c,s)
Primary factors							
(5) Labor [o]	V1LAB(o,i)						V1LAB_I(o)
(6) Capital [1]	V1CAP(i)						V1CAP_I
(7) Land [1]	V1LND(i)						V1LND_I
Other expenses							
(8) Production taxes [1]	V1PTX(i)						V1PTX_I
(9) Other costs [1]	V1OCT(i)						V1OCT_I
(10) Total expenditure (sum rows 1–9)	V1TOT(i)	V2TOT(i)	V3TOT	V4TOT	V5TOT	V6TOT	Σ_i(V1TOT(i) + V2TOT(i)) +V3TOT + V4TOT + V5TOT + V6TOT

7.2.1 The Columns of the Absorption Matrix

Each column represents the expenditures of an agent, with the agents arranged into several groups. The first set of columns shows the expenditures of the industries, or intermediate expenditure. Typically a large number of industries are identified in input–output tables produced by official statistical agencies: the Australian input–output tables identify 115 industries while, the US tables identify 71 in ordinary years and 389 in the benchmark years.

The remaining columns account for final demand. The second column block shows investment demand. This is typically represented as a single column in official input–output tables, but for the purposes of CGE modelling, the investment column is split into i columns corresponding to the industries identified in the first column block. This treatment enables investors to have varying expenditure profiles across industries, capturing the difference between dwellings investment, for example, an intensive user of residential construction, and manufacturing investment, for which imported machinery and equipment is an important input. Furthermore, in dynamic modelling, the links between industry rates of return, investment and capital stocks are crucial. Without splitting investment expenditure by industry, the data would be unable to support the capital accumulation mechanism of a dynamic CGE model.

The third, fourth and fifth columns account for final demand by households, the rest of the world (exports) and government respectively. Data in each of these columns may be disaggregated if desired. For example, the US Census data identifies data for household deciles which could be used to split the single household column into ten columns. The export column may be split by destination. This is particularly useful if there are large growth disparities between trading partners. The government column may also be split into levels of government, for example, federal and state governments.

7.2.2 The Rows of the Absorption Matrix

Several types of commodities are represented in the rows. Firstly there are produced commodities, or goods and services, for example manufactured goods, health services or construction. These commodity classifications typically align with the industries, as is the case in TERM, but this is not a necessary feature of a CGE database. The goods and services are represented in the first two row blocks, with domestic goods and services in the first block and imports in the second. Flows in these first two row blocks are valued at basic prices. For domestic goods and services this is equivalent to the prices received by producers. For imported goods, the basic value is equal to the cost, insurance, freight (c.i.f) value plus tariffs.

Margin commodities are shown in row (3) of Table 7.1. Examples of margin commodities include retail trade, transport, insurance or gas pipelines—commodities which facilitate the delivery of other commodities from producers to purchasers. By assumption, all margin commodities are produced in the domestic economy. Row block 3 is very large, with room to record margin sales of many types on all base flows of both domestic and imported commodities. Margins are assumed to be used by all agents except "change in inventories" (column 6), the dummy agent responsible for inventory accumulation.

Indirect taxes, also treated as a commodity in this framework, are shown in the fourth row block. Indirect taxes constitute a payment made by purchasers but not received by producers. In this sense, indirect taxes are similar to margin payments. The difference is that indirect taxes are collected by government and do not correspond explicitly to the production of any services, such as transport services. Like margins, indirect taxes are assumed to be paid by all agents except inventory accumulation.

Payments to the factors of production labor, capital and land are placed in row blocks 5, 6 and 7. Payments to factors appear only in the first column. Direct payments to factors made by any other agents (households, for example) are channeled through industries to ensure that this convention is upheld. Thus the imputed rental of owner-occupied dwellings, typically the largest single expenditure item of the household sector, is treated as a purchase of "dwelling ownership", a commodity produced by a dummy industry. The imputed rental payment is a payment to capital (row 6) of the dwelling ownership industry in the first column block. Similarly, payments made to labor by domestic households hiring staff would be treated as purchases of a dummy "domestic household services" commodity produced by a dummy industry of the same name, and the payments would be included in row 5 of column 1.

Production taxes, which are shown in the eighth row block, are part of industry costs only. Unlike indirect taxes, production taxes are not linked to the purchase of any particular commodity. An example of a production tax would be a subsidy (a negative tax) to the manufacturers of air-conditioners.

Finally, row 9 includes other costs, which in practice is a small catch-all residual term.

Table 7.1 contains all of the data required to furnish a simple CGE model in which there is a one-to-one correspondence between industries and commodities and there is no explicit accounting for income. A model of this type has a square or balanced input–output structure, that is, every industry must produce a single commodity, and every commodity must be produced by a single industry. In this case, the column totals in column block 1 (industry costs) equate to the corresponding row totals in row block 1 (domestic commodity sales revenue) for non-margin commodities. For margin commodities, domestic sales revenue includes basic sales of margin commodities from row block 1 plus margin sales from row block 3.

7.3 The Income Matrix

If the columns of the absorption matrix (Table 7.1) represent the expenditure profiles of the agents, it is possible to conceive of a table of the same structure that represents the income or sales profiles of the agents. Table 7.2 is an "income matrix" according to this concept. Data in this table may be used to support the explicit modeling of income in a CGE context. Note that the naming convention is similar to that used in the absorption matrix, with the letter "Y" introduced to indicate income where appropriate.

Row blocks 1–9 of the income matrix correspond to rows blocks 1–9 of the absorption matrix. A further set of rows in Table 7.2 under the subheading "Transfers" capture flows that are not associated with the items identified in row blocks 1–9. Income taxes and welfare payments are included in this section.

Reading across each row in the income matrix, we see the supply structure of each commodity. For the database to be balanced, for the row blocks 1–9, the row totals in the income matrix equate to the corresponding row totals in the absorption matrix. For the remaining rows in the income matrix, which are not reflected in the absorption matrix, the row totals are zero.

The column totals in the income and absorption matrices bear out the relationship between income, expenditure and savings for each agent. The column totals in the absorption matrix represent total expenditure by each agent. Rows 1–12 of each column of the income matrix represent the income structure of each agent, with total income recorded in row 13. Total expenditure is recorded in row 14, carried over from the absorption matrix. Savings, at row 15 of the income matrix, is equal to the difference between total income and total expenditure. Aggregate saving, the total of row 15, is equal to zero.

We now turn to a row-by-row description of the income table. Row block 1 shows that income from commodity sales accrues to the industries. The MAKE matrix in column 1 is equivalent to Supply tables in published input–output accounts (for example, BEA (2016)). If the MAKE matrix is diagonal, this implies that every industry produces a single commodity and every commodity is produced by a single industry. In practice, this is seldom the case; instead many industries may supply, or produce, more than one commodity type, and commodities may be supplied by more than one industry. For example the Australian supply table for 2013–2014 (ABS 2016) shows that 13% of production is recorded in the off-diagonal cells, that is, 13% of products are produced by industries other than their main industry.

Consistent with the absorption matrix, margin commodities appear in both row blocks 1 and 3. Basic flows of margin commodities appear in row block 1 and flows for margin purposes appear in row block 3. MAKM represents industry supplies of margin commodities. In practice, MAKM is usually aggregated into the MAKE matrix. Note that the margin row block is depicted as having m rows although it has $c{*}s{*}m$ rows in the absorption matrix. The adding-up condition is for the m rows in block 3 is therefore

Table 7.2 Income matrix

	(1) Industries [i]	(2) Investors [i]	(3) Households [1]	(4) Rest of World [1]	(5) Government [1]	(6) Change in inventories [1]	(7) Total sales (sum columns 1 to 6)
Goods and services							
(1) Domestic [c]	MAKE(c,i)						V0BAS(c,*dom*)
(2) Imported [c]				Y4CIF(c)	V0TAR(c)		V0BAS(c,*imp*)
(3) Margins [m]	MAKM(m,i)						$\Sigma_c\Sigma_s$V0MAR(c,s,m)
(4) Indirect taxes [c* s]					Y5TAX(c,s)		V0TAX(c,s)
Primary							
(5) Labour [o]			Y3LAB(o)	Y4LAB(o)			V1LAB_I(o)
(6) Capital [1]			Y3CAP	Y4CAP	Y5CAP		V1CAP_I
(7) Land [1]			Y3LND	Y4LND	Y5LND		V1LND_I
Other							
(8) Production taxes [1]					Y5PTX		V1PTX_I
(9) Other Costs [1]			Y3OCT	Y4OCT	Y5OCT		V1OCT_I
Transfers							
(10) from HOU [1]			-V34TR -V35TR	V34TR	V35TR		ZERO
(11) from ROW [1]			V43TR	-V43TR -V45TR	V45TR		ZERO
(12) from GOV [1]			V53TR	V54TR	-V53TR -V54TR		ZERO
(13) Total income (sum rows 1–12)	Y1TOT(i)	ZERO	Y3TOT	Y4TOT	Y5TOT	ZERO	Σ_iY1TOT(i) + Y3TOT + Y4TOT + Y5TOT
(14) Total expenditure (= absorption table row 10)	V1TOT(i)	V2TOT(i)	V3TOT	V4TOT	V5TOT	V6TOT	Σ_i(V1TOT(i) + V2TOT(i)) + V3TOT + V4TOT + V5TOT + V6TOT
(15) Saving (row 13 minus row 14)	ZERO	-V2TOT(i)	V3SAV	V4SAV	V5SAV	-V6TOT	ZERO

$$\Sigma_i \mathrm{MAKM}(m, i) = \Sigma_c \Sigma_s \mathrm{V0MAR}(c, s, m)$$

Row block 2 shows that the income of sales of imports valued at cost, insurance freight prices accrues to the rest of the world (column 4). Tariffs on imports accrue to the government (column 5). The row totals in row block 2 are therefore equal to the basic values (c.i.f. value plus tariffs) used in the absorption matrix.

Row 4 shows that all indirect taxes are assumed to accrue to the government (column 5). In a single-region model this seems obvious. However, it is conceptually possible for taxes to accrue to other agents. For example, in EU member states, agricultural subsidies are paid by the EU and not by the region's own government. In this case subsidies (negative taxes) may be recorded against the rest of the world (column 4). Dixon (2006) uses a single-region CGE model in an analysis of the effects on Ireland of changes to the Common Agricultural Policy (CAP), and records CAP subsidy payments in the rest of the world column. In federations such as the United States, which have state governments and a federal government, column 5 would be partitioned into several columns to represent the various governments, and taxes collected would be recorded in the appropriate columns.

Rows 5, 6 and 7 record factor income. Factor income may accrue to the household sector, to the rest of the world, or to the government. Labor income (row 5) is assumed to accrue to domestic households (column 3, Y3LAB) or, for foreign workers, to the rest of the world (row 4, Y4LAB). There is no entry in row 5, column 5, which would represent labor income accruing to government. Note that taxes on labor income are recorded in row 10 (transfers from households to government). Remittances by domestic workers to the rest of the world (perhaps to family members) are also recorded in row 10, column 4 (transfers from households to rest of the world).

Rental income on capital and land (rows 6 and 7) is assumed to accrue to domestic households (column 3, Y3CAP and Y3LND), the rest of the world (column 4, Y4CAP and Y4LND) and in the case of public corporations, government (column 5, Y5CAP and Y5LND). Note that the items Y5CAP and Y5LND are not used record taxes on capital income, which are kept in rows 10–12, column 5 (transfers to government). Although undistributed earnings may exist in practice, the database convention is to record all earnings against the final demand sectors. Investment of retained earnings by industries is channeled through the final owners of the assets, that is, the household, government or rest of the world sectors.

Production taxes, like indirect taxes, are recorded as government income (row 8, column 5).

Other costs may accrue to any of domestic households, rest of the world and government (row 9, columns 3, 4 and 5). The treatment of other costs will depend on the application at hand.

Rows 10–12 cover transfers between agents. Note the departure from the previous convention of rows representing commodities; here the transfers are from the agent named in the row title to the agent named in the column title. There are no corresponding rows in the absorption matrix. While there is some appeal in adding similar rows to Table 7.1 to record transfers as expenses, Table 7.1 as it stands looks exactly like the ORANI-G representation of a CGE database. To preserve the link between Table 7.1 and the ORANI-G database, outward transfers are instead recorded as negative items in the income table. This means that every transfer is recorded twice: for example, transfers from households to government, V35TR, is recorded as a positive item in row 10, column 5 (government income), and a negative item in row 10, column 3 (negative income to households).

Transfers from households to government, V35TR, are mainly payments of income tax. Indirect taxes are included in V3TAX (row 4) and household purchases of government services are included in V3BAS (row 1). Transfers from government to households, V53TR, are mainly welfare payments.

Transfers from households to the rest of the world, V34TR, are remittances such as gifts or donations. Transfers from the rest of the world to households, V43TR, include gifts and donations and also include capital and labor income earned overseas, net of taxes paid to foreign governments. Note that capital and labor income earned by foreigners in the domestic economy is recorded in rows 5–7 (Y4LAB, Y4CAP and Y4LND).

Transfers from the rest of the world to government, V45TR, include income taxes (taxes on foreign-owned labor, capital and land) and incoming foreign aid. Transfers from the government to the rest of the world, V54TR, include outgoing foreign aid.

Row 13 records the total income of each agent. Total expenditure in row 14 is carried over from the absorption table, enabling the derivation of agent savings in the final row. Each item has a real-world interpretation. Household saving is represented by V3SAV (row 15, column 3). Rest of the world saving, V4SAV (row 15, column 4) is equivalent to the current account deficit. Government saving, V5SAV (row 15, column 5) is equivalent to government net lending if positive, or net borrowing if negative.

At this stage, note that there are no entries in rows 1 to 12 of columns 2 or 6, representing investment and inventories. Investment is funded by the collective savings of all of the other agents. Calculating "savings" as income minus expenditure, *negative* V2TOT is recorded in column 2, row 15. (Similarly, negative V6TOT is recorded in column 6, row 15.) If all other balance conditions have been met, that is, all row totals in the income matrix equate to the corresponding row totals in the absorption matrix, total net savings, the total of row 15, is equal to zero. That is, total investment (Σ_iV2TOT(i)) is equal to total domestic saving (V3SAV + V5SAV − V6TOT) plus the current account deficit (V4SAV).

In practice, the only balancing conditions that are hard-wired into a CGE model database are the balancing conditions on domestically produced goods and services. These are (1) that total industry costs equate to total industry revenue, i.e. V1TOT(i) = Σ_cMAKE(c,i) + Σ_mMAKM(m,i), and (2) that total sales of domestic goods and services equate to total supplies, i.e. V0BAS(c,*dom*) = Σ_iMAKE(c,i) and $\Sigma_c\Sigma_s$V0MAR(c,s,m) = Σ_iMAKM(m,i).

The remaining balancing conditions are assured by calculations within the model. For example, to ensure balancing in row 2 (imports), the model code will carry a formula such as Y4CIF(c) = V0BAS(c,*imp*) − V0TAR(c). Balancing in the factor markets can be assured by defining share coefficients, say ROWCAPSH(i) and GOVCAPSH(i) for rental returns on capital to the rest of the world and government respectively. The model code would then carry formulae such as Y4CAP = Σ_i(V1CAP(i) * ROWCAPSH(i)); Y5CAP = Σ_i(V1CAP(i) * GOVCAPSH(i)); and Y3CAP = Σ_i(V1CAP(i) * (1 − ROWCAPSH(i) − GOVCAPSH(i))). In this example it would be necessary that the values for the share coefficients fell in the appropriate ranges, that is 0 < ROWCAPSH(i) < 1, 0 < GOVCAPSH(i) < 1, and 0 < (ROWCAPSH(i) + GOVCAPSH(i)) < 1 for all industries *i*.

The structure of the absorption-income matrix framework easily lends itself to identifying multiple agent types within each column block. Multiple household types, trading partners, and levels of government can all be represented by appropriately partitioning the columns. The same principles of balance between expenditure, income and savings apply within each partition.

7.4 Comparison with SAM

Taken together, the absorption and income matrices suggest an alternative layout of the information contained in a Social Accounting Matrix (SAM), a data framework established by Pyatt and Round (1985) and popularized at the World Bank. The absorption and income matrices represent the data in three dimensions: agents (columns), commodities (rows) and type of flow (expenditure in Table 7.1 and income in Table 7.2). The SAM presents this data in a two-dimensional format in which columns represent expenditure and rows represent income. The SAM is square, with every row having a corresponding column. Commodities, such as goods and services, taxes and factors, sit alongside agents such as industries and households. This is illustrated in the simple SAM depicted in Table 7.3, which ignores production taxes, other costs, margins, land, stocks and the occupation dimension of labor. For comparison, the items from the absorption-income framework are placed in this SAM.

For agents, the columns show expenditure. The shaded columns shown in the SAM are similar to the columns of the absorption matrix, with the addition of transfers to other agents. Savings are also included as an expense item. As a result, for households, rest of the world and government, the column totals—V3TOT*, V4TOT* and V5TOT* respectively—differ from the corresponding column totals in the absorption matrix. It is straightforward to show that row totals are equivalent to column totals for all agents, for example, V3TOT* = Y3TOT*.

The agents' rows, also shaded, are equivalent to the columns in the income matrix. The row totals Y3TOT*, Y4TOT* and Y5TOT* differ from the corresponding total income recorded in the income matrix (Table 7.2, row 13) because outward transfers are not subtracted.

For commodities, which are in the unshaded rows and columns, the rows are equivalent to the rows of the absorption matrix. Like the absorption matrix, for each commodity, row shares are equivalent to sales or usage shares. Note that where these rows intersect with commodity columns, there are no entries. These cells are marked "-x-".

The commodity columns are equivalent to the rows in the income matrix. The column shares therefore show the supply structure of each commodity or factor. For example, the column shares in the "labor" column show the shares of labor sourced from domestic households and from the rest of the world.

Readers may note that the final "Investors" column block consists of only one investor, instead of the *i* investors identified in the absorption-income framework. While it would be possible to identify *i* investors as columns of the SAM, in keeping with the requirement that a SAM is square, it would then also be necessary to disaggregate savings, or funds available to investors, into *i* dimensions. This additional data requirement, while interesting, creates a burden that is potentially unnecessary for many CGE models. In building a SAM, the issue is often avoided by aggregating investors into a single agent, as in Table 7.3. This is not ideal. Investment data by industry is an important element of many CGE models in the ORANI tradition, but bilateral funder-to-industry investment data is not necessary. The absorption-income framework offers greater flexibility, because while it is possible to accommodate data for investment by funding agent, it is not necessary. The investment-savings constraint operates in aggregate regardless of the level of disaggregation of either investment or savings.

An attraction of the SAM layout is that the balancing conditions—agent income = agent expenditure, and commodity sales = commodity supplies—are easily verified by checking that every row total equates to its corresponding column total. These conditions are also easily verified in the absorption-income framework by verifying that every row and column total in the absorption table equates to its corresponding row or column total in the income table, and the extra rows in the income table sum to zero.

A second attraction of SAM is that it organizes all of the data into a single table. The cost of this arrangement is that SAM contains many redundant cells. In particular, it makes no sense to have entries in cells where commodities intersect with each other. Intersections between rows and columns for agents may contain transfers (for example, from households to rest of the world). Transfers need to be recorded only once, unlike in the income table where each transfer is recorded as a negative and a positive entry.

Unlike SAM, the income-absorption framework does not attempt to force an essentially three-dimensional database (agent * commodity * flow direction) into a two-dimensional table. While some cells in the absorption-income framework are left empty by convention, all cells have a meaningful interpretation. With less redundancy, the absorption-income framework offers a more compact presentation of the traditional SAM.

7.3 A social accounting matrix

	(1) Industries [i]	(2) Goods & services: Domestic [c]	(3) Goods & services Imported [c]	(4) Households [1]	(5) Rest of world [1]	(6) Government [1]	(7) Sales Taxes [c,s]	(8) Labor [1]	(9) Capital [1]	(10) Investors [1]	(11) Total income/usage (sum columns 1 to 10)
(1) Industries [i]		MAKE(c,i)									Y1TOT(i)
(2) Goods & services: Domestic [c]	V1BAS (c,*dom*,i)	-x-	-x-	V3BAS (c,*dom*)	V4BAS(c)	V5BAS (c,*dom*)	-x-	-x-	-x-	Σ_iV2BAS (c,*dom*,i)	V0BAS (c,*dom*)
(3) Goods & services: Imported [c]	V1BAS (c,*imp*,i)	-x-	-x-	V3BAS (c,*imp*)		V5BAS (c,*imp*)	-x-	-x-	-x-	Σ_iV2BAS (c,*imp*,i)	V0BAS (c,*imp*)
(4) Households [1]					V43TR	V53TR		Y3LAB	Y3CAP		Y3TOT*
(5) Rest of world [1]			Y4CIF(c)	V34TR		V54TR		Y4LAB	Y4CAP		Y4TOT*
(6) Government [1]			V0TAR(c)	V35TR	V45TR		Y5TAX (c,s)		Y5CAP		Y5TOT*
(7) Sales Taxes [c,s]	V1TAX (c,s,i)	-x-	-x-	V3TAX (c,s)	V4TAX(c) *s=dom only*	V5TAX (c,s)	-x-	-x-	-x-	Σ_iV2TAX (c,s,i)	V0TAX (c,s)
(8) Labor [1]	V1LAB(i)	-x-	-x-				-x-	-x-	-x-		V1LAB_I
(9) Capital [1]	V1CAP(i)	-x-	-x-				-x-	-x-	-x-		V1CAP_I
(10) Funds available to investors [1]		-x-	-x-	V3SAV	V4SAV	V5SAV	-x-	-x-	-x-		V3SAV+ V4SAV+ V5SAV
(11) Total expenditure/supplies (sum rows 1 to 10)	V1TOT(i)	V0BAS (c,*dom*)	V0BAS (c,*imp*)	V3TOT*	V4TOT*	V5TOT*	V0TAX (c,s)	V1LAB_I	V1CAP_I	Σ_iV2TOT (i)	

7.5 Data Conventions for CGE Modelling

Building on the conceptual description of the absorption and income tables, this section provides some suggestions for suitable conventions to adopt in preparing data for CGE modelling. Topics addressed in this section are the treatment of government income and expenditure, including subsidized services, effective subsidies to industries, and revenue collection, and dummy industries.

7.5.1 Government-Funded or Subsidized Services

Services such as school education, health care, and child care are often heavily subsidized. Conceptually, government-funded services can be represented in the absorption-income tables in several ways. Consider a unit of service that costs $100 to produce and uses only labor and capital inputs. The service is consumed by households. For every $100 consumed, households receive a rebate of $40. Some possible representations of this transaction in the absorption/income tables are:

1. The industry producing the service receives a production subsidy (V1PTX = −$40), and the service is purchased at the subsidized price by households (V3BAS = $60); or
2. Households receive a sales subsidy on purchases of the service (V3BAS = $100, V3TAX = −$40); or
3. The subsidized component of the service is treated as a purchase by government (V3BAS = $60, V5BAS = $40); or
4. The service is purchased by households (V3BAS = $100), accompanied by a transfer payment from government to households (V53TR = $40).

All other things equal, each of the above treatments is consistent with a balanced income-absorption database. Treatment in official input–output tables may reflect literally the way in which the subsidy is administered. For example, option 4 gives the most intuitive representation of subsidized medical care implemented via a rebate system. However, for CGE modelling, the most suitable treatment will reflect the purpose served by the model database in the implementation of the model.

Recall that household decision-making is generally modelled as a constrained optimization problem. For any of the common functional forms for the utility function, including Cobb–Douglas, Stone–Geary, CDE or CES, the Johansen method requires household budget shares to parameterize the household demand functions. Household budget shares, at purchasers' prices, are provided by the database. Options 1, 2 and 3 return the correct budget share based on $60 spent by households on this service.

Another consideration is the appropriate calculation of GDP at market prices and at factor cost. Under all options, the contribution of this service to GDP at factor cost is $100, the cost of production. However, under options 1 and 2, where the government contribution is treated as a subsidy, the contribution of this service to GDP at market prices is $60, whereas under options 3 and 4, it is $100. Similarly, welfare calculations based on aggregate absorption will value the service at $100 under options 3 and 4, and at $60 under options 1 and 2.

Given that subsidized medical treatment is likely to be welfare-improving, option 3 is the preferred convention for the treatment of data in models such as USAGE-TERM. This is not to suggest, however, that all subsidized activities should be treated in this way. Unlike subsidies on health or education, subsidies to industry sectors such as manufacturing or agriculture are generally not considered to be welfare-enhancing. To avoid over-estimation of the contribution of these sectors to GDP or welfare, option 1 is the more suitable treatment for these subsidies. While there is no hard and fast rule determining how subsidized activities should be treated, as a general guide, option 3 is more suitable for non-market services, and option 1 for all other activities. A useful reference is the OECD definition of non-market services,[1] which includes activities such as education, health, social welfare and cultural activities.

7.5.2 Government Investment and Effective Subsidies

The income-absorption framework offers no obvious place for government-financed investment in public goods. By convention in models such as USAGE-TERM, public goods such as roads are treated as though all industries own a share in them, which has a uniform, positive impact on industry rates of return. However, in some cases publically-funded infrastructure is advantageous to a single industry or group of industries. For example, a road connecting a mine to a port in an otherwise remote and unpopulated region is not a public good so much as it is a production subsidy to the mining sector. In an instance such as this, the modeler may decide to estimate the increase in mining value-added attributable to the road, and treat this as a production subsidy (a negative value for V1PTX).

7.5.3 Payments to Government

Broadly categorized, the revenue of a regional or federal government can be classified as indirect taxes (import tariffs, taxes on production, and sales taxes), transfers (such as income taxes) or revenue from sales of goods and services, including returns on government-owned resources. While some revenue sources, such as sales taxes, are relatively straightforward to classify, others require more judgement. These judgements should be made with reference to the role of the

[1]https://stats.oecd.org/glossary/detail.asp?ID=1814.

model database in supporting the model's theories. In Chap. 8, Madden (2017) describes this process with reference to the detailed Long-Term Revenue Analysis data for Florida (Florida Revenue Estimating Conference 2011).

Consider fees for driver licenses, an example of government revenue for which there are several potential representations in the absorption-income tables. Driver license fees might be represented as

1. a tax on the activity of driving;
2. a household purchase of an administrative service provided by government; or
3. a transfer from household to government.

Under each of these options, the government net budget position should be the same. For the government, options 1 and 3 involve an income entry (V3TAX and V35TR respectively) and an equivalent purchase of administrative services, such as the operation of driver testing services (V5BAS). Under option 2, households purchase this service directly (V3BAS), with the same net effect on the government budget. If the government is thought to "profit" through the sales of driver licenses, this is reflected in all three options as supernormal profits in the administrative service activity, which is owned by government. Returns to government from this activity are recorded in the income table at Y5CAP.

In a model such as USAGE-TERM, treating license fees as a tax on the activity of driving (in accordance with option 1) will mean that driver license fees are linked to changes in the amount of driving. The fees will represent a wedge between the private cost of driving (such as operating and maintaining a motor vehicle) and households' valuation of driving, which must also include driver license fees. To successfully implement this option, "driving" must be identified as a model activity. Data for driving, as well as for a myriad of other activities subject to government fees, may be difficult to obtain and add unwanted dimensions to the absorption-income tables, leading to longer solution times for the model.

Driver license fees are treated as a direct purchase of an administrative service under both options 2 and 3. Under option 2, the purchase is made by households; under option 3 it is made by government with an accompanying transfer from households to government. Option 2 brings the purchase of driver license fees into the household consumption bundle, meaning that changes in the purchase of driver license fees will be determined by the model in accordance with the utility-maximizing behavior of households. Driver license fees will have no direct or appropriate link with driving, unless treated explicitly with a nested Leontief utility function. The obvious drawbacks to this are that the modification to the utility function may prove unwieldy (especially in a model which uses variable aggregation), and, as for Option 1, "driving" needs to be a separately identified activity.

Option 3 provides the simplest treatment. Minor revenue sources such as driver license fees are simply bundled up into public administration and funded by a lump-sum transfer from households. Model results for the lump-sum transfer are typically determined by indexation to real or nominal GDP or population.

Expenditure on administrative services would be determined by the government's expenditure function, rather than the household's expenditure function as in option 2.

A simple example such as driver licensing fees illustrates a range ways government revenue can be represented in the absorption-income table framework. Similar principles need to be borne in mind when classifying more complex sources of government revenue. For example, land transfer duties (also known as conveyance duty or stamp duty) are levied in some jurisdictions on purchases of land, dwellings or other buildings. The duties are calculated as an ad valorem tax on the value of the asset purchased. However, Freebairn (2016) argues that the duty is better represented as a specific tax on property transfers. For example, the cost of moving house (movers' costs, legal fees and so forth) may realistically be as little as one-fiftieth of the value of the dwelling. A 2% duty on the purchase of a dwelling is therefore equivalent to a tax of 100% on the act of moving house. As a result, although the headline rate of tax may appear low, estimates of the marginal excess burden of conveyance duties are high (e.g. Cao et al. 2015). To appropriately capture the distortionary effect of land transfer duty in a CGE model as though it is a tax of 100% on the act of moving house, a separate activity ("moving house") would need to be identified in the model database and appropriately taxed.

As with subsidies, there is no hard and fast rule in determining the appropriate treatment for the many sources of government revenue. The more important sources of revenue, as judged by the modeler for reasons of size, distortionary effect or relevance to a particular project, may require the inclusion and estimation of associated activities, such as driving a car, or moving house. Other sources may be treated as transfers or direct purchases of government services by households.

7.5.4 Dummy Industries

Dummy industries are activities that do not exist in the sense of conventional industries, but nonetheless produce output of economic value. Two common uses of dummy industries are for capital-intensive, owner-operated activities, and for bundled activities.

The most important example in the first category is the ownership of dwellings. Owner-occupied dwellings account for a large proportion of household consumption of dwelling services, yet payment for these services does not appear explicitly in conventional household accounts. To capture this, the database should include an "ownership of dwellings" industry which produces dwelling services by using capital services, in other words, the value of housing rental, including imputed rent on owner-occupied housing. The industry is typically very capital intensive, with payments to labor of zero in some model databases (for example, Adams et al. 2015). The output of this dummy industry is purchased by households.

The importance of ownership of dwellings as a separate activity cannot be understated. It is typically the largest single expenditure item for households. While most household expenditure in developed economies is labor intensive, ownership of dwellings is usually the most capital intensive activity in the economy. Economic shocks, especially at the regional level, are borne out through changes in the prices of dwellings. Residents of declining regions may experience the double blow of unemployment and deteriorating house prices if they are owner-occupiers. Similarly, residents of booming regional economies may find much of this economic success capitalized in the value of their homes. Appropriate treatment of dwelling ownership in the model database is crucial if the full extent of regional economic developments is to be captured appropriately.

Adams et al. (2010) treat several other activities in a similar manner. The expenditure profiles for the dummy industries private transport, private heating and private electricity each consist of rental returns to a privately owned capital good (a vehicle, a heating appliance or an electrical appliance), and intermediate inputs such as fuels and maintenance. In a model such as USAGE-TERM, which uses Leontief technology in intermediate inputs, moving these items from the household account into a dummy industry means that there is no inappropriate price-induced substitution between, for example, electricity and electrical appliances.

An example of a bundled activity that may be represented as a dummy industry is tourism. Tourism is typically not treated as a separate activity in official input–output tables. However, a dummy "tourism" activity may be constructed, consisting of intermediate inputs such as entertainment, accommodation and restaurant meals. Payments to factors are not recorded under the dummy activity as they are already recorded under the component activities. Transport may be treated as a margin on the tourism activity. Instead of consuming entertainment, accommodation and restaurant meals, the activity "tourism" is consumed by the final consumer. Domestic tourism, consumed by households, and inbound foreign tourism, an export, may be represented by a single dummy industry or two separate industries if their cost structures are very different. Travel margins for domestic and inbound foreign tourists may differ significantly even if the base tourism activity is similar. Households may also import tourism. The usual substitution between imported and domestic varieties applies, capturing the idea that as tourists, the domestic household sector in the US makes a choice between skiing domestically in Colorado and importing tourism services by visiting the French Alps.

In a model with Leontief technology in intermediate inputs, the use of dummy industries for bundled activities is an effective way of safeguarding against inappropriate price-based substitution without needing to change the underlying structure of the household utility function.

In the many instances where multiple options exist for the treatment of data, the modeler should first consider whether the absorption-income tables are balanced. As illustrated, there are often multiple ways of representing data which satisfy the balancing conditions. It is necessary but not sufficient for a successful CGE model to have a balanced database. Therefore the modeler also needs to consider the underlying purpose of the data in the economic model. Is it to provide household consumption shares? Should there be distortions in agent decision-making? Should certain commodities be treated as complements or substitutes? The absorption-income tables cannot answer these questions, but they do at least provide a framework in which the basic balancing requirements of the database are immediately obvious.

7.6 Other Data Requirements

The absorption-income tables represent flows pertaining to a particular time interval, typically a single year. A dynamic CGE model also requires some data on stocks, such as industry capital stocks, and the stock of net foreign liabilities. Being stocks and not flows, these items do not sit naturally in the absorption-income framework.

The dynamic capital accumulation mechanism in MONASH-style models requires industry capital stocks, investment, and the rate of depreciation. Investment is read from the absorption matrix but data on capital stocks and depreciation are not part of the absorption-income framework and need to be recorded separately.

Industry investment in MONASH-style models is determined according to a positive function describing the relationship between the industry rate of capital growth and the expected rate of return. The inverse-logit specification of this relationship (Dixon and Rimmer 2002) is calibrated to an estimated trend rate of capital growth and "normal" rate of return. These parameters do not belong in the income-absorption framework and need to be recorded separately.

While not central to the operation of a CGE model, demographic data such as population, working age population, participation rate and unemployment rate provide useful links between employment and population. The unemployment rate may play a role in the MONASH-style sticky wage adjustment mechanism, although the original specification (Dixon and Rimmer 2002) was based on a comparison of employment in base and policy simulations. These data items must be recorded outside the absorption-income framework.

The stock of net foreign liabilities, another stock item, is also required in some CGE models (for example, Adams et al. 2015). Payments to foreign owners of assets are recorded in Y4CAP for equity and V34TR and V54TR for interest payments. To update interest payments in a dynamic simulation, data for the stock of foreign debt and the interest rate may be required. These data are recorded outside the absorption-income framework.

7.7 Extending to Multiple Dimensions

Conceptually, the database described in the absorption and income tables could be extended to capture a region with several economies. A single country divided into several regions may be treated as though it is made up of several regional economies, linked through trade in commodities and factor markets.

In the database, for an r-region economy, every domestic agent is reproduced r times, leading to $r*i$ industries, $r*i$ investors, r households, r governments, and r stocks. It may be necessary to add in an extra layer of government, for example, a multi-region economy may have r regional (state) governments and a single federal government. Although the federal government is a single entity, it also operates in every region, so the federal government is also represented as having r dimensions.

Every domestically produced commodity is also reproduced r times, to represent the region in which the commodity is produced. Therefore there are $r*c$ domestic goods and services, with attendant taxes and margins, and r types of labor, capital and land. Depending on the level of complexity required, margins may be recorded in their actual region of production. The margin on any domestic good or service would be of r-cubed dimension: region of base commodity production, region of margin production, and region of use. To simplify the database, margins may be assumed to be produced in a region linked to the base commodity flow (perhaps the region of production or the region of use.

To extend just the absorption table to incorporate a multi-regional database, with the margins assumed to be produced in a region linked to the base commodity flow, and no extra level of government added, the number of columns increases from $2i + 4$ to $(2i + 3)r + 1$. The number of rows increases from $(4 + 2m)i + 5$ to $((2 + m)i + 5)r + (2 + m)i$. For a 100-industry model with 5 margins, turning a single-region database into a 10-region database increases the number of cells in the absorption table by a factor of 55.

The TERM model methodology devised by Horridge (2012) reduces the data requirement by many orders of magnitude and never requires the database to be derived in full as suggested in this section.

7.8 Conclusions

A CGE model that is relevant to policy makers requires a highly detailed, multi-dimensional database. Even a single-region model with many industries—100 is typical in policy-focused research—will require a database with several hundred thousand elements. The data is subject to many constraints: commodity and factor markets must clear and income, savings and expenditure must balance for every agent. It is therefore advisable that the data is arranged in a framework that clearly illustrates these requirements.

The absorption-income framework described in this chapter will aid modelers in building the balanced database required for CGE model applications. The market clearing and budget balancing conditions are easily verified by checking that the corresponding row and column totals equate in the two tables. While the SAM has long been used for this purpose, the absorption-income framework offers an alternative, more flexible framework for organizing the same data.

It is a necessary but not sufficient condition for a CGE model to be underpinned by a balanced database. There is often more than one way to represent flows of funds, particularly when government intervention is involved. When looking for the most suitable methods for treating data, the guiding principles are to consider the role of the data in the model—for example, to provide cost shares—and to consider the implications for macro calculations such as GDP and welfare. Taxes and subsidies imply the existence of allocative inefficiency, where direct government purchases and transfers do not.

The main complexities of data for CGE model remain in the input–output table, or absorption matrix. However, the absorption matrix on its own has no way of measuring national income as distinct from GDP, which is a problem if there is significant foreign ownership of factors. By recording income attribution, both the income table and the SAM make a small but useful marginal contribution in this regard.

References

Adams PD, Dixon JM, Horridge JM (2015) The Victoria University Regional Model (VURM): Technical documentation, Version 1.0. Centre of Policy Studies working paper G-254

Adams P, Dixon J, Giesecke J, Horridge M (2010) MMRF: Monash Multi-Regional Forecasting Model: a dynamic multi-regional model of the Australian economy. CoPS working paper G-223

Australian Bureau of Statistics (2016) Australian national accounts: input-output tables, 2013–14 (Cat. No. 5209.0) Commonwealth of Australia

BEA (Bureau of Economic Analysis) (2016) Input–output accounts data. https://www.bea.gov/industry/io_annual.htm. Accessed 2 Feb 2017

Cao LY, Hosking A, Kouparitsas M, Mullaly D, Rimmer X, Shi Q, Wende S (2015) Understanding the economy-wide efficiency and incidence of major Australian taxes. Canberra: Treasury working paper 2015–2001

Dixon JM (2006) The 2003 Mid Term Review of the common agricultural policy: a computable general equilibrium analysis for Ireland. Ph.D thesis, Trinity College Dublin

Dixon P, Rimmer M (2002) Dynamic general equilibrium modelling for forecasting and policy: a practical guide and documentation of MONASH. North-Holland, Amsterdam

Florida Revenue Estimating Conference (2011) Long-term revenue analysis FY 1970–1971 through FY 2020–2021, Office of Economic & Demographic Research, Tallahassee, vol. 27 (Fall) http://edr.state.fl.us/Content/conferences/longtermrevenue/archives/2011longtermrevenueanalysis.pdf

Freebairn J (2016) Taxation of Housing. Aust Econ Rev 49:307–316

Horridge M (2012) The TERM model and its database. In: Wittwer G (ed) Economic modeling of water: the Australian CGE experience. Springer, Dordrecht, pp 13–36

Horridge M (2014). ORANI-G: a generic single-country computable general equilibrium model. http://www.copsmodels.com/oranig.htm. Accessed 16 Dec 2016

Madden J (2017) Fiscal accounts in regional CGE modeling. In Wittwer G (ed) Multi-regional dynamic modeling of the U.S. economy. Springer, Dordrecht

Pyatt G, Round J (eds) (1985) Social accounting matrices: a basis for planning. The World Bank, Washington D.C.

Chapter 8
Fiscal Accounts in Regional CGE Modeling

John Madden

Abstract Assessing the budgetary effects of regional economic shocks, whether the shocks are fiscal or more general, has long been an important issue in regional economic analysis. Capturing such budgetary effects in a CGE model requires a full set of government financial accounts to be incorporated within the model. In this chapter we consider the nature of such fiscal accounts and how they might be implemented in a multiregional CGE model of the United States, USAGE-TERM. We commence with a description of such accounts and discuss how these government-finance accounts are linked to a set of income accounts that incorporate a standard CGE input–output data base. An illustrative example of a single-region CGE model of the US state of Florida, which contains comprehensive modeling of two tiers of government, is described. This is followed by discussion of a number of issues relating to converting certain government components of U.S. data into an appropriate form for CGE modeling. We conclude with a consideration of establishing multiregional fiscal accounts for the USAGE-TERM model.

Keywords Computable general equilibrium (CGE) · Regional policy · Fiscal federalism · Multiregional modeling · Government accounts

8.1 Introduction

Fiscal policy analysis has formed a major area of CGE research for many years at both the national and regional levels. Early examples are Shoven and Whalley (1972) and Keller (1980), while Madden et al. (1983) and Morgan et al. (1989) provide early instances of multiregional CGE modeling of fiscal issues in federal systems. The degree of fiscal detail incorporated in regional CGE models has varied from small illustrative or specific-purpose models with a restricted range of fiscal instruments (e.g. Groenewold et al. 2003) to large-scale general-purpose CGE

J. Madden (✉)
Centre of Policy Studies, Victoria University, Melbourne, VIC, Australia
e-mail: john.madden@vu.edu.au

G. Wittwer (ed.), *Multi-regional Dynamic General Equilibrium Modeling of the U.S. Economy*, Advances in Applied General Equilibrium Modeling,
DOI 10.1007/978-3-319-58866-7_8

models with a full treatment of two or more tiers of government revenues, expenses and transfers.

There are many examples of regional CGE models analyzing the effects of government fiscal instruments which carry detailed aspects of (federal) fiscal systems (see Partridge and Rickman (1998) and Giesecke and Madden (2013) for literature reviews). While specialized models will continue to play an important role in examining regional fiscal issues, a large proportion of CGE analysis is undertaken with general-purpose models. While many regional CGE applications may not involve fiscal shocks, there is frequently an interest in budgetary impacts. For instance, in modeling the effects of a major project, modelers frequently wish to impose an assumption of long-run budget neutrality. It is for such reasons that the incorporation into large-scale general-purpose multiregional CGE models of a comprehensive treatment of multiple tiers of government finances is the focus of the current chapter.

General-purpose regional CGE models can be expected to include modeling of taxes and government expenditure, but the degree of detail and comprehensiveness varies. Early examples of quite comprehensive treatments of central and regional (state/provincial) governments within a federal economic system are for Canada (Whalley and Trela 1986) and Australia (Madden 1990). The latter model, entitled FEDERAL, was succeeded by MMRF (Naqvi and Peter 1996) and FEDERAL-F (Giesecke 2002).[1] MMRF, which is now known as VURM, has become the workhorse of Australian CGE modeling and has been in continuous use on a very wide range of policy issues for over two decades.[2] VURM contains very detailed government (and income) accounts, including a detailed treatment of environment and energy taxes (Adams et al. 2015).

In the case of the United States, probably the best known CGE model with extensive treatment of (multi-tiers) of government is the DRAM model of California (Berck et al. 1996).[3] Other US single-state CGE models with extensive modeling of two or more tiers of government include OTIM (Legislative Revenue Office 2001) and the dynamic Florida State Model, hereafter FSM (Griffith et al. (2013).[4] FSM was constructed for the Florida Legislature's Office of Economic and Demographic Research (EDR) and has been in use by EDR for the past 5 years to model a range of policy issues.

---

[1]FEDERAL was initially entitled TASMAIN and its theoretical structure was first outlined in Madden (1987). See Madden (1993) and Dixon et al. (1993) for early FEDERAL applications. FEDERAL-F is a dynamic version of FEDERAL. For a full description of the theoretical structure of FEDERAL-F, see Giesecke (2000).

[2]MMRF/VURM applications have ranged across studies in the areas of tax, trade, labor markets, productivity, environment, energy, agriculture, mining, transport and major projects/events, etc. There are a number of MMRF derivative models, notably the B-Maria model of Brazil (Haddad 1999).

[3]A fiscal federalism feature captured by DRAM is the interaction between state and federal taxes.

[4]OTIM stands for Oregon Tax Incidence Model and is based on DRAM (Dynamic Revenue Analysis Model). For FSM, see also Giesecke et al. (2012).

FSM is a single-region dynamic version of the national model, ORANI-G, developed by Dixon et al. (1982) and modified by Horridge (2000). In the first step of constructing FSM, it was developed as a comparative-static regional model by the use of techniques developed by Giesecke (2011) for constructing an ORANI-G style model of Los Angeles County. The next steps in the development of FSM were to make it dynamic, and then to enhance the fiscal and household income components of the model so as to allow the detailed revenue forecasting and scenario analysis required by EDR.

FSM provides a starting point for developing the fiscal component of the multiregional USAGE-TERM model (Horridge 2012). USAGE-TERM is also a dynamic CGE model which has its origins in ORANI-G. It does not contain, however, the comprehensive fiscal accounting that was added to FSM.

In the rest of this chapter we cover the major issues involved in introducing a government financial module into a large-scale multiregional CGE model of the United States, with particular reference to USAGE-TERM. We commence in Sect. 8.2 by discussing the main elements of a set of government accounts and how they link to an income account of the type presented in Table 7.2 of the previous chapter of this book (Dixon 2017). We then move into an applied setting with a discussion of how the government accounts module is implemented in the Florida example and how the accounts are linked with the other parts of FSM. Sect. 8.3 deals with various issues which emerge when fitting official data sets into the requirements of a CGE model. Lastly, we consider issues related to government accounting within a multiregional setting.

8.2 Framework for CGE Fiscal Accounting

8.2.1 A General Set of Government Accounts

The basic form of government financial accounts can be seen in the 5th column (Government) of Table 7.2 of the previous chapter. The entries found in the first 12 rows of column 5 are the revenue items, with row 13 showing aggregate revenue. Row 14 of Table 7.2 shows total government expenditure, while the final row gives government savings or the budget balance (=total income less total expenditure).[5]

In Table 8.1 we show the items from column 5 of Table 7.2 in a more standard government budget format. The revenue and expenditure items are shown in the left hand column, with the associated Table 7.2 income matrices shown in the right hand side column.

In practice, large-scale fiscal oriented CGE models are likely to contain more budget categories than those shown in Table 8.1. Tables 7.2 and 8.1, however, can

[5]Since government expenditure shown here is confined to current consumption, the budget balance is the government's net operating balance. See Adams et al. (2015, p. 4.16), for a discussion of budget balance concepts.

Table 8.1 Basic government financial account items

Item	Row block (see Table 7.2, Chap. 7)
Government revenue	
Taxation revenue	
Tariffs on international imports	V0TAR
Commodity taxes	Y5TAX
Production taxes	V1PTX
Income and other direct taxes	V35TR + V45TR
Net income from government enterprises	Y5CAP + Y5LND
Government expenditure	
Government consumption	V5TOT
Transfers payments	V53TR + V54TR

be used to illustrate a number of general features about CGE modeling of government finances. For instance, it can be seen from Table 7.2 that transfer payments are recorded twice. Thus, transfer payments by households to government (e.g. income taxes and other direct taxes such as fees and fines) and transfer payments by government to households (e.g. unemployment benefits, social security payments) appear both in the government and household income columns.Thus, in installing a government financial module into a CGE model like USAGE-TERM, which presently includes only those fiscal variables that relate to activity variables (i.e. government consumption expenditure and indirect taxes), it is necessary also to update the household income area of the model to include the effects of direct taxes and transfers on household income.

A second task associated with introducing transfer payments to, from, and where applicable, between governments is the need to introduce theory into the model explaining the value of these transfers. In non-fiscal CGE models, such as ORANI-G, the only items of government income are usually tax revenues, which are a function of tax rates and the underlying tax bases, the latter in turn being determined within the standard model (e.g. commodity sales, imports). In fiscal models, however, new equations may need to be introduced to link certain fees, fines and transfers to economic/demographic drivers. Sometimes there is no clear specific driver within the model, and revenue for that item is linked to a more general economic driver. For instance, changes in nominal speeding-fines revenue might be linked to movements in population size and a price index, probably the CPI. For other items, such as unemployment benefits/insurance, there are more specific economic drivers; in this case the nominal value of unemployment benefits payments is normally linked to the level of unemployment and the benefits rate.[6]

In a federal system, intergovernmental grants from the federal government, particularly in countries where there is a substantial degree of vertical fiscal

[6]A complication in the case of the United States arises through time limits on unemployment compensation.

imbalance, can form the largest component of state government revenues. The nominal level of federal grants to individual states is often modeled similarly to our speeding fines example; i.e. movements in grants are linked to movements in a state's population and a (local) price index. A more sophisticated approach would be to endogenize the federal grants to individual states by incorporating an actual grants distribution formula into the model.

We see that Tables 7.1 and 7.2 provide a framework for increasing the fiscal and regional dimensions of the model. So far in this chapter, in order to make our discussion general, we have abstracted from the dimensions of each matrix. Take for instance the matrix V1TAX, commodity taxes on intermediate demands, in Table 7.1. For a national model with a single government, this matrix has three dimensions: commodity by source (domestic, import) by industry user. For a multiregional model, however, with separately specified governments, the dimensions of V1TAX would increase to at least 5: commodity by source (domestic regions, international imports) by industry by region of purchase by government.[7] In FSM, as discussed in the next section, a further commodity tax type dimension is added.

8.2.2 An Illustrative Example: Florida State Model

FSM was constructed in three stages. The first stage followed the method outlined in Giesecke (2011) for the construction of a comparative-static CGE model for a single region of the United States using IMPLAN data. In the second stage, the model was made into a recursive dynamic one through the addition of stock-flow relationships and lagged labor-market adjustment. At this point FSM could be considered as a single-region counterpart to the multiregional USAGE-TERM model. FSM's essential innovation is in the third stage, the development of its government finance module.

The major features of the fiscal component of FSM are:

(i) Explicit treatment of 38 types of Florida state government revenue[8];
(ii) Government consumption expenditure disaggregated to 8 classes of expenditure;
(iii) Government expenditure modeled as being driven by revenue receipts reflecting Florida's constitutional requirement for a balanced budget[9];
(iv) A revenue-allocation matrix that maps each of the 38 revenue items to the 8 classes of state government expenditure, reflecting the actual practice of Florida's State Government.

---

[7]For a detailed discussion of government accounting in a dynamic multiregional CGE model with a federal government, see Sect. 7.4 of Giesecke and Madden (2013).

[8]Two additional state government receipts are passed on to local government.

[9]Most U.S. state governments have a balanced budget requirement. Holcombe (2015) says that the Florida "State government has been very diligent about meeting this requirement". State government expenditure is set on the basis of estimates by the Revenue Estimating Conference (see http://www.edr.state.fl.us/content/conferences/revenueimpact/, accessed 2 February 2017).

FSM models 38 Florida state government revenue sources which are identified in Florida Revenue Estimating Conference (2011a). These items were decomposed into 6 broad categories of revenue: (i) commodity taxes; (ii) production taxes; (iii) taxes on labor; (iv) taxes on capital; (v) direct taxes on households; and (vi) intergovernmental grants.

Fourteen types of revenue were allocated to commodity taxes and contributed almost a third of total state government revenue. Of these Florida's Sales and Use tax was by far the largest category, comprising just over 60% of the 14 sales taxes' contribution (or almost 20% of all Florida Government revenue).[10] The next broad category, production taxes, is a minor revenue group. Six revenue sources (e.g. inspection fees, severance taxes) were allocated to it; these sources contributed only just over a quarter of 1% to total income. The three revenue sources treated as taxes on labor made up over 1% of total revenue (with the unemployment compensation tax comprising the bulk of this).[11] Four revenue sources were treated as taxes on capital, contributing close to 3% to total revenue (with corporation income tax being dominant among these four revenue types). Neither taxes on labor nor capital include income taxes on individuals, Florida being one of 7 U.S. states which do not levy a state income tax. Six revenue sources were various sorts of licenses, fees and fines, and were treated as direct taxes on households. These 6 sources contributed just over 6.5% of total revenue.[12] The last revenue source was federal government grants which comprised over a quarter of all Florida State Government revenue.

For the initial 2009 FSM data base, production taxes and commodity taxes were allocated across industries and commodities respectively on the basis of information in Florida Revenue Estimating Conference (2011b) and other information supplied by EDR as to the industries/commodities on which these taxes fell. This allocation was carried out at the 436 industry/commodity level, prior to subsequent aggregation. Labor and capital taxes were allocated in a uniform way across all industries.

Each tax matrix in FSM was given a government dimension: Florida State; and Federal/Local.[13] The Federal/Local tax rows were initially computed as a residual. Any resultant negative entries which arose out of incompatibilities between our state government tax estimates and the IMPLAN total tax estimates were generally set to zero. A modified RAS procedure (which maintained compatibility with Florida revenue totals) was subsequently undertaken to restore balance.

---

[10]Florida Revenue Estimating Conference (2011a, p. 147) states that "Florida's sales and use tax is a 6% levy on retail sales of most tangible personal property, admissions, transient lodgings, commercial rentals, and motor vehicles".

[11]Since 2012 the unemployment tax has been renamed the reemployment tax.

[12]Some of these revenue types were treated as direct taxes because there was no clear revenue base for them in terms of FSM variables (e.g. fines, forfeitures and judgments, donations, miscellaneous revenues). Some revenues treated as direct taxes might be considered as sales by government (e.g. Article V fees), but their value did not justify special treatment.

[13]The Federal/Local sub-matrices may be split into separate federal and local components in an update of FSM.

A feature of FSM is that for commodity taxes it maintains a tax type dimension. That is, rather than amalgamating the 14 different commodity tax types levied by the State government, these are treated separately within the model. Despite significantly expanding the sizes of the commodity-tax (VnTAX) matrices, this has an important benefit of the model being able to provide results by the revenue types shown in Florida Revenue Estimating Conference (2011a). For simulations undertaken with the aggregated 69-sector version of FSM, the extra size of the tax matrices does not have a noticeable effect on computing time.

Like most other U.S. States, Florida has a balanced budget requirement. In FSM this balanced-budget requirement is instituted via a system of hypothecating income from each of the 38 revenue types to eight broad types of state government expenditure: Education, Human services, Criminal justice and corrections, Natural resources, Transportation, General government, Judicial branch, and Grants to local government. A mapping of the allocation from revenue to expenditure classes was done on the basis of information in the 2010 Florida long-term revenue analysis (Florida Revenue Estimating Conference 2011a).

A small number of revenue types are allocated to only one expenditure category (e.g. Gross receipt taxes are hypothecated to Education, Citrus inspection fees and licenses revenue is entirely allocated to Natural resources, while all three taxes on labor are allocated to General government). Most revenue types, however, are allocated to five or more categories. Since Education (30%), Human services (37%) and General government (13%) make up over 80% of State government expenditure, these items on average are allocated the large portion of revenues. However, for individual revenue items, the different expenditure classes may be allocated greater or lesser shares than their all-revenue share (e.g. 78% of Lottery revenues are allocated to Education, while 86% of Tobacco taxes are allocated to Human Services).

In allocating State revenues to State government consumption expenditure classes, it was first necessary to exclude from the Human services' revenue allocation an amount of social security payments to be transferred to persons. These transfers, consisting of Medicaid and unemployment insurance, then appear in the household income part of FSM. Finally it was necessary to decompose 7 of the 8 expenditure categories into individual FSM commodity purchases (the 8th category is distributed to local government). We delay discussing this matter to Sect. 8.3.2 below, so that it can be put into the context of some wider issues relating to government industry/commodity classification.

8.3 Adapting Fiscal Data for CGE Modeling

8.3.1 Indirect Tax Data

Chapters 2–6 and 10 describe the estimation of the USAGE-TERM data base, using the national USAGE data base and various regional statistics, such as regional employment and payroll bills, international trade by port, etc. A key input to the estimation of the USAGE data base itself is the national I/O data produced by the U. S. Bureau of Economic Analysis (BEA).[14] The IMPLAN regional input-output tables, which are the chief data source for the FSM data base, are similarly based on the BEA national I/O tables and by and large carry the BEA conventions on to the regional level.

Looking at Table 7.1 of Dixon (2017) it can be seen that commodity flows are shown in basic prices,[15] with associated indirect taxes shown in separate matrices. The BEA I/O data, however, is in producer prices which includes indirect taxes. It is thus necessary to separate out the indirect tax component of the producer price, so as to show the basic price and indirect tax components separately as in Table 7.1.

The natural step in performing this task would be to use the indirect tax row vector provided in the producer-price table to estimate a tax rate for each industry's output. After converting these to commodity tax rates, with the aid of the MAKE matrix—and assuming for each commodity uniform tax rates across purchasers—an initial estimate could be made for the separate basic value and tax component of each commodity flow.[16] Dixon and Rimmer (2002) noticed, however, that indirect taxes were being credited to industries (like wholesale and retail) which collected the taxes rather than those industries which produced the commodities subject to the taxes. As noted by Giesecke (2011, p. 338), using this treatment in a CGE model would result in incorrect computations of welfare effects and in tax shocks generating "perverse industrial composition effects".

Consequently, in creating the initial USAGE data base, Dixon and Rimmer (2002) had to engage on a major multi-stage estimation procedure to correctly classify indirect taxes in order to generate a proper row block of commodity taxes and then remove these taxes from the BEA commodity-flow and MAKE matrices. This task was aided by three sets of tax data supplied by BEA, including a list of taxes classified by around 50 US tax types and some 7000 wholesale tax figures categorized by commodity and user. The lengthy many-step estimation procedure required to generate I/O Use and Make tables in basic price terms is described in detail by Dixon and Rimmer (2002).

In developing the data base for LA County using IMPLAN data, Giesecke (2011) also needed to devise an estimation technique for turning IMPLAN's producer-price tables into basic-price tables. While this was still a complex task, he was greatly aided by making use of USAGE tax rates as part of his procedure. This same procedure was used to develop the input-output component of the FSM data base (Giesecke et al. 2012; Griffith et al. 2013).

---

[14]BEA national input-output tables can be accessed at the BEA web page: https://www.bea.gov/iTable/index_industry_io.cfm. The latest 389-industry benchmark I/O tables are for 2007 (BEA 2013). Annual updates at the 71-industry level are available for 1997–2015.

[15]For domestic commodities, the basic price is that which accrues to the producer, while for imports it is the landed duty paid price.

[16]One complication that has to be handled is that the tax row in the producer price table includes both taxes on industry sales and production taxes on its primary factor inputs.

8.3.2 Government Activities

In Sect. 8.2.2, we discussed how Griffith et al. (2013) computed the expenditure of the Florida Government on 8 different classes of expenditure as a function of the level and pattern of 38 classes of State Government revenue. However, the IMPLAN I/O table, from which FSM's core data base is derived, does not show sales of government commodities of this type to state and local government consumption expenditure. In this section we first outline the treatment of government industries/commodities in the BEA and IMPLAN I/O frameworks, and the issues it raises for CGE modeling, before proceeding to explain how government expenditure is modelled in FSM.

Excluding government-owned enterprises, there are three government sector industries/commodities in the 2007 national I/O tables: Federal general government (defense), Federal general government (nondefense) and State and local (S&L) general government. The Make matrix shows that nearly all (around 95%) of the output of each of the two federal government industries is made up of their own commodity. Most of their remaining output is Scientific research and development services. Almost 80% of S&L general government output consists of the same-named commodity, S&L general government, with their other main commodity outputs being Hospitals (7%), Junior colleges, colleges, universities, and professional schools (4%) and Scientific research and development services (2%).[17] Each of the three general government commodities is sold to just one purchaser, their respective government consumption expenditure. Thus, for instance, S&L general government is sold entirely to S&L government consumption expenditure.

The commodity, S&L general government, thus bundles together most of the activities of sub-national governments, such as education, health, law and order, community services and general government administration. For certain model applications such a high degree of aggregation might not be of importance, particularly if there is not a large difference in capital/labor ratios between activities. However, for other types of model applications, such as sector-specific analysis where government plays a major role (e.g. health, education), separate treatment of these individual government activities is likely to be important. For a general-purpose fiscal model, it would seem sensible that the model contains not too dissimilar a level of (dis)aggregation for publicly-provided commodities as it does for privately-provided ones.[18]

[17] A further 1% of S&L general government's output is Funds, trusts and other financial vehicles, while the remaining 7% of output is spread across some 60 other commodities, such as Waste management, other health-related activities, etc.

[18] At the 389-industry level, the national I/O table does not just separately identify the health sector, but also decomposes it into ten separate non-government industries: Offices of physicians, offices of dentists, Offices of other health practitioners, Outpatient care centers, Medical and diagnostic laboratories, Home health care services, Hospitals, Nursing and community care facilities, and Residential mental retardation, mental health, substance abuse and other facilities.

At the national level we may be able to achieve such a disaggregation of government industries/commodities by first performing a simple split of each government industry's columns and commodity rows on the basis of figures for major classes of Federal and State & local government expenditure provided in the National Income and Products Accounts (NIPA) in Table 3.17 of BEA (2017). We could then use the cost pattern of the corresponding (or similar) private industries as a guide to estimating the newly disaggregated government industries' input structures so that they more closely reflected their type of activity (e.g. education, health, public order). It would then be necessary, for each disaggregated government industry, to rebalance their new columns, so as to maintain their row and column totals. Thus, for each input, the row total summed over the new sub-industries should be equal to the value of their parent industry's purchase of that input. There would also be a requirement for consequential adjustments to the new commodities' sales rows and to the Make matrix.

The treatment of government industries in IMPLAN I/O data, however, differs from that of the BEA's current I/O tables, and instead would seem to follow a former BEA treatment when its I/O table had a SIC-based industry classification rather than its current NAICS-based structure. IMPLAN features six administrative government employment and payroll industries (hereafter "payroll" industries). These industries have no intermediate inputs, only compensation of employees and gross operating surplus.[19] There are also six categories of government final demand, of which 4 are consumption expenditure: two federal (defense and non-defense), and two S&L (education and non-education). The columns for these four types of government demand contain purchases of a wide range of standard commodities as well as their respective payroll commodities.

In using the IMPLAN I/O table to develop the FSM model, Griffiths et al. (2013) split the S&L consumption expenditure columns into one for State government and another for Local government. They then further split the first of these new columns into the 7 Florida government expenditure categories listed in Sect. 8.2.2. For the new State-government (education) current government expenditure column, the IMPLAN S&L expenditure pattern for education was used. However, for each of the 6 new non-education columns, the pattern of expenditure on commodities (including payroll commodities) was little altered from the IMPLAN pattern for the S&L current consumption expenditure (non-education). The method of using commodity patterns from related private-industries, discussed earlier in this section, together perhaps with the use of superior data from State government departments, could be used to improve on the current FSM estimates for future versions of the model.

While Griffith et al. (2013) thus created 7 individual state government consumption expenditure columns, they retained the IMPLAN government payroll industries/commodities. A useful further step would be to introduce a set of 7

[19]These "payroll" industries are termed "administrative" by IMPLAN because they do not include government enterprises. There are two industry/commodities for each tier of government (federal, state, local). There is both a defense and non-defense federal employment and payroll industry. The lower level government industries are split into education and non-education industries.

government industries, each of which produced one of the 7 categories of Florida's S&L government expenditure. Dixon and Rimmer (2002) showed that such a step could readily be done when they developed the initial USAGE model's data base, using BEA's 1992 SIC-based I/O table. The BEA 1992 table contained 35 different types of government final demands. Fourteen of these were for current consumption expenditure (12 of which were S&L expenditures), while a further 14 were for investment expenditure in each of the same areas as covered by the consumption categories.[20] Dixon and Rimmer (2002) used the expenditure patterns of these government expenditure columns to replace the payroll industries with a larger and more useful set of new government industries. They did this by first moving the commodity purchases from each of 28 government expenditure columns into intermediate input columns for 28 new industries. Next, the 28 new industries' purchases of "payroll" commodities were reassigned from intermediate purchases to their purchases of labor and capital. The now-empty "payroll" commodity rows were then replaced by 28 rows for sales of the 28 new commodities produced by the new government industries. The sales of the 14 new "current-consumption" commodities were allocated to a single government current consumption column, which replaced the 14 previous government current consumption columns. For a regional model with more than one tier of government, two or more government current consumption columns would be required. The commodity sales of the 14 new investment-related industries were allocated to 14 investment-demand columns for assembling the capital to be used by the 14 new "current-consumption" industries.[21]

The extensive disaggregation of government current demands in the 1992 SIC-based tables no longer exists for BEA I/O tables, following the adoption of the new NAICS industry structure. However, the commodity pattern of the S&L government industries developed for the initial USAGE model, despite the age of the data, could serve as a useful input into a better estimation of the expenditure patterns of the major areas of government demand.[22]

8.4 Multiregional Fiscal Accounts

Although FSM conceptually contains three tiers of government, it only includes the very detailed treatment of revenues and expenditure for the one government of interest, namely the Florida State Government. In a multiregional model where there is a less confined interest in a single government, the task of constructing a very detailed government finance module is likely to become more complex.

[20]The remaining 7 columns were for investment in S&L government enterprises.

[21]It was also necessary to implement consequential changes to the Make matrix.

[22]The 1992 commodity pattern for different categories of government consumption could be updated in line with changes over time in the commodity purchase patterns for intermediate inputs by corresponding private industries such as health and education.

Nevertheless, the discussion in 8.2.1 suggests a feasible framework for developing a multiregional CGE model with many governments—a federal government operating in all regions, and at least one regional government operating in each region. The model could be specified so that all governments could have the same theoretical specification of revenue sources and expenditure by type. However, the data base could be used to restrict some governments' use of certain revenue sources and limit the commodities on which they could spend. Thus, for particular governments, restrictions on using some types of revenues (e.g. income tax receipts for some state governments and for all local governments) and on some types of expenditure (e.g. defense expenditure by all regional governments) could be instituted by zero entries in relevant parts of the data base, reflecting that such revenues and expenditures are not applicable for those governments.

Thus, in the multiregional data base, only the Federal government would have non-zero tax bases in all regions. Regional governments would effectively be modeled as only being able to tax agents which operated in its region and to tax only those commodity flows which either originated and/or were purchased in its region. This idea could be extended, so that a more detailed government-finance treatment of just one region within the multiregional model could be accomplished.

Multiregional models might incorporate just two regions (e.g. the two-region FEDERAL model, Madden 1990) or many regions (as in Horridge et al. 2005). Regions may be a combination of states/provinces, or of sub-state regions (e.g. counties), or a combination of both (e.g. a number of sub-state regions in one state, and then all other states as a residual region, or aggregated state). In the latter example, the State government revenues from, and State government expenditures in, the counties within the state of focus would be aggregated in forming the state government accounts. Similarly, the Federal government accounts would aggregate across that government's operations in all states.

The larger the number of regions, the more computing limitations will constrain the degree of sectoral disaggregation and the degree of detail in the government finance module.

There are also more extensive problems with the availability of data at the regional level. Nevertheless, the procedures outlined in Chap. 10 by Wittwer (2017) enable regions to be specified for quite small areas. Similarly, if one starts by assuming tax rates across regions are reasonably alike, and that there are similar patterns of expenditures across regions, it is possible that one can form reasonable local government accounts for small regions. The availability of data from the U.S. Census Bureau survey of governments should greatly assist for improving the estimation of the government component of U.S. multiregional CGE models. U.S. Census Bureau (2005) publishes data for individual counties, and for some municipal governments, on major classes of government revenue and expenditure. U.S. Census Bureau (2016) provides data for recent quarters at the state level.

8.5 Concluding Comments

Regional economists now have a number of options for undertaking regional CGE analysis which captures the detailed effects of fiscal and other policies on government finances.

In this chapter we discuss how detailed modeling of a state government's finances, including important institutional features, are incorporated within the single-region dynamic CGE model of the State of Florida, FSM.

We also adumbrate how the multiregional dynamic CGE model of the United States, USAGE-TERM, might be further enhanced by extending its treatment of government finances. USAGE-TERM is a powerful analytical tool which captures the price-responsive behavior of regional agents, their interregional interactions, and regional and national resource constraints. Incorporation of a full set of government accounts into USAGE-TERM, which already contains a large number of fiscal variables, would further enhance its usefulness to policy-makers in undertaking evidence-based research.

The choice of regional CGE model does involve trade-offs. Dynamic CGE models with many regions, industries and occupations, and which contain detailed institutional features of state government finances, can become very large indeed. This carries costs in terms of solution times, particularly for simulations over many time periods. Also at the small-area level, regional data tend to be scarce. Nevertheless, there is sufficient local data and very good estimation techniques that allow for successful modeling of small regions. Also, the USAGE-TERM model is flexible so that more detailed modeling of government finance can be introduced through offsetting reductions in other dimensions, such as the number of regions and/or industry sectors.

References

Adams PD, Dixon J, Horridge JM (2015) The Victoria University Regional Model (VURM): technical documentation, version 1.0. Centre of Policy Studies working paper G-254. Victoria University, Melbourne

Berck P, Golan E, Smith B (1996) Dynamic revenue analysis for California: report. California Department of Finance, Sacramento

Bureau of Economic Analysis (2013) Benchmark input–output account of the U.S. economy, 2007, December

Bureau of Economic Analysis (2017) National income and product accounts, Section 3, Government current receipts and expenditure. https://www.bea.gov/iTable/iTable.cfm?reqid=16#reqid=16&step=1&isuri=1. Accessed 27 Jan 2017

Dixon J (2017) Enhancing the links between income sources, user expenditures and taxes in a CGE data base. In: Wittwer G (ed) Multi-regional dynamic general equilibrium modeling of the U.S. economy. Springer, Dordrecht

Dixon P, Rimmer M (2002) MONASH-USA: creating a 1992 benchmark input-output database. Centre of Policy Studies, Monash University, May 2001 (revised June 2002)

Dixon PB, Madden JR, Peter M (1993) Simulations of the economic effects of changing the distribution of general revenue assistance among the Australian states. Econ Rec 69:367–381
Dixon PB, Parmenter BR, Sutton J, Vincent DP (1982) ORANI: a multisectoral model of the Australian economy. North-Holland, Amsterdam
Florida Revenue Estimating Conference (2011a) Long-term revenue analysis FY 1970-71 through FY 2020-21. Office of Economic & Demographic Research, Tallahassee, vol. 27 (Fall). http://edr.state.fl.us/Content/conferences/longtermrevenue/archives/2011longtermrevenueanalysis.pdf. Accessed 27 Jan 2017
Florida Revenue Estimating Conference (2011b) Florida tax handbook: including fiscal impact of potential change 2011. State of Florida, Tallahassee
Giesecke JA (2000) The theoretical structure of the FEDERAL-F model. CREA paper TS-08. Centre for Regional Economic Analysis, University of Tasmania, Hobart
Giesecke JA (2002) Explaining regional economic performance: an historical application of a dynamic multi-regional CGE model. Pap Reg Sci 81:247–278
Giesecke JA (2011) Development of a large-scale single U.S region CGE model using IMPLAN data: a Los Angeles County example with a productivity shock application. Spat Econ Anal 6:331–350
Giesecke JA, Madden JR (2013) Regional computable general equilibrium modeling. In: Dixon PB, Jorgenson DW (eds) Handbook of computable general equilibrium modeling. Elsevier, Amsterdam, pp 379–475
Giesecke JA, Griffith M, Madden JR (2012) Development of a large-scale dynamic fiscal CGE model of Florida using IMPLAN data. In: Ninth Biennial National IMPLAN user's conference, Bloomington, MN, June
Griffith M, Madden JR, Giesecke JA (2013) A dynamic computable general equilibrium (CGE) model of Florida. Report for the Office of Economic and Demographic Research, Florida Legislature
Groenewold N, Madden JR, Hagger AJ (2003) The effects of interregional transfers: a political-economy CGE approach. Pap Reg Sci 82:535–554
Haddad EA (1999) Regional inequality and structural change. Ashgate, Aldershot
Holcombe RG (2015) Florida's fiscal policy: responsible budgeting in a growing state. Mercatus working paper, George Mason University, Arlington, February. https://www.mercatus.org/research
Horridge JM (2000) ORANI-G: a general equilibrium model of the Australian economy. Preliminary working paper No. OP-93. Centre of Policy Studies and Impact Project, Monash University
Horridge M (2012) The TERM model and its database. In: Wittwer G (ed) Economic modeling of water: the Australian CGE experience. Springer, Dordrecht, pp 13–36
Horridge M, Madden J, Wittwer G (2005) Using a highly disaggregated multi-regional single-country model to analyse the impacts of the 2002–03 drought on Australia. J Policy Model 2:285–308
Keller WJ (1980) Tax incidence: a general equilibrium analysis. North-Holland, Amsterdam
Legislative Revenue Office (2001) The Oregon Tax Incidence Model (OTIM). Research report number 1-01, State of Oregon, Salem OR
Madden JR (1987) The structure of the TASMAIN model. IAESR working paper No. 11/1987. The Institute of Applied Economic and Social Research, University of Melbourne
Madden JR (1990) FEDERAL: A two-region multi-sectoral fiscal model of the Australian economy, PhD thesis, University of Tasmania, Hobart
Madden JR (1993) The economics of vertical Fiscal imbalance. Australian Tax Forum 10:75–90
Madden JR, Challen DW, Hagger AJ (1983) The Grants Commission's relativities proposals: effects on the state economies. Aust Econ Pap 22:302–321
Morgan W, Mutti J, Partridge M (1989) A regional general equilibrium model of the United States: tax effects on factor movements and regional production. Rev Econ Stat 71:626–635
Naqvi F, Peter MW (1996) A multiregional, multisectoral model of the Australian economy with an illustrative application. Aust Econ Pap 35:94–113

Partridge MD, Rickman DS (1998) Regional computable general equilibrium modeling: a survey and critical appraisal. Int Reg Sci Rev 21:205–248

Shoven JB, Whalley J (1972) A general equilibrium calculation of the effects of differential taxation of income from capital in the U.S. J Public Econ 1:281–322

U.S. Census Bureau (2005) 2002 Census of Governments, vol. 4, No. 3, Finances of County Governments: 2002. Washington DC

U.S. Census Bureau (2016) Quarterly summary of state and local government tax revenue http://www.census.gov/govs/qtax/. Accessed 2 Feb 2017

Whalley J, Trela I (1986) Regional aspects of confederation. University of Toronto Press, Toronto

Wittwer G (2017) Preparing a dynamic database for dynamic CGE modeling. In: Wittwer G (ed) Multi-regional dynamic general equilibrium modeling of the U.S. economy. Springer, Dordrecht

Part III
Model Preparation

Chapter 9
Preparing a Database for Dynamic CGE Modeling

Glyn Wittwer

Abstract This chapter describes the preparation of a multi-regional database for aggregated dynamic simulations with USAGE-TERM, a multi-regional model of the U.S. economy. The need for aggregation arises because the master database is far too large for the model ever to be run with full dimensions, necessitating aggregation for every model application.

Keywords National database modifications · CGE database aggregation · Database updates · Dynamic regional baseline

9.1 Recap of the TERM Approach

The broad philosophy of the TERM approach to sub-national, multi-regional CGE modeling is to make the most of scarce data and to undertake model simulations with an aggregated version of the full database. Several key assumptions underpin the approach to devising a TERM database.

A starting assumption is that technologies for a particular industry are identical in all regions of an economy. If we know of examples where this is clearly not the case, and where we believe it matters in the context of scenario analysis, we split the national database first. An example concerns different forms of electricity generation. California, for example, generates a larger than average share of electricity from hydroelectric plants and a smaller than average share from coal-fired plants. We can represent California's electricity generation base more appropriately if we split the national databasc into different types of electricity generation, as discussed in Chap. 6. Then, when we split the national database using regional shares, our database reveals differences between California and other states.

G. Wittwer (✉)
Centre of Policy Studies, Victoria University, Melbourne, VIC, Australia
e-mail: glyn.wittwer@vu.edu.au

G. Wittwer (ed.), *Multi-regional Dynamic General Equilibrium Modeling of the U.S. Economy*, Advances in Applied General Equilibrium Modeling,
DOI 10.1007/978-3-319-58866-7_9

The common sourcing assumption used in the TERM and GTAP models helps overcome the curse of dimensionality. In TERM, the USE matrix includes the commodity, region of destination and user, but not the region of origin. The TRADE matrix includes the commodity, the origin and the destination but not the user. By assuming that all users in a given region source a given commodity from all regional origins in common proportions, the USE plus TRADE matrix provide the transactions data with a many-fold decrease in size over a single matrix that details the sales of commodities by region of origin, region of destination and the user. Chapter 2 details the theory that enables the dimension saving of the TERM approach. The common sourcing assumption is used across a number of data matrices in the TERM database.

An advantage of the TERM approach concerns the relatively modest data requirements. The use of identical industry technologies in all regions is discussed above. Previously, the absence of inter-regional trade data has been cited as a barrier to development of multi-regional CGE databases. Section 9.2.2.1 details how available data on production, consumption and international trade are used to estimate inter-regional trades in the TERM approach.

TERM databases are designed for many applications. A counter-intuitive approach is that the multi-regional database creation is undertaken at a maximum level of disaggregation. In many instance, this eases rather than complicates the task of estimation. For example, we may not have ready estimates of Washington state's share of national agricultural activity, but we are confident that its share of national tropical fruit production is zero.

Since the master database of USAGE-TERM is massive, containing 512 sectors and 70 regions in its state-based form, and 121 sectors and 436 regions in its congressional district form, it is necessary to aggregate the database for each specific application of the model. An aggregation of the state-based model to 30 sectors and 5 regions results in a database that is more than 4000 times as small as the master database. The exponent of solution time with respect to database size is approximately 1.7. This implies that if a dynamic aggregation of 30 sectors and 5 regions requires 4 min to solve in a 20 year model run, the master database would require more than 1.3 million times ($=4000^{1.7}$) as long to solve, implying a solution time approaching a decade.

This example shows that aggregation of the master database for a particular option is not optional; it is compulsory as part of the TERM approach to practical policy analysis. Moreover, in order to undertake dynamic TERM modeling, in addition to aggregating the core database as in comparative static analysis, we require a method of aggregating the dynamic components of the model.

9.2 From National to Regional, USAGE to USAGE-TERM

This chapter outlines the complex task of adapting, updating and splitting a national dynamic CGE model for multi-regional dynamic analysis. The starting point is the 2005 USAGE database. USAGE is a dynamic CGE model of the national U.S. economy (Dixon and Rimmer 2012; Dixon et al. 2012).

We make several modifications to the national USAGE database in preparation for splitting into regions. The MAKE matrix of the database is diagonalized so that each industry corresponds with a single commodity. The database is split where required (Sect. 9.2.1). Next, we require estimates of regional shares of national industry output, household consumption, industry investment and international trade. These are used to create the master USAGE-TERM database (Sect. 9.2.2). In the final stage, the USAGE-TERM 2005 database is aggregated and updated to 2013 (Sect. 9.2.3).

9.2.1 Adjustments to the National Database

9.2.1.1 Diagonalization of the MAKE Matrix

In practice, firms may produce a variety of products that appear as different commodities in the national input-output table. Some industry processes are genuinely multi-product. In sugar production, bagasse is a by-product that can generate electricity. If the electricity is used entirely by the sugar mill, there may be no need to record the electricity as an output. But if co-generated electricity is exported to the grid, there is a case for treating the sugar mill as multi-product. The MAKE matrix in the CGE database records the commodity outputs of each industry, and will in this case record both electricity and sugar commodities being produced by the sugar refinery industry.

Another example may arise from vertical integration, in which a firm is involved in both processing and retailing. Meat products production may be attributed to abattoirs, which obviously belong in the meat products industry. Retail supermarket chains may have their own final meat processing plants and consequently, meat products may appear as an output of the retail trade industry.

The problem with multi-product representation is that it may mask the direct links between inputs and outputs. For example, a jump in the world price of sugar should induce a supply response in the sugar industry. It may be hard to explain a change in electricity generation, a by-product, arising from this.

We can choose to diagonalize the MAKE matrix, which records the commodity output of each industry. Supposing 80% of meat products output is attributed to the meat products industry (which we will assume produces no other commodity) and 20% to the retail trade industry in the original MAKE matrix. If we realign the cost structures on a commodity by commodity basis so as to diagonalize the MAKE matrix, the new cost structure of the meat products industry will include all the costs of the original meat products industry, plus a contribution from the retail trade industry that expands the meat products industry total costs by 25%. The revised meat products industry will include a contribution from the cost structure of the retail trade industry, and will be altered to reflect some inputs that are specific to retail trade. If the retail trade commodity is not produced by any industry other than retail trade, the retail trade cost structure will shrink by a proportion equal to meat product's share of total retail trade output in the original database. In the revised cost structure of the database that includes a diagonal MAKE matrix, livestock inputs into retail trade production will remain, though smaller by a proportion equal to meat product's share of original retail trade's total output value. To diagonalize the MAKE matrix, we first calculate the share of commodity c in total production for industry i ($\mathrm{MShr}_{c,i}$):

$$\mathrm{MShr}_{c,i} = \frac{\mathrm{MAKE}_{c,i}}{\mathrm{MAKE}_{\bullet,i}} \tag{9.1}$$

The diagonalized MAKE matrix rMAKE is calculated as:

$$\mathrm{rMAKE}_{c,i} = \sum_k \mathrm{MShr}_{c,k}.\mathrm{MAKE}_{c,k} \quad \text{for } c = i, \text{else } 0 \tag{9.2}$$

Revised intermediate input costs $\mathrm{rINT}_{c,i}$ for commodity c into industry i are based on original intermediate costs $\mathrm{INT}_{c,k}$:

$$\mathrm{rINT}_{c,i} = \sum_k \mathrm{MShr}_{i,k}.\mathrm{INT}_{c,k} \tag{9.3}$$

Revised primary factor costs $\mathrm{rPRIM}_{p,i}$ for factor p into industry i are based on original primary factor costs $\mathrm{PRIM}_{p,k}$:

$$\mathrm{rPRIM}_{p,i} = \sum_k \mathrm{MShr}_{i,k}.\mathrm{PRIM}_{p,k} \tag{9.4}$$

9.2.1.2 Additional Sectors in the National Database

Before preparing a multi-regional database, there are sectoral splits we undertake on the CGE database. Even though the national database includes around 500 sectors which is sufficient detail across much of the economy, there are still two areas in which we improve the representation. The first area is in agriculture. As is elaborated in Chap. 2, USAGE-TERM represents agriculture by commodity rather than by farm type. This requires splits of the national CGE database so that, for example, the grains industry in the national USAGE database is split into wheat, rice and corn. One virtue of this particular split is that these three grains have markedly different regional distributions (see Table 2.2).

The other major split is of the electricity sector. In the case of USAGE-TERM, electricity is split into different types of generation, with a single sector covering transmission and distribution. The structure of electricity generation is changing rapidly, as renewable generation costs fall, and as underground coal mining becomes less competitive. Chapter 4 describes the process of gathering data in detail. A disaggregation of electricity so as to represent electricity generation by fuel type enhances the capability of USAGE-TERM. The split of electricity might be the starting point for devising satellite greenhouse gas accounts, so as to deal with greenhouse gas abatement scenarios, and devising feasible regions for electricity trading, following the approach elaborated by Adams and Parmenter (2013).

Figure 9.1 summarizes the alterations made to the national USAGE database in preparation for splitting into USAGE-TERM.

9.2.2 *Estimating Regional Shares of National Output*

Table 9.1 outlines data sources used to obtain regional shares of national activity. Data sources are discussed in detail in Chaps. 3–6. In the case of industries, these are shares of national output. In the case of international trade, these are regional sales shares by commodity.

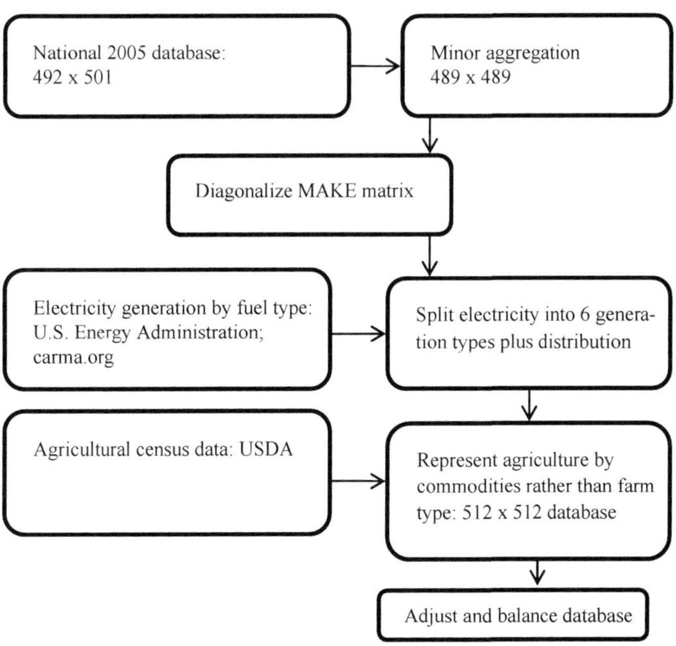

Fig. 9.1 National database amendments

Table 9.1 Data sources used in preparation of USAGE-TERM database

Source	Task
BEA national accounts data (60 + sectors)	http://www.bea.gov/regional/downloadzip.cfm (1) Check 2005 database against national accounts (2) State shares in 2013 of national activity (3) Update of regional database to 2013
U.S. Census Bureau 2010 census	http://www2.census.gov/econ2010/CBP_CSV/ Annual payroll bills, number employed to estimate regional shares of national activity for 400+ out of 512 sectors
USDA data	http://quickstats.nass.usda.gov/?source_desc=CENSUS (1) National targets for split of initial CGE database (2) State/county shares of national activity by crop or livestock activity
U.S. Energy Information Administration; Carbon Monitoring for Action (carma.org)	http://www.eia.gov/electricity/annual/html/epa_03_01_a.html http://www.carma.org (1) Split of initial CGE database into electricity generation by fuel type (2) State shares of national activity by type of generation
U.S. Department of Health and Human Services: Medicaid and Medicare data	http://www.cms.gov/NationalHealthExpendData/downloads/resident-state-estimates.zip (1) Split "SLGOther" into state production shares (2) Government expenditure shares
National Center for Education Statistics	http://nces.ed.gov/quicktables/result.asp?SrchKeyword=state+level+expenditure&topic=All&Year=2010 State shares of "SLGovEduc"
U.S. Census Bureau	http://usatrade.census.gov/ International merchandise trade by port used to estimate international state export and import shares

The USAGE-TERM master database has two versions. The first is the 512 sector, 70 region version (expanded to 82 regions to enable preparation of a database for modeling of the Californian drought in Chap. 11) based mainly on states. Table 9.2 lists the regions of this version. Data are available at the county level from the census and agricultural census (see Fig. 9.2), so that we can devise a bottom-up database with some sub-state detail. The states with the largest populations have been split into more than one region. These include California, Florida, Illinois, Michigan, Missouri, New York, Pennsylvania, Ohio and Texas. States with large populations remaining as single regions are New Jersey (9.4 million population), Georgia (9.2 million), North Carolina (9.0 million) and Virginia (7.1 million).

A second version of the USAGE-TERM master database is the 121 sector, 436 region version based on congressional districts. This is detailed in Chap. 10.

Figure 9.2 outlines the database jobs that use available regional shares of national activity in order to devise a multi-regional CGE database for USAGE-TERM. A close inspection of Fig. 9.2 reveals that there are areas for improvement in data collection. First, state-based national accounts expenditure data would improve the regional household consumption shares.

Table 9.2 Regions of the master database in 512 sector, 70 region version

Alabama	PalmBeachFL	RoMissouri	PhladlphiaPA
Alaska	Georgia	StLouisCtyMO	RhodeIsland
Arizona	Hawaii	Montana	SouthCarolin
Arkansas	Idaho	Nebraska	SouthDakota
SanFranCtyCA[a]	RoIllinois	Nevada	Tennessee
RoCalifornia	ChicagoCtyIL[b]	NewHampshire	RoTexas
LosAngelesCA	Indiana	NewJersey	DallasTX
OrangeCA	Iowa	NewMexico	HarrisTX
RiversideCA	Kansas	RoNewYork	TarrantTX
SacramentoCA	Kentucky	NewYorkCity[d]	Utah
Colorado	Louisiana	RoOhio	Vermont
Connecticut	Maine	CuyahogaOH	Virginia
Delaware	Maryland	ColumbusOH[e]	Washington
DC	Massachusett	Oklahoma	WestVirginia
RoFlorida	RoMichigan	Oregon	Wisconsin
BrowardFL	DetroitCtyMI[c]	NorthCarolin	Wyoming
HillsbrghFL	Minnesota	NorthDakota	
MiamiDadeFL	Mississippi	RoPnnsylvnia	

Composite county sub-state regions are as follows
[a]SanFranCtyCA = Alameda, Contra Costa, Marin, Napa, San Francisco, San Mateo, Santa Clara, Solano, Sonoma
[b]ChicagoCtyIL = Cook, Du Page, Will, Kanel, McHenry, De Kalb, Grundy
[c]DetroitCtyMI = Wayne, Oakland, Macomb
[d]NewYorkCity = New York, Nassau, Suffolk, Kings, Queens, Bronx, Richmond
[e]ColumbusOH = Franklin, Delaware, Fairfield

At present, regional consumption shares are based on estimated regional labor earnings shares obtained from census data and national accounts. We could also infer expenditures from household income data available at the congressional district level.[1] The congressional district data, however, are aggregates without commodity composition detail and are based on income-side rather than expenditure-side data. If state level data were available for broad commodity b, regional household consumption shares could be modified as follows. Using a mapping from commodity c to broad commodity b, $\mathrm{R003}_{cr}$, the share of consumption of c in region r ($\mathrm{R003}_{cr}$) could be calculated as:

$$\mathrm{R003}_{cr} = POP_r/POP_{st(r)} * \left(\mathrm{V3\_state}_{b(c),st(r)}/\mathrm{V3NAT}_{b(c)}\right) \tag{9.5}$$

In (9.5), V3_state refers to the expenditure figure for broad commodity b in state st. V3NAT is the expenditure for broad commodity b implied by adding up the mapping from c in the national CGE database. That is, state level data would be

[1]See http://www2.census.gov/acs2011_1yr/CD113/ accessed 27 January 2017.

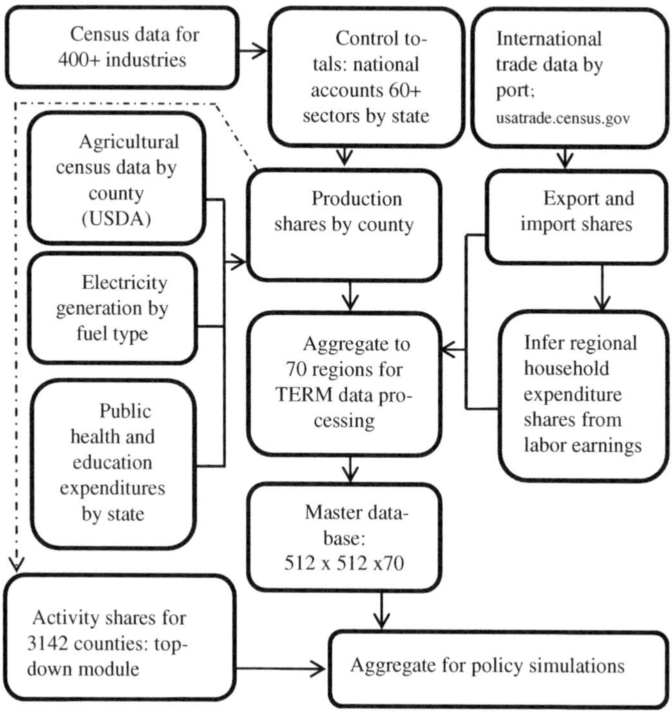

Fig. 9.2 USAGE-TERM database jobs

normalized to fit the national data. 40 states plus DC have a one-to-one mapping to region *r*. The remaining 29 regions *r* map to the remaining 10 states *st*. Hence, there is a need to include $POP_r/POP_{st(r)}$ in (1), which is the sub-state share of the state-wide population, so that sub-state shares are allocated on the basis of population shares. An alternative would be to base aggregate consumption on household income data available at the congressional district level.

Another area in which regional data are not readily available is international trade in services. United States Census Bureau data are confined to international merchandise trade. International trade in services is represented in the national USAGE database. A default assumption in the absence of further data is that regional international export shares follow industry activity shares and regional international import shares follow population shares. More detailed estimates concerning education and tourism exports are outlined in Chaps. 5 and 6.

9.2.2.1 The Master Database for USAGE-TERM

Estimation of a master database for USAGE-TERM follows the procedure elaborated in Horridge (2012). The regional shares of national activity, that is of industry production, industry investment, household consumption, government consumption, international exports and international imports, are used to calculate total supplies and total demands for each bottom-up region.

The absence of inter-regional trade data is often cited as a barrier to developing a multi-regional CGE database. There are no custom posts between sub-national regions, and so there is no systematic recording of merchandise trade. Freight movement data might provide some information on inter-regional trade volumes, but fall a long way short of being a reliable estimator of inter-regional trade values by commodity. Rather than use lack of data to justify representing small regions in a bottom-up CGE framework, we need to find a defensible method for estimating such trades. Horridge (2012) explains the estimation procedure used in TERM models to devise a TRADE matrix of $n \times n \times 2$, where n is the number of sub-national bottom-up regions from either domestic or import origins (= 2).

The rows of this matrix correspond to region of origin and columns correspond to region of use. Locally consumed production is designated by diagonal elements. As shown in Fig. 9.3 we already have estimates of the row totals (supply by commodity and region) and the column totals (demand by commodity and region).

Since inter-regional trade data are deficient or non-existent, Horridge's approach is to use the gravity formula (i.e., trade volumes follow an inverse power of distance) to construct trade matrices consistent with row and column totals. Horridge defended the use of the gravity formula in the case of production concentrated in a few regions (e.g., almonds in California), because the gravity hypothesis does little. Working with a highly disaggregated database increases the number of commodities with a high concentration of production in a small number of regions.

In the case of USAGE-TERM, and in the Australian case, international merchandise exports and imports by port are based on actual data. This confines the gravity assumption in the case of international exports and imports to assigning movements between sub-national regions. The gravity assumption concentrates inter-regional trades of eventually exported goods between origins and ports that are relatively proximal. Similarly, imported goods are likely to be sourced as inter-regional exports from relatively nearby ports.

For a particular commodity we may start with the usual gravity formula:

$$V_{r,d} = \frac{\lambda_r \, \mu_d \, V_{r,\bullet} \, V_{\bullet,d}}{D^2_{r,d}} \quad r \neq d \tag{9.6}$$

where

$V_{r,d}$ value of flow from origin r to destination d (corresponding to matrix TRADE in Fig. 9.3),
$V_{r,\bullet}$ production in r (known, corresponding to MAKE_I in Fig. 9.3),
$V_{\bullet,d}$ demand in d (known, corresponding to USE_U in Fig. 9.3),
$D_{r,d}$ distance from r to d.

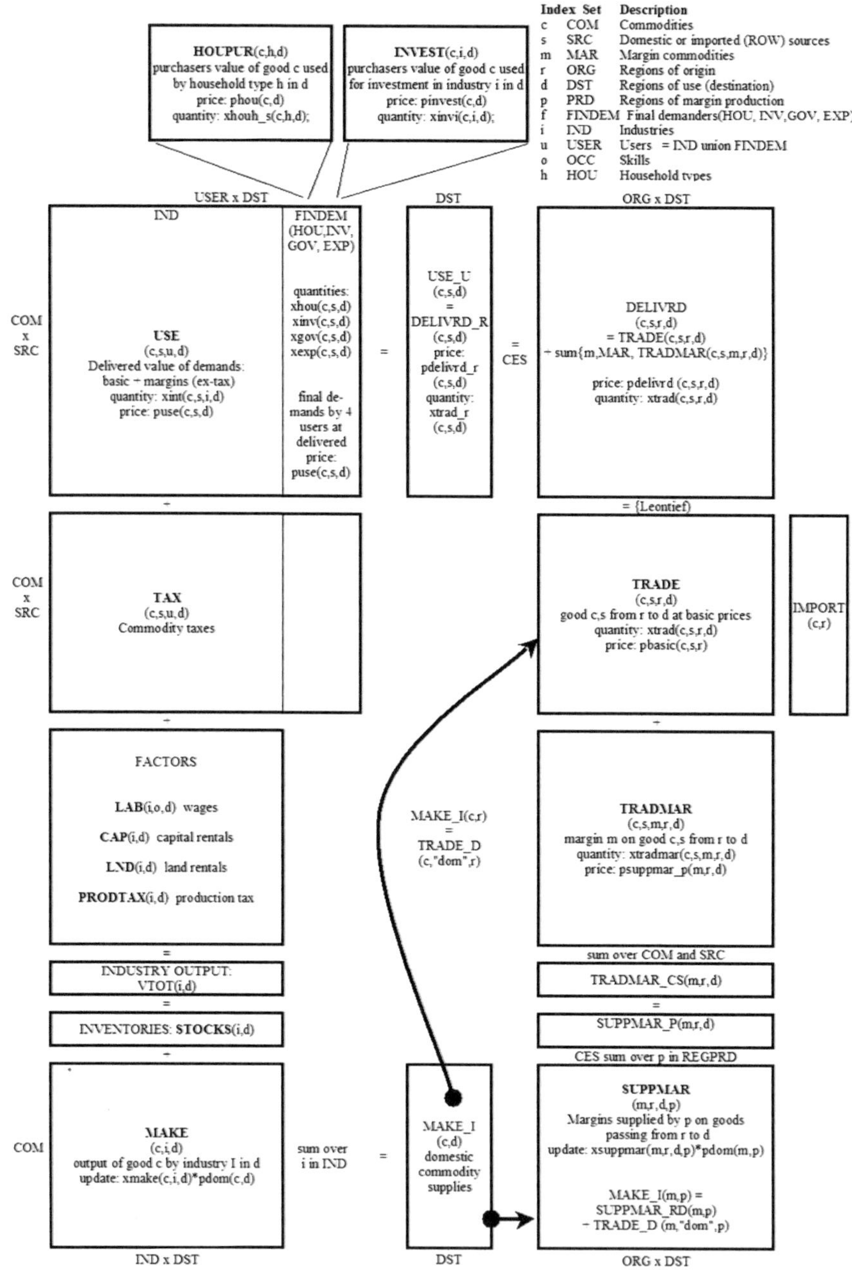

Fig. 9.3 Horridge's diagram of the USAGE-TERM flows database

The λ_r and μ_d are constants chosen to satisfy:

$$S_r V_{r,d} = V_{\bullet,d} \text{ and } S_d V_{r,d} = V_{r,\bullet}$$

Due to implausible results for some commodities arising from Eq. 9.2, Horridge modified the gravity formula to estimate the TRADE matrix in TERM as follows:

$$\frac{V_{r,d}}{V_{\bullet,d}} \propto \frac{\sqrt{V_{r,\bullet}}}{D_{r,d}^{k}} \quad r \neq d \tag{9.7}$$

where K is a commodity-specific parameter valued between 0.5 and 2, with higher values for commodities not readily tradable.

The locally-supplied demand in d as a share of local production ($V_{d,d}/V_{\bullet,d}$, the diagonal elements of the domestic sub-matrix of TRADE) is calculated as

$$\frac{V_{d,d}}{V_{\bullet,d}} = \text{MIN}\left\{\frac{V_{d,\bullet}}{V_{\bullet,d}}, 1\right\}.F \tag{9.8}$$

where F is a commodity-specific parameter valued between 0.5 and 1, with a value close to 1 if the commodity, such as elementary schools or hairdressers, is not readily tradable. The smaller are the regions, the fewer are the local commodities.

The initial estimates of $V_{r,d}$ are scaled (using a RAS procedure) so that:

$$\sum\nolimits_r V_{r,d} = V_{\bullet,d} \text{ and } \sum\nolimits_d V_{r,d} = V_{r,\bullet}$$

Transport costs as shares of trade flows increase with distance:

$$\frac{T_{r,d}}{V_{r,d}} \propto \sqrt{D_{r,d}} \tag{9.9}$$

where $T_{r,d}$ is represented by the matrix TRADMAR in Fig. 9.3.[2]

The key to using the gravity assumption is to work with the fully-disaggregated database. That is, we do not aggregate the national USAGE database before splitting it into regions.[3] We work with the full sectoral representation of the national database and indeed, as mentioned in Sect. 9.2.1, split it further so as to align agricultural commodities with available farm output data, and to represent different forms of electricity generation by region. We know, for example, that California produces virtually all the nation's output of a number of horticultural

[2]Section 10.2.1 provides a gravity formula suitable for use on congressional districts, in which there may be a very high degree of tradability between geographically close regions.

[3]This is the case with the 70 region version of USAGE-TERM. The 436 region database discussed in Chap. 9 is aggregated to 121 sectors before the regional split. We regard this as a sufficiently large number of sectors so as not to overburden the common sourcing assumption while keeping the master database creation task computationally manageable.

products. We therefore know that many cells in the TRADE matrix equal 0. The greater the sectoral disaggregation we use for devising the multi-regional database, the smaller the burden on the gravity assumption.

9.2.3 Preparing an Updated and Aggregated USAGE-TERM with a Dynamic Baseline

Dixon et al. (2012) details the dynamic approach to CGE modeling. There are several key attributes of dynamic CGE modeling. Such models capture links between flows and stocks, including investment flows and capital stocks, and trade balance flows and net foreign liability stocks. Dynamics also apply to lagged adjustment processes. For example, USAGE-TERM includes a theory of sticky wages applied at the regional level (Wittwer and Verikios 2012). This theory allows inter-regional real wage differentials to arise in response to changes in regional labor market conditions.

Dynamic modeling enables us to consider important short- and long-term consequences in a formal framework. If, for example, we model an infrastructure project, we would model substantial investments in the early years of the project that give rise to increased employment and aggregate consumption in the short term. However, at the same time, there would be a real appreciation of the domestic currency and a movement towards deficit in the trade balance. The investment impacts cannot justify the project, as there are longer term consequences. The increased deficit in the trade balance relative to forecast will build up net foreign liabilities relative to forecast. What matters is whether the marginal benefits of the operational phase of the project are sufficient to cover the marginal costs.

We can calculate welfare (*dWELF*) at the national level based on the time profile of deviations in aggregate private and public consumption, net of changes in net foreign liabilities in the final year of the simulation:

$$dWELF = \sum_{d}\sum_{t}\frac{dHOUTOT_{dt} + dGOV_{dt}}{(1-r)^{t}} - \frac{dNFL_{z}}{(1-r)^{z-t0}} \tag{9.10}$$

dHOUTOT and *dGOV* are the deviations in real household and government spending in region *d* and year *t*; *dNFL* is the deviation in real net foreign liabilities in the final year *z* of the simulation (*t0* is the initial year of the simulation); and *r* is the discount rate. Welfare is calculated at the national level rather than regional level, because regional level welfare measures are complicated by inter-regional migration. If *dWELF* is positive, it indicates that in the CGE framework, the marginal benefits of a given project exceed the marginal costs.

To make the national welfare calculation comparable with national accounts values, notably GDP, we may choose to report annualized welfare. We do so by multiplying *dWELF* by the discount rate.

9.2.3.1 Matching the USAGE Update to Updating Variables in USAGE-TERM

Figure 9.4 summarizes the tasks taken to update an aggregated USAGE-TERM database and prepare a dynamic baseline for it. To update a database, we must choose a suitable array of exogenous variables to shock. Dixon and Rimmer (2002, Chap. 5) details closure choices in various contexts, including historical updates or forecasts. The updating of USAGE-TERM is based closely on the closure and shocks used to update Mini-USAGE to 2010 (Dixon and Rimmer, 2012). We update USAGE-TERM to 2013.

The major concern in updating from 2005 to 2013 is to capture the impacts of the marked real depreciation of the U.S. dollar against other currencies. In particular, a real depreciation alters the structure of the economy, slowing growth in

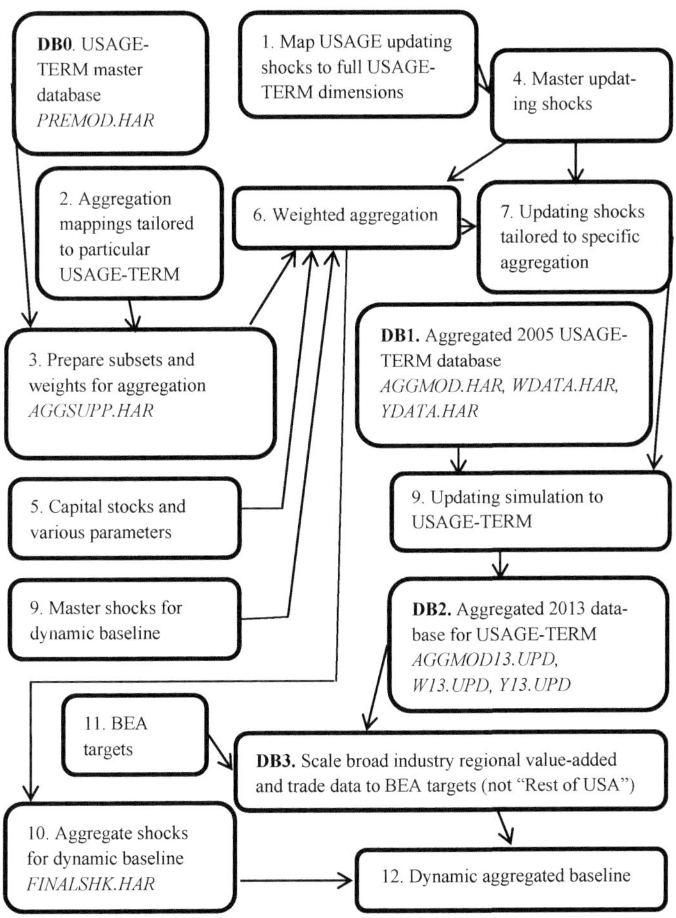

Fig. 9.4 Tasks in preparing an aggregated database and baseline

Table 9.3 Summary of macro shocks to update database from 2005 to 2013

Population (ascribed at regional level)	9.08	Government consumption	7.25
Aggregate employment	−0.88	Export Volume	34.05
Public investment	−7.77	Import Volume	6.05
Private investment	−6.37	Nominal exchange rate ($US/foreign)	11.1
Aggregate consumption	12.25	CPI	19.3
Real wage	−0.8		

Imposed at national level (unless otherwise stated)
Source Bureau of Economic Analysis; World Bank

consumption and imports, while accelerating export growth. The impacts at the sectoral level are governed by the degree of trade exposure or dependence on household consumption in a particular industry. The GFC resulted in a collapse in housing investment, reflected by a marked decline in private investment. The only region-specific shocks imposed on the update are for observed population growth. Table 9.3 summarizes the macro shocks.

9.2.3.2 Creating a Shocks File for the Master Database

The process of updating the model to 2013 is combined with that of preparing ingredients for a dynamic baseline. Both the updating task and dynamic baseline require regional and industry (IND)/commodity (COM) mappings for a particular aggregation (task 2 in Fig. 9.4), the preparation of subsets of COM and IND (task 3), unweighted aggregations of capital stock values (task 5) and weighted aggregations of parameters and updating/baseline shocks (task 6). The updating procedure requires the preparation of master updating shocks (task 4), a weighted aggregation to produce specific aggregation shocks (task 7) and the updating simulation (task 8). The updated database (DB2) is scaled to broad industry (21 sector) value-added targets for 2013 from the Bureau of Economic Analysis, obtained by navigating through http://www.bea.gov/regional/index.htm. Similarly, broad regional international export and import data from https://usatrade.census.gov/ are used to adjust regional values of international trade.

The dynamic baseline starts with the updated, scaled database (DB3) and uses shocks prepared in task 9 and aggregated in task 10. If we were to omit the updating procedure and instead rely on the dynamic aggregated baseline for updating from 2005, then we would not require tasks 6, 10, 11 and 12, as we could proceed with DB1 (the 2005 database) to task 13. Essentially, tasks 11 and 12 in this case would have been undertaken in tasks 6 and 9.

There is a particular reason for avoiding a faithful year-by-year update of the database from 2005 to 2013. The GFC, the effects of which became apparent around 2008, resulted in a collapse in the housing market, a high number of foreclosures of existing dwellings, firm closures and job losses. The task of modelling the GFC in a CGE framework is not routine. Dixon and Rimmer (2011) added a theory of excess capacity to the national USAGE model to capture the impacts of recession. If excess capacity is not part of the modelling, the GFC leads to immediate price adjustments inconsistent with observation. The U.S. economy was stuck in a deep unemployment trough in which idle capital, precipitated by foreclosures and housing evictions, was a feature. For the purpose of modeling policy scenarios into the future, a one-off update of the USAGE-TERM database from 2005 to 2013 without explicit modelling of the economic crisis around 2008 is sufficient.

The main reason for choosing an update in a single simulation, as we have, is to update without using the specialist dynamic software RunDynam (see Wittwer and Verikios 2012, pp. 52–54). Since the updating procedure is part of a variable aggregation task that might be applied to many aggregations, it is convenient to include a single updating model run as part of a batch of data processing jobs, run using GEMPACK software within a DOS box. In Fig. 9.4, this corresponds with tasks 2 to 12 being run using a single DOS command. Preparation prior to running the DOS command includes a one-off computation of master shocks. Each new aggregation then requires specific mappings from the full 512 sectors and 70 regions (or 121 sectors and 436 congressional districts in the second master database) to the target aggregated sectors and regions.

There are several one-off tasks involved in preparing an updated, aggregated database suitable for dynamic modeling. The task requires a master file of updating shocks corresponding to the full dimensions of the master database, either 512 × 70 or 121 × 436. These are mapped from the 74 industries and 76 commodities of the Mini-USAGE update (Dixon and Rimmer 2012). The master updating shocks are never run in their full dimensions. Rather, they are aggregated from the master sectors and regions to the target aggregated sectors and regions using database weights (task 10, Fig. 9.4).

Another one-off step is to prepare Bureau of Economic Analysis value-added targets at the industry level. Let IND be the industry dimension of the master database and IndNatAc the 21 industry sectors of the latest available state level national accounts data. The IndNatAc data are downloaded for each state. These are mapped to the IND dimension to create a matrix of IND × IndNatAc × State data (task 11, Fig. 9.4).

In a subsequent step, prior to the preparation of DB3, a matrix of IND × IndNatAc × State data can be aggregated to any industry aggregation (IndAgg) so long as IndAgg maps to IndNatAc. That is, we can aggregate industry value-added targets cleanly provided no sector in IndAgg is more aggregated than the corresponding IndNatAc sector. In practice, we often aggregate the 21 IndNatAc sectors because, for example, we may not wish to represent two of the 21, wholesale trade and retail trade, separately in a specific aggregation.

Task 3, the preparation of subsets, is a potentially tedious step that has been automated. For example, USAGE-TERM includes a subset of COM referred to as "traditional exports". These sectors have individual national export demand curves, whereas the remaining commodities have grouped export demand curves.

The manual way of defining subsets as traditional exports is to write down each element in model code. An alternative is to define subset elements using a parameter in a database. We define subset elements in a master database as those elements with a parameter value of 1.0, with remaining commodities then set to zero. Using export values as weights, an aggregation of the master database to target dimensions results in an aggregated set of traditional exports. An example from USAGE-TERM of TABLO code for this approach to devising subsets in aggregation procedures is as follows[4]:

Coefficient (parameter)(all,c,COM) IsIndivExp(c) # > *0.5 For individual exports#*;
Read IsIndivExp from file REGSETS header *"Sxpr"*;
Set TEXP # *Individual export commodities* # = (all,c,COM: IsIndivExp(c) > 0.5);
Write (Set) TEXP to file Summary header *"TEXP"*;
Set NTEXP = Com - TEXP;

The set denoted by REGSETS in the TABLO code of USAGE-TERM contains information on the subsets listed in Table 9.4.

An array of TABLO-generated programs aggregates the USAGE-TERM master database to sectors and regions of choice for a particular study. One program, TERMSET.TAB, contains a WAGG header used in Weighted AGGregation of the master shocks (task 4, Fig. 9.4). WEIGHTS.HAR calculates database weights from the master database PREMOD.HAR. The dimensions of these weights match those of updating shocks in the master shocks file.

9.2.3.3 Aggregating the Database and Shocks Files for the Historical Update and Dynamic Runs

Some of the tasks shown in Fig. 9.4 are one-off, being required to produce master shocks that are subsequently aggregated. These include tasks 1–3, 6, 7 and 11. The remaining tasks are aggregation specific and therefore need to be repeated for each new aggregation. The procedure is automated through the use of a batch file. The batch file invokes the use of individual TABLO-generated programs plus AGGHAR[5] to complete the task of preparing aggregation-specific ingredients for dynamic simulations.

The following files (as labelled in the USAGE-TERM code) are aggregated in this procedure (all tasks below refer to Fig. 9.4):

INFILE The main CGE database (master DB0, aggregated DB1 and DB2);
REGSETS Sets and subsets, the latter defined using parameters (task 3);
WDATA Contains starting levels for various macro, debt and labour market variables (tasks 5 and 6);

[4]This notation was first used in GEMPACK in the ORANIG model (see http://www.copsmodels.com/oranig.htm).

[5]See http://www.monash.edu.au/policy/gpwingem.htm.

Table 9.4 Mappings & subsets for updates and dynamic simulations

Header	Dimension	Coefficient	Name
CPSC	IND	CapScor	CPSC = 1 if zero capital in industry, else 0
ELED	IND	ElecDScor	ElecDist = 1, else 0
ELEG	COM	ElecGScor	Electricity generation sectors = 1, else 0
EXPS	COM	Exportshare	Defines Set AllExp, exclusive exporters = 1. Used in update
GOVI	IND	GovtInvScor	Government investment industry: used in update.
GOVS	COM	GovtSpScor	Commodities that government spends: used in update
IMP2	Ocom	ImpKnow2	Commodities with known import values: used in update
MCOM			Specific mapping for aggregation from master database
MIND			Specific mapping for aggregation from master database
MREG			Specific mapping for aggregation from master database
NOOK			Commodities excluded from mapping from Mini-USAGE
OCC			Set OCC Skills
REG			Set REG
REGD			Set DST regions of use
REGP			Set PRD regions of production
REGS			Set ORG Regions of origin
RMAP			Mapping from sub-state regions to states
SNIV	IND	NoInvScor	Industries, usually public, that don't follow RoR rule in baseline
STAX			Set STATEX aggregated states or composite states
SXPR	COM	TexpScor	Set of export commodities with individual export demands

YDATA Contains data concerning investment and capital (tasks 5 and 6);
Update shocks Updating from 2005 to 2013 (task 8) and scaling to BEA targets (task 12); and
Annual shocks for dynamic runs FinalShk.har (task 10).

9.2.3.4 A Consumption Function for a Dynamic Regional Model

A dynamic model enables us to capture links between stocks and flows over time. In the consumption function, we need to distinguish between income earned in a region and the disposable income of the representative household. Of relevance in calculating income available for consumption is the link between trade balance deficits, net foreign liabilities and interest payments to foreigners. We start by tying regional aggregate household consumption to wages plus a share of national gross operating surplus (*NatGOS*) net of payments to foreigners (*r* is the nominal interest rate and *NFL* national net foreign liabilities).

$$NatGOS = \sum_{i}\sum_{d}(LND_{id} + CAP_{id}) \tag{9.11}$$

$$APC_d = HOUTOT_d \,/\, LAB_d + LAB_d \,/ \sum_{e} LAB_e(NatGOS - r.NFL) \tag{9.12}$$

LND_{id} refers to land rentals and CAP_{id} to capital rentals in industry i and region d. $VHOUTOT_{,d}$ is aggregate household consumption and LAB_d aggregate labor earnings in region d. $APC_{,d}$ is the average propensity to consume. NFL is national net foreign liabilities and r the nominal interest rate. The payment to foreigners is $r.NFL$ which in turn depends on initial year NFL and subsequent trade balances.

Equation 9.6 indicates that we assign *NatGOS* net of payments to foreigners to specific regions based on the region's share of national labor earnings.

9.3 Summary

This chapter brings together two key ideas in utilizing the database of a multi-regional CGE modeling. The first is that having created a master database, tailored aggregations are necessary when it comes to running a TERM-based model. The second is that dynamics are becoming an increasingly important tool in CGE modeling. Therefore, it is highly desirable to make the tailored aggregation of the multi-regional model dynamic.

Updating a CGE database is often necessary. National official input-output tables may not be released until a number of years after the year they depict, with economic circumstances altering in the interval. For example, the structure of the US economy changed between 2005 and 2013 as a consequence of the GFC. Notably in this interval, there was a decline in national employment and a downturn in investment. With a real depreciation of the U.S. exchange rate, there was an upswing in exports as a share of GDP. The updating procedure is outlined in Sect. 9.2.3.1.

Modelers have several choices when it comes to updating. One is to update the model using year-by-year dynamic baseline. Another is to use the updating procedure to prepare the baseline of the model to start in a later year than otherwise. A more time-consuming option is to develop a core national CGE database from the latest available national input-output tables, followed by a regional split.

USAGE-TERM will be limited as a practical tool unless it is possible to prepare dynamic ingredients for a tailored aggregation of the model. Section 9.2.3 outlines the procedure by which such ingredients are prepared.

References

Adams P, Parmenter B (2013) Computable general equilibrium modeling of environmental issues in Australia: economic impacts of an emissions trading scheme. In: Dixon P, Jorgenson D (eds) Handbook of computable general equilibrium modeling. North-Holland, Amsterdam, pp 553–657

Dixon P, Rimmer M (2002) Dynamic general equilibrium modelling for forecasting and policy: a practical guide and documentation of MONASH. North-Holland, Amsterdam

Dixon P, Rimmer M (2011) You can't have a CGE recession without excess capacity. Econ Model 28:602–613

Dixon P, Rimmer M (2012) USAGE 2.0: historical simulations for 1998 to 2009. Centre of Policy Studies Mimeo. https://www.copsmodels.com/archivep.htm. Accessed 27 Jan 2017

Dixon P, Koopman R, Rimmer M (2012) The MONASH style of computable general equilibrium modeling: a framework for practical policy analysis. In: Jorgenson D, Dixon P (eds) Handbook of computable general equilibrium modeling, Elsevier, pp 23–103

Horridge M (2012) The TERM model and its database. In: Wittwer G (ed) Economic modeling of water, the Australian CGE experience. Springer, Dordrecht, pp 13–36

Wittwer G, Verikios G (2012) Introducing dynamics to TERM. In: Wittwer G (ed) Modeling of water, the Australian CGE experience. Springer, Dordrecht

Chapter 10
Top-Down Extensions to Represent Counties and Congressional Districts and Moving to Bottom-Up

Mark Horridge and Glyn Wittwer

Abstract The TERM implementation of a multi-regional model enables users to run with more sectors and regions than earlier multi-regional CGE models. But a trait of multi-regional modeling is that there is always interest in regions smaller than those captured by the model. In addition, in policy debates, political regions are of interest. A top-down representation, which takes simulation results and distributes outcomes to small regions based on industry activity shares, provides a way of representing county level or congressional district outcomes in USAGE-TERM. From top-down data, it is possible to devise a bottom-up master database for more regions than the standard USAGE-TERM database.

Keywords Top-down versus Bottom-up modeling · County representation · Congressional districts

10.1 Introduction

In any CGE model, it is possible to represent outcomes for regions smaller than those captured in the core theory of the model via relatively modest modifications. The ORANI model included a top-down module that supplemented national results from the core model with a state dimension (Dixon et al. 1982, Chap. 6).[1] The present chapter starts by outlining a top-down module devised for the TERM suite of models, which enables the user to distribute provincial or state-level bottom-up

[1]An international example of sub-national representation has been developed for GTAP. See http://www.copsmodels.com/archivep.htm TPMH0100. Accessed 28 Jan 2017.

M. Horridge · G. Wittwer (✉)
Centre of Policy Studies, Victoria University,
300 Flinders St, Melbourne, VIC 3000, Australia
e-mail: Glyn.wittwer@vu.edu.au

M. Horridge
e-mail: mark.horridge@vu.edu.au

G. Wittwer (ed.), *Multi-regional Dynamic General Equilibrium Modeling of the U.S. Economy*, Advances in Applied General Equilibrium Modeling,
DOI 10.1007/978-3-319-58866-7_10

results to small regions. The approach was developed in Bandung, Indonesia, in September 2006 by the authors.

The internet age has seen substantial advances in downloadable data. The quality and abundance of small-region data available online would have been unthinkable little more than a decade ago. In Australia, the Australian Bureau of Statistics provides detailed industry employment data for over 1300 small regions online. In the U.S. context, the U.S. Census Bureau provides county level detail on employment for over 400 industries. Table 9.1 in Chap. 9 lists the online data sources used in preparing USAGE-TERM. The onus is on modelers to maximize their use of such data, though this may be time consuming.

Computer programs are an integral part of both national and multi-regional CGE database preparation. Among the advantages of programming is reproducibility. After the onerous task of program coding, the process of updating a CGE database is relatively straightforward when updated data inputs become available. Another advantage of programming is to provide an audit trail. That is, all assumptions used in preparing a multi-regional database are contained within the programs. As an example, a typical weak point in a CGE database concerns international trade in services. Should better data become known to the database practitioners concerning aspects of international trade such as tourism or education exports, the programs can be amended to reflect new data. When better data become available, all old inputs are used to run the database creation programs again. In addition, new inputs reflecting newly available data are added to the programs: relatively crude earlier estimators of, in our example, tourism or education exports may be superseded by improved data.

In many instances, the shares used in preparation of the bottom-up master database of USAGE-TERM are aggregated to the 70 regions from the 3000+ county level. This aggregation uses national accounts data at the state by broad industry level to provide control totals. Rather than discard the county level inputs via this aggregation, the county level data can be used in a top-down manner, so that bottom-up solutions can be distributed to the county level. Typical county level impacts that can be reported through a top-down technique include employment, real income and real household consumption.

10.1.1 Top-Down Versus Bottom-Up Modeling Combinations

What do we mean by 'top-down' and 'bottom-up'? The early ORANI model (from which USAGE-TERM descends) included regional representation (see Dixon et al. 1978; Dixon et al. 1982). ORANI used a 'top-down' method of computing regional results which essentially consisted of a series of regional input-output models driven by the national CGE model. Within national models of the ORANI style, regional activities are represented by regional shares of national production, household consumption, investment, government consumption and international exports. Industry technology is assumed to be the same in all regions.

Industries are designated as one of two types, "national" or "local". "Local" industries are assumed not to be traded between regions. Changes in regional "local" industries are driven by changes in regional incomes. This implies that the regional shares of "local" industries are endogenous. Examples of local industries might include elementary schools, childcare centers, hairdressers, restaurants, retail trade and housing. Regional "national" industries, on the other hand, produce goods and services that are tradable between regions. For these industries, regional output shares are exogenous (and usually not shocked), so regional output changes by the same percentage as the national industry. The local industry treatment enables a national CGE model to capture regional economic multiplier effects. That is, if an industry expands in a simulation, regions which have a greater-than-national percentage share of the expanding industry in overall activity will have a greater-than-national percentage increase in local industry activities.

Only changes in regional quantities are modelled in the top-down representation. All prices follow results generated by the national model. In a top-down framework, the regional outcomes of national policy shocks, such as tariff reductions, can be modeled. Indeed, the national dynamic USAGE model of the U.S. economy includes a top-down representation of the states (Dixon et al. 2007).

The top-down framework can accommodate certain region-specific shocks. For example, government demand can be shifted between regions, and the regional distribution of national industries can be altered. But it cannot model policies that would induce price variations between regions. For example, a new tobacco tax which applied only to Florida should cause the Florida cigarette price to rise more than the national average-but the top-down approach does not allow this.

USAGE-TERM is a bottom-up multi-regional model in which such shocks can be imposed. In "bottom-up" models, demands, supplies, prices and quantities are computed for each region separately. The theory of "bottom-up" models at the regional level is much the same as that which applies at the national level in CGE models such as ORANI (Dixon et al. 1982). That is, industries minimize the costs of producing outputs. The levels of output are chosen to satisfy demands, which reflect prices and incomes. Rates of return on industry capital determine industry investment. Each region has its own consumption function linking the spending of a representative household to regional income. That is, the full theory that applied in national CGE models is applicable at the regional level. The regions are linked by inter-regional trade matrices and accompanying equations that assume imperfect substitutability.

The TERM methodology enables us to represent an economy in a bottom-up, multi-regional framework. Now, the top-down representation in a model such as USAGE-TERM applies at a lower level than in a national model. Instead of having a national model such as USAGE with top-down state representation, we have in USAGE-TERM a bottom-up representation of states (and some sub-state regions) with a top-down representation of counties. Having gone this far, the next possibility is to use the top-down methodology to map state- and county-level results to the congressional district level.

10.1.2 Congressional Districts

Congressional districts change once a decade as regional population shares change. For example, New York State's share of the national population has shrunk while Florida's has grown over the past 50 years. In 1953, New York had 43 congressional districts and Florida only 8 (Table 10.1).

As of the decade starting in 2013, both states have 27. A full explanation of the mechanisms driving changes in state population shares over time is beyond the scope of this chapter. Such shifts reflect several dimensions of structural change. The decline of manufacturing as a share of GDP has contributed to a decline in the population shares of states in the north east. Sun Belt states appear to have had more rapid population growth than others: they suffered disproportionally from the GFC but this provided little more than a hiccup in the overall trend. Immigration patterns are also an influence, with proximity to the Mexican border and the Caribbean islands driving up the Hispanic Latino proportion of a state's population. But for our purposes, it is sufficient to understand that regional and state shares of national population and economic activity change over time.

An extension to the top-down module of USAGE-TERM has been prepared that includes regional representation using the 2013 congressional districts. This is based on mappings from counties to congressional districts using http://mcdc.missouri.edu/websas/geocorr12.html.

Aligning regional data with sub-national political boundaries is a non-trivial task. This is particularly so if electorates or congressional districts change so as to even out populations. Statistical collection regions may cross political boundaries, no matter how small the collection regions. In the United States, the ease with which congressional districts map to counties varies according to state. There are several rules of thumb. Away from the cities, east of the Rockies, there are many counties per congressional district. Yet even east of the Rockies, large cities tend to have many congressional districts per county. This is so in Houston, Dallas, Miami, Philadelphia, Detroit, New York and Chicago. West of the Rockies, there are fewer counties per congressional district.

Table 10.2 shows the number of counties and the number of congressional districts in each bottom-up region in the master database of USAGE-TERM. The regions are ordered on the basis of the number of counties per congressional district, as shown in the 3rd column of the table. Relatively remote, sparsely populated states without any cities of half a million or more people have the highest average number of counties per congressional district. This is so for the first 10 states shown in Table 10.2, all of which average more than 20 counties per congressional district. The first state in the table including a city of more than half a million people is Kentucky (i.e., Louisville), the 11th region listed in the table.

At the other end of the scale, the larger metropolitan areas have many congressional districts per country, starting with the San Francisco City (SanFranCtyCA) region, with 9 counties and 13 congressional representatives. Los Angeles County is the extreme case, with the county containing 9 congressional

Table 10.1 Changing congressional representation, 1953–2013

	1953	1963	1973	1983	1993	2003	2013
Alabama	9	8	7	7	7	7	7
Alaska	1[a]	1	1	1	1	1	1
Arizona	2	3	4	5	6	8	9
Arkansas	6	4	4	4	4	4	4
California	30	38	43	45	52	53	53
Colorado	4	4	5	6	6	7	7
Connecticut	6	6	6	6	6	5	5
Delaware	1	1	1	1	1	1	1
Florida	8	12	15	19	23	25	27
Georgia	10	10	10	10	11	13	14
Hawaii	1[a]	2	2	2	2	2	2
Idaho	2	2	2	2	2	2	2
Illinois	25	24	24	22	20	19	18
Indiana	11	11	11	10	10	9	9
Iowa	8	7	6	6	5	5	4
Kansas	6	5	5	5	4	4	4
Kentucky	8	7	7	7	6	6	6
Louisiana	8	8	8	8	7	7	6
Maine	3	2	2	2	2	2	2
Maryland	7	8	8	8	8	8	8
Massachusetts	14	12	12	11	10	10	9
Michigan	18	19	19	18	16	15	14
Minnesota	9	8	8	8	8	8	8
Mississippi	6	5	5	5	5	4	4
Missouri	11	10	10	9	9	9	8
Montana	2	2	2	2	1	1	1
Nebraska	4	3	3	3	3	3	3
Nevada	1	1	1	2	2	3	4
New Hampshire	2	2	2	2	2	2	2
New Jersey	14	15	15	14	13	13	12
New Mexico	2	2	2	3	3	3	3
New York	43	41	39	34	31	29	27
North Carolina	12	11	11	11	12	13	13
North Dakota	2	2	1	1	1	1	1
Ohio	23	24	23	21	19	18	16
Oklahoma	6	6	6	6	6	5	5
Oregon	4	4	4	5	5	5	5
Pennsylvania	30	27	25	23	21	19	18
Rhode Island	2	2	2	2	2	2	2
South Carolina	6	6	6	6	6	6	7

(continued)

Table 10.1 (continued)

	1953	1963	1973	1983	1993	2003	2013
South Dakota	2	2	2	1	1	1	1
Tennessee	9	9	8	9	9	9	9
Texas	22	23	24	27	30	32	36
Utah	2	2	2	3	3	3	4
Vermont	1	1	1	1	1	1	1
Virginia	10	10	10	10	11	11	11
Washington	7	7	7	8	9	9	10
West Virginia	6	5	4	4	3	3	3
Wisconsin	10	10	9	9	9	8	8
Wyoming	1	1	1	1	1	1	1
DC	1[a]	1[a]	1[a]	1[a]	1[a]	1[a]	1[a]

Source http://en.wikipedia.org/wiki/List_of_United_States_congressional_districts. Accessed 27 Jan 2017

[a]Non-voting members

districts of its own combined with another 9 that cross into neighboring counties/USAGE-TERM regions. The Los Angeles case presents difficulties that we overcome using the method explained below.

To estimate a top-down industry by congressional district wages bill or value-added matrix requires several steps. In the case of a wages bill matrix, the starting point is the corresponding industry by county matrix from the top-down database of USAGE-TERM (Fig. 10.1, step 1). To use these data, a mapping from counties to congressional districts is necessary. This is downloadable from the Missouri Census Data Center (step 2). Mappings are required between the regional codes and the USAGE-TERM county names (step 3).

The next decision concerns the choice of a three dimensional matrix, linking industries (512), congressional districts (436) and regions. If we choose counties, the final dimension has 3142 elements and the resulting wages bill matrix is 700 million cells (=512 × 436 × 3142). This was not possible to compute with earlier versions of GEMPACK, but is now. This simplifies the task of estimating congressional district activities. GEMPACK writes the matrix to a file using a sparse storage format which stores only non-zero entries. All but 600,000 of the 700 million cells are zero, ensuring that this matrix is only 4.9 megabytes in size.

Our initial procedure used congressional district population shares of county value-added to estimate congressional district value-added:

$$VA_{i,d,c} = \frac{Pop_{d,c}}{Pop_{\bullet,c}} . VA_{i,\bullet,c} \tag{10.1}$$

where $VA_{i,\bullet,c}$ refers to value-added initially available for industry i (512) by region c (3142) and $Pop_{d,c}$ is the population in congressional district d (436) by county c (3142).

Table 10.2 Counties and congressional districts in USAGE-TERM regions

	Counties	Congressional districts	Ratio		Counties	Congressional districts	Ratio
SouthDakota	66	1	66.0	NewHampshire	10	2	5.00
Montana	56	1	56.0	RoNewYork	55	12	4.58
NorthDakota	53	1	53.0	Nevada	17	4	4.25
Nebraska	93	3	31.0	Washington	39	10	3.90
Alaska	27	1	27.0	RoPnnsylvnia	66	18	3.67
Kansas	105	4	26.3	Delaware	3	1	3.00
Iowa	99	4	24.8	Maryland	24	8	3.00
Wyoming	23	1	23.0	RoFlorida	63	22	2.86
Idaho	44	2	22.0	Hawaii	5	2	2.50
Mississippi	82	4	20.5	RhodeIsland	5	2	2.50
Kentucky	120	6	20.0	NewJersey	21	12	1.75
Arkansas	75	4	18.8	Arizona	15	9	1.67
WestVirgini	55	3	18.3	RoCalifornia	45	28	1.61
RoMissouri	113	7	16.1	Connecticut	8	5	1.60
Oklahoma	77	5	15.4	Massachusett	14	9	1.56
Vermont	14	1	14.0	DC	1	1	1.00
Virginia	135	11	12.3	StLouisCtyMO	2	2	1.00
Georgia	159	14	11.4	ColumbusOH	3	3	1.00
NewMexico	33	3	11.0	SanFranCtyCA	9	13	0.69
Minnesota	87	8	10.9	ChicagoCtyIL	7	13	0.54
Louisiana	64	6	10.7	NewYorkCity	7	16	0.44
Tennessee	95	9	10.6	DetroitCtyMI	3	7	0.43
Indiana	92	9	10.2	PhladlphiaPA	1	3	0.33
Alabama	67	7	9.6	RiversideCA	1	4	0.25

(continued)

Table 10.2 (continued)

	Counties	Congressional districts	Ratio		Counties	Congressional districts	Ratio
Colorado	64	7	9.1	SacramentoCA	1	4	0.25
Wisconsin	72	8	9.0	HillsbrghFL	1	4	0.25
RoIllinois	95	11	8.6	PalmBeachFL	1	4	0.25
RoTexas	251	30	8.4	CuyahogaOH	1	4	0.25
Maine	16	2	8.0	MiamiDadeFL	1	5	0.20
RoMichigan	80	10	8.0	BrowardFL	1	6	0.17
NorthCarolin	100	13	7.7	DallasTX	1	6	0.17
Utah	29	4	7.3	TarrantTX	1	6	0.17
Oregon	36	5	7.2	OrangeCA	1	7	0.14
SouthCarolin	46	7	6.6	HarrisTX	1	9	0.11
RoOhio	84	15	5.6	LosAngelesCA	1	18	0.06

The "Congressional district" columns include districts straddling more than one region (i.e., the sum of these columns exceeds 436). For example, Los Angeles County has 9 congressional districts entirely within the county. Another nine congressional districts cross into other USAGE-TERM regions

Source http://mcdc.missouri.edu/websas/geocorr12.html

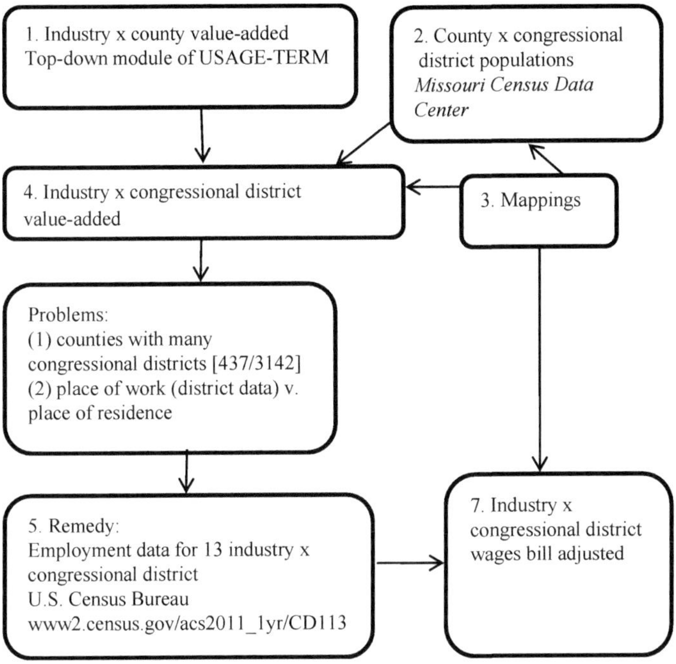

Fig. 10.1 Preparing the value-added matrix for congressional districts

We obtain congressional district estimates of industry activity by summing across the county dimension:

$$\mathrm{VA}_{\mathrm{i,d,\bullet}} = \sum_{\mathrm{c}} \mathrm{VA}_{\mathrm{i,d,c}} \tag{10.2}$$

In cases in which many counties map to a single congressional district, we might think that this provides a final estimate. But we have additional data, namely employment by 13 broad industries in each congressional district, which we can use to modify these data. Both census industry by county employment data and broad industry congressional district employment data are based on place of residence. However, differences arise in the district totals. We assume that the broad sector totals obtained from district data are superior to those obtained by using a matrix of population in district by county to obtain estimates of regional employment (see Eqs. (10.5)–(10.6)).[2]

Another avenue by which district employment data will modify our estimates from (10.2) concerns that of many districts being contained in a single county.

[2]The broad sector totals may be superior in district data than county data, but the latter's advantage concerns the composition at the disaggregated sector level.

Consider the case of Maricopa County in Arizona. For example, 6.6% of Arizona's 1st congressional district (AZ-01) population, 39.9% of the state's 3rd district (AZ-03) population and 8.9% of the state's 4th district (AZ-04) population live within Maricopa County. County level data spread to congressional districts will capture part of the industrial composition of these regions, when added to the contributions from other counties. A problem arises with the 5th to 9th districts (AZ-05, AZ-06, AZ-07, AZ-08 and AZ-09), which are located entirely within the county. If we were to stop with (10.1), the industries composition of each of these districts would be identical.

The U.S. Census Bureau has data available on employment in 13 broad industries by congressional district.[3] These data enable us to depict differences in composition between the districts of the city-based counties listed in column (b) of Table 10.2.

We expect that the most substantial industry level activity revisions on the basis of congressional district employment data will be in the cities of Phoenix in Arizona (i.e., AZ-05 to AZ-09 above), Los Angeles and San Diego in California, Miami and Palm Beach in Florida, Chicago in Illinois, Detroit in Michigan, Dallas and Houston in Texas, Seattle in Washington state and New York.

To modify the value-added estimates for congressional districts, we calculate 13 sector shares of national employment ($EmpSh_{j,d,\bullet}$) from industry j by region d employment $Emp_{j,d,\bullet}$:

$$EmpSh_{j,d,\bullet} = \frac{Emp_{j,d,\bullet}}{Emp_{j,\bullet,\bullet}} \tag{10.3}$$

We multiply $EmpSh_{j,d,\bullet}$ by the national wages bill LAB_i (i.e., 13 j sectors mapped to the full 512 i industries):

$$LABcd_{j,d,\bullet} = EmpSh_{j,d,\bullet} \sum_{i \in j} LAB_i \tag{10.4}$$

Equation (10.5) follows the calculation of (10.1): $WageBill_{i,\bullet,c}$ is the initial matrix of industry wage costs by county. At this point, we use wage bills rather than value-added for scaling purposes, as the labor-intensity of production may vary between the finely disaggregated i industries. We would miss such differences if we used only value-added data.

$$Wage - 13_{j,d,c} = \sum_{i \in j} \frac{Pop_{d,c}}{Pop_{\bullet,c}}.WageBill_{i,\bullet,c} \tag{10.5}$$

[3]See http://www2.census.gov/acs2011_1yr/CD113/. Accessed 27 Jan 2017.

The 13 j industries in WageBill-$13_{j,d,c}$ are summed across the county dimension c to provide a numerator for scaling value-added estimates calculated in (10.6). Finally, $VA^*_{j,d,\bullet}$ is a rescaled estimate of value-added by district:

$$VA^*_{i,d,\bullet} = VA_{i,d,\bullet} \cdot \frac{LABcd_{j(i),d,\bullet}}{Wage - 13_{j(i),d,\bullet}} \quad d \in \text{district} \tag{10.6}$$

Table 10.3 shows how the congressional district data modified the value-added estimates for districts AZ-05 to AZ-09. Equations 10.1 and 10.2 resulted in the broad sector value-added estimates shown in the 1st column of the table. Since Maricopa Country data were imposed on each of AZ-05 to AZ-09, the industry structures of these five districts were initially identical. We see in Table 10.3 that the average of each adjusted industry activity is not equal to the initial activity. This is because Maricopa County extends into other districts mentioned above which have, for example, much higher primary activities (i.e., agriculture, mining, forestry and fishing) than AZ-05 to AZ-09. In utilizing district employment data, we push down the primary activities from initial levels for each of these Phoenix-based districts.

In summary, it is quite possible to devise defensible estimates of disaggregated industry activities by congressional districts. We need to be aware of the difference between employment numbers provide by the census at the county level and those for districts. The processing of congressional district employment share estimates is fully programmed. The programming ensures that when congressional districts change again, as they do once a decade, we can use available data on the revised districts to re-estimate the congressional district industry activities within USAGE-TERM.

Table 10.3 Modifications in Maricopa County using congressional district data

Value-added $m	Initial all	AZ-05	AZ-06	AZ-07	AZ-08	AZ-09
Primary	209	276	211	181	133	197
Transport and utilities	1340	1166	1323	1926	942	1091
Construction	1087	1373	906	1106	904	1314
Manufactures	1763	1631	2305	1330	1715	1662
Wholesale trade	1533	1349	1773	1180	1473	1587
Retail trade	1594	1627	1402	1624	1570	1847
Information technology	842	809	994	509	851	965
Finance, insurance, leasing	2992	2687	4041	1994	2982	3126
Professional, scientific & waste management srvc	3264	3024	4037	2806	2362	3733
Education and health	2430	2537	2670	1720	2338	2758
Other services	632	3348	4350	3355	2730	5050
Art, recreation, dining, accommodation	992	761	1225	913	1049	975
Public administration	3074	3032	1956	2695	4746	2435

10.2 Congressional Districts in a Bottom-Up Representation of USAGE-TERM

One certainty in regional CGE modeling is that clients can always think of a new regional representation which they require. No particular regional representation in a master database can cover all possible scenarios. A state level representation is unsatisfactory for many applications: for example, California's economy is in the top 10 in the world, with GDP comparable to that of Canada. The GDP of Texas is comparable to that of Australia, the 12th largest national economy in the world.[4] As discussed above, even the county level representation in California is deficient, since Los Angeles County has a larger population than all but eight states of the union. But at the other end of the scale, the Dakotas, Montana and Alaska each contain fewer than one million inhabitants.

When dealing with scenarios such as investment in urban infrastructure, a master database based on 436 congressional districts may be better than one based on states or the 70 regions of the original USAGE-TERM model. Yet when dealing with a mining boom in the Dakotas, a master database based on 70 regions may be insufficient not because it fails to split urban regions sufficiently, but because it does not concentrate sufficiently on the set of counties within which the boom occurs.

At issue is how best to use available data to create a master database with appropriate regional representation for a particular group of scenarios. For a state, we need to recognize that a top-down representation is inadequate if we wish to ascribe supply shocks specific to a small region. But it follows that if we wish to devise scenarios concerning parts of Los Angeles County, even a county level bottom-up master database would be deficient: the county is represented separately in the standard 70-region USAGE-TERM master database.

A next step is to introduce some flexibility in how we might devise regions in a bottom-up master database. In theory, if we have the industry shares for congressional district top-down representation, we have gone a substantial way towards devising the requirements for a bottom-up master database based on 436 congressional districts. Census data (see footnote 2) fill many of the data gaps. Census data on employment from this site are used in Eq. (10.6).

The census data also provide the total number of employed and unemployed persons by congressional district, enabling us to include both labor supply and total employed by region in the model. Such data are used in the regional labor market theory of the model, based on the assumption of sticky wages (Wittwer et al. 2005).

The congressional district data are sufficient to provide a platform for further modeling studies. For example, data are available on the distribution of income across congressional districts. Demographic details are available, plus data on housing, housing fuel type and health insurance coverage. These data would be useful in regional CGE studies concerned with household income distribution.

---

[4]See http://www.imf.org/external/country/index.htm. Accessed 27 Jan 2017.

Table 10.4 Matching ports to congressional districts

Port	Congressional district	USAGE-TERM 70 region
MobileAL	AL-01	Alabama
AnchorageAK	AK-00	Alaska
NogalesAZ	AZ-02	Arizona
SanFrancCA	CA-13	SanFranCtyCA
LosAngelesCA	CA-44	LosAngelesCA
SanDiegoCA	CA-53	RoCalifornia
WashingtonDC	DC-01	DC
TampaFL	FL-14	HillsbrghFL
MiamiFL	FL-24	MiamiDadeFL
SavannahGA	GA-01	Georgia
HonoluluHI	HI-01	Hawaii
ColumSnakeID	ID-00	Idaho
ChicagoIL	IL-04	ChicagoCtyIL
NewOrleansLA	LA-01	Louisiana
BostonMA	MA-07	Massachusett
BaltimoreMD	MD-03	Maryland
PortlandME	ME-01	Maine
DetroitMI	MI-13	DetroitCtyMI
MinneapolMN	MN-05	Minnesota
DuluthMN	MN-08	Minnesota
StLouisMO	MO-01	StLouisCtyMO
GreatFallsMT	MT-00	Montana
WilmingtonNC	NC-07	NorthCarolin
PembinaND	ND-01	NorthDakota
NewYorkNY	NY-10	NewYorkCity
OgdensburgNY	NY-21	RoNewYork
BuffaloNY	NY-26	RoNewYork
ClevelandOH	OH-11	CuyahogaOH
PhiladelphPA	PA-01	PhladlphiaPA
ProvidenceRI	RI-01	RhodeIsland
CharlestonSC	SC-01	SouthCarolin
ElPasoTX	TX-16	RoTexas
HoustonTX	TX-18	HarrisTX
FortWorthTX	TX-24	DallasTX
LaredoTX	TX-28	RoTexas
PortArthurTX	TX-36	RoTexas
NorfolkVA	VA-03	Virginia
StAlbansVT	VT-00	Vermont
SeattleWA	WA-07	Washington
MilwaukeeWI	WI-04	Wisconsin

Greater use of existing data may enable us in future research to come up with more sophisticated estimates of congressional district shares of national consumption by commodity.

The TERM methodology requires a distance matrix in order to use the gravity assumption to distribute trades between supplies and demands for commodities. A distance matrix is generated again using U.S. census data which provide latitude and longitude coordinates: see http://www.census.gov/geo/maps-data/data/gazetteer2013.html.

Table 10.4 shows the mapping of international ports to districts and regions. In the TERM methodology, international trade flows are recorded at the point of export or import rather than by export origin or import destination. For example, imports into Los Angeles that are destined for use in Nevada appear in USAGE-TERM as an international import to Los Angeles, and an inter-regional export from Los Angeles to Nevada.

10.2.1 A Suitable Gravity Assumption for Small Regions

The first implementation of TERM relied on an estimation of inter-regional trade matrices in which trade volumes were an inverse power of distance. As noted in Sect. 10.1.1, some commodities were designated as strictly local.

If we start splitting the database into smaller regions, the distribution of trades between regions requires a rethink. In cities, it might be that the only strictly local commodity is housing. In this context, price disparities between regions dominate allocation ahead of inter-regional housing trades. This seems defensible, given that price disparities between suburbs a few miles or even a few streets apart can be stark.

The aim of modifying the gravity formula is to replicate the inter-regional trade pattern in a database with a fine level of regional disaggregation that we previously obtained with a coarser level of regional disaggregation. That is, we wish to observe a similar trade pattern when either master database is aggregated to the same regions. If we do not modify the gravity assumption, a master database with a fine level of regional representation may understate inter-regional trades relative to a master database with fewer regions.

For other "local" commodities, it is more appropriate to think that the definition of "local" switches from a single region to a cluster of adjacent regions in the context of intra-city congressional districts. Therefore, we require a distance exponent that enables high tradability between closely located regions, but which tends to the usual degree of tradability (i.e., as in databases with less regional disaggregation) as the distance increases. For example, a customer may travel several miles for a haircut or grocery shopping but is unlikely to travel 100 miles—unless there is no closer source of supply.

The usual TERM gravity formula, as described in Horridge (2012) and Sect. 9.2.2.1, is:

$$\frac{V_{r,d}}{V_{\bullet,d}} \propto \frac{\sqrt{V_{r,\bullet}}}{D^{k}_{r,d}} \quad r \neq d \tag{10.7}$$

where

$V_{r,d}$ value of flow from r to d
$V_{r,\bullet}$ production in r
$V_{\bullet,d}$ demand in d
$D_{r,d}$ distance from r to d

where K is a commodity-specific parameter valued between 0.5 and 2, with higher values for commodities not readily tradable.

Diagonal cells of the trade matrices are set according to: $\frac{V_{d,d}}{V_{d,\bullet}}$ = locally-supplied demand in d as share of local production

$$= \min\left\{\frac{V_{d,\bullet}}{V_{\bullet,d}}, 1\right\} F \tag{10.8}$$

where F is a commodity-specific parameter valued between 0.5 and 1, with a value close to 1 if the commodity is not readily tradable.

The revised formula to allow for local trade between near regions is based on a modified distance variable $D^{m}_{r,d}$.

Let $A = 1 + 0.5{*}D_{r,d}$ and $B = A + 400/(10-3){*}(D_{r,d}-3.0)$

$$\begin{aligned} D^{m}_{r,d} &= A && \text{for } D_{r,d} <= 3, \\ &= A + B && \text{for } D_{r,d} > 3,\ D_{r,d} < 20, \\ &= A + B + 10 * (D_{r,d} - 20) && D_{r,d} > 20 \end{aligned}$$

D is measured in units of approximately 6 miles each, computed from latitude and longitude coordinates. The revised gravity formula is

$$\frac{V_{r,d}}{V_{\bullet,d}} \propto \frac{\sqrt{V_{r,\bullet}}}{D^{m}_{r,d}} \tag{10.9}$$

The modified distance variable ensures that all commodities (other than housing and tourism exports, which are excluded from the modified formula) are tradable between proximal regions r and d (i.e., $D_{r,d}$ <=3, about 18 miles), but the degree of tradability declines beyond this distance.

In summary, there are several ways of altering the tradability between regions as region size changes. One is to alter the gravity formula, using Eq. (10.9) instead of (10.7) as shown above. Another is to alter the list of local commodities. Within Eq. (10.8), we can vary F. In practice, we may compare aggregations of a more finely disaggregated database (e.g., 436 congressional districts) with an aggregation from a less disaggregated master database (e.g., 70 state and sub-state regions) to calibrate Eq. (10.9). This requires inspection of the respective TRADE matrices.

10.2.2 Choosing a Manageable Number of Sectors

Having obtained activity shares for production, current consumption and international trade by congressional district, next we need to settle on a manageable number of industries and commodities. To replicate the 512 sectors of the USAGE-TERM 70 region database would require a very large database, the preparation of which may be beyond the capabilities even of GEMPACK software. Whereas the 70 region master database is 0.56 GB, a corresponding 436 region master database would probably exceed 13 GB. By increasing the number of regions by six-fold, the database size would increase by more than 25-fold. A pragmatic approach is to reduce the number of sectors. Initially, we erred on the side of conservatism, and settled for 59 sectors. The choice of sectors will depend on the nature of regional study of interest. Since a congressional district representation is likely to concentrate more on cities than rural areas, some aggregation of primary industries appears reasonable. In the original master database representing 512 industries, agriculture is represented by 31 different sectors. This was reduced to two in the 59 industry master database for congressional district representation. The 11 mining industries in the 512 sector database were reduced to 2 in the 59 sector version. Among manufactures, the 46 industries covering food, beverages and tobacco products in the original database were represented by a single industry.

An alternative approach to keeping a larger number of sectors in a database with many regions relies on a feature of TERM master databases. A single matrix showing the supply of margins (SUPPMAR) increases its share of the total database size as the number of regions grows, as this matrix grows with the cube of the number of regions. In the case of the 59 sector, 436 region master database of USAGE-TERM with 4 margins, which depicts economic activity by congressional district, the SUPPMAR matrix accounts for 78% of the total database size. Its size depends on the number of regions and margins in the database, and is independent of the number of non-margin industries/commodities. For this reason, doubling the number of sectors from 59 to around 120, while retaining 4 margins, will result in the size of the master database increasing by only one-third, from 1.7 to 2.3 GB, in the header array file generated by GEMPACK. If the number of margins doubles to 8, the resulting master database will exceed 4 GB, with the SUPPMAR matrix alone being around 2.5 GB. The 436 congressional district master database at present includes 121 sectors and 4 margins.

Our choice so far in limiting ourselves to a master database of 2.3 GB is one of management. If we chose to enlarge the master database to 8 GB, this would enable us to represent 300 sectors and 8 margins for each congressional district. But generating the master database would take many hours of computation instead of an hour or so. Aggregation of the master database would be cumbersome, as it would strain existing software. Having gone to this trouble, we would question the purpose of having 300 sectors. The congressional district representation is mainly about splitting up large urban centers. For many of the potential modeling tasks that might utilize the flexibility arising from 300 sectors, sub-state representation other than by congressional district might be more useful. For the time being, we have two master database representations. The 512 sector, 70 region master database is most useful for scenarios that do not involve large cities directly. The other master database based on congressional district is preferable for urban analysis. Since major urban regions are dominated by services rather than primary or even secondary industries, the relatively limited sectoral choice in the 436 region version will not in most circumstances hinder modeling analysis. However, we should not assume that these two master databases are suitable for all scenarios. Section 10.3 outlines another potential approach.

10.3 Towards Variable Disaggregation of USAGE-TERM

The 121 sector representation of congressional districts may be suitable for some CGE simulations but deficient for others. Supposing an urban CGE study is to examine transport options. The congressional district representation would generally be preferable to the original 70 region database. There may be limitations: For example, the 121 sectors of the congressional district database include a single sector covering road and rail transport. We may wish to generate a new master database that has the relevant sectors fully disaggregated (i.e., with rail transport, road transport and urban passenger transport represented separately), and some aggregation of other sectors to keep the database size manageable.

If congressional district representation is necessary for some projects, and sub-state representation necessary for others, maybe the variable disaggregation approach should go further. To proceed with this approach, we should first take stock of the strengths and weaknesses of available data at the county and congressional district levels respectively.

County data are probably superior in industries that are relatively labor-intensive, in those cases in which census data are available. This is because census data provide employment numbers by industry: Such data become a less reliable estimator as the labor intensity of industry production decreases. Agricultural census data provide more crop types and livestock activities than are represented in the 512 sector version of USAGE-TERM. The agricultural census data are therefore a useful estimator of regional agricultural industry outputs, although such data may be somewhat dated (only 2007 output data were available at the county level in 2014). Electricity generation data are available from carma.

org.[5] Overall, estimates of industry activities are available at the county level at a level of disaggregation not approached by congressional district data.

Yet when it comes to regional income data, income distribution data, employment levels, unemployment rates and broad occupational detail, congressional district data are superior to county data. As an example, it appears to be easier to estimate regional household aggregate consumption at the congressional district level than the county level, as congressional district data include per capita income and income distribution by households. While industry incomes are estimated at the county level, they are not equivalent to household incomes, as capital may be owned by inhabitants of other nations or other congressional districts. For this reason, in the top-down module of USAGE-TERM (i.e., used in aggregations of the 70 region master database), county level nominal household consumption is tied to nominal labor earnings rather than nominal regional GDP.

One approach to variable disaggregation would be to disaggregate one state at a time, while leaving remaining states as single regions. But each disaggregation would require careful decision making. Consider California: would it be sufficient to prepare a master database consisting of the state's 53 congressional districts plus the 50 remaining U.S. states (including the District of Columbia) as separate regions? Certainly, this is computationally feasible: with 400 industries/commodities and 6 margins, such a database would be no bigger than the original USAGE-TERM database (i.e., 512 industries/commodities, 70 regions and 9 margins). A concern with congressional district representation is that some predominantly rural regions may be dominated by urban economic activity. However, three congressional districts in California remain substantially agricultural. These are CA-20, CA-16 and CA-21, each with agriculture's contribution to regional GDP exceeding 20%.

But for some modeling projects, this regional representation may remain deficient. For example, Chap. 12 details modeling with a modified version of the master database that splits California's Central Valley into 12 separate counties. The modified master database relied on top-down county shares provided by the core master database, while theoretical modifications followed Dixon et al. (2012).

How many regions could we represent with the full 512 sector, 9 margin database before exceeding the size of the 121 sector, congressional district representation? In theory, as many at 168 regions could be represented.

The upside of implementing a variable disaggregation approach is that we could devise combinations of congressional districts and counties with the necessary detail of a core CGE database without feeling constrained by dimensionality. The downside is that beyond a certain point, the task of maintaining and updating a stable of master databases, rather than the existing two master databases, could itself become cumbersome.

---

[5]Indeed, carma.org data provide latitude and longitude coordinates for power generating plants that can be matched to either counties or congressional districts.

For this reason, we are exploring the possibility of partitioning the SUPPMAR and TRADMAR matrices in generating the master database. As an example, if we succeeded in reducing to one-tenth the existing size of these matrices via splitting the dimensions of each further, the size of a 512 sector, 436 region database would be around 5.8 GB. This may be computable with high memory PCs. Such an advance would enable us to prepare a single master database. It remains to be seen whether this would provide optimal database management.

10.3.1 Estimating Regional Activity on a Journey-to-Work Basis

There are many examples in which regional economic activity is best estimated on the basis of place of work. Downtown city precincts are important economic hubs in which place-of-residence data underestimate their economic importance. If our modeling scenarios are to include such precincts, we can supplement our district data with U.S. Census Bureau employment data by zip code on a place-of-work basis.[6] Indeed, some zip codes refer specifically to work places, notably airports. After processing U.S. Census Bureau data, we find that employment numbers in some congressional districts are little more than 100,000 on a place of work basis, whereas in New York's 12th congressional district (NY-12), employment exceeds 1.1 million. By contrast, the broad sector-by-district employment data compiled on a place-of-residence basis indicate a range of district employment levels from a maximum of half a million workers to little more than 200,000. The latter is in FL-11, reflecting a high proportion of retirees in the population.

Where necessary, based on zip code data, we could realign the shares of national activity so as to represent congressional districts using a place of work rather than a place of residence basis.

Our preference is to locate consumption activities where people live rather than where they work. Therefore, this will provide a sharp difference in some instances between regional production and regional household consumption activities, particularly in large cities.

Given that transport infrastructure is a major policy issue in urban centers, a possible future direction might be to devise a matrix of employment that includes both the place of residence and place of work. Again, we would require a methodology that estimates the two locations for workers based on journey-to-work and place-of-residence census data. One objective of such detail might be to have estimates of typical distances that workers commute. This would bring

---

[6]The link https://www.census.gov/econ/cbp/download/ contains the relevant data. The link http://www2.census.gov/geo/relfiles/cdsld13/natl/natl_zccd_delim.txt provides a mapping from zip codes to congressional districts (accessed 5 September 2014).

multi-regional CGE modeling a little closer to transport models, thereby enhancing the capability of CGE models in analyzing the costs and benefits of major urban transport infrastructure projects.

References

Dixon P, Parmenter B, Sutton J (1978) Spatial disaggregation of ORANI results: a preliminary analysis of the impacts of protection at the state level. Econ Anal Policy 8:35–86

Dixon P, Parmenter B, Sutton J, Vincent D (1982) ORANI: a multisectoral model of the Australian economy. Contributions to economic analysis, vol 142, North-Holland, Amsterdam

Dixon P, Rimmer M, Tsigas M (2007) Regionalising results from a detailed CGE model: macro, industry and state effects in the U.S. of removing major tariffs and quotas. Papers Reg Sci 86:31–55

Dixon PB, Rimmer MT, Wittwer G (2012) The theory of TERM-H_2O. In: Wittwer G (ed) Economic modeling of water, the Australian CGE experience. Springer, Dordrecht

Horridge M (2012) The TERM model and its database. In: Wittwer G (ed) Economic modeling of water, the Australian CGE experience. Springer, Dordrecht, pp 13–36

Wittwer G, Vere D, Jones R, Griffith G (2005) Dynamic general equilibrium analysis of improved weed management in Australia's winter cropping systems. Aust J Agric Resour Econ 49: 363–377

Part IV
Model Applications

Chapter 11
Modeling California's Drought

Glyn Wittwer

Abstract The drought of 2012–2015 in California imposed severe stress on the state's water resources. USAGE-TERM is a multi-regional CGE model that represents 12 key irrigation counties in California as separate economies. Water trading between irrigators would help California cope with drought. In particular, sales of water from producers of annual crops to producers of perennials may lower the costs of maintaining plantations, given the high fixed costs arising from the alternative of drilling new wells.

Keywords Drought impacts · Impediments to water trading · Aquifer depletion

11.1 Background

By 2015, California entered its fourth consecutive year of drought. This imposed water-shortage stress on farmers and other users. In the spring of 2015, Governor Brown ordered a 25% reduction in urban water use. This created some resentment among urban communities who reason that agriculture is the largest user of water and therefore should bear the burden of restrictions. Indeed, surface water allocations to irrigators have been cut in the wake of the drought. One response by farmers has been to increase use of groundwater and invest in new bores to extract water. This has potentially adverse consequences: some wells in Central Valley have run dry (James 2015).

Historically, water management in California has been dominated by engineering solutions. Vast diversions of water to satisfy agricultural and urban needs are part of the folklore of the state and have played an integral part in the state's economic development. Economic instruments to allocate water have played little

G. Wittwer (✉)
Centre of Policy Studies, Victoria University,
300 Flinders St, Melbourne, VIC 3000, Australia
e-mail: Glyn.wittwer@vu.edu.au

G. Wittwer (ed.), *Multi-regional Dynamic General Equilibrium Modeling of the U.S. Economy*, Advances in Applied General Equilibrium Modeling,
DOI 10.1007/978-3-319-58866-7_11

or no role. In response to the current water crisis, there are signs of the belated introduction of economic signals. The usual rules that tie water usage to land ownership are, in some instances, being by-passed. There has been some diversion of water from annual cropping to supplying the needs of perennials. Livestock feed is being imported from other regions as diminished water availability reduces on-farm feed inputs.

A version of USAGE-TERM has been developed in order to analyze the impacts of drought. It includes provision for water trading between irrigators and regions. This chapter outlines the theoretical and database modifications required to USAGE-TERM. Drought simulations using this model and insights gained from the modeling conclude the chapter.

This chapter concentrates on agriculture rather than other users. It is the case in drought that although large cities may suffer water restrictions, often accompanied by considerable publicity, it is often regional communities off of the main water grids whose water supplies are most vulnerable to drought. Although it would be possible with further research effort to model urban and regional non-agricultural water use, it is outside the quantitative scope of this chapter.

11.2 Modifying the USAGE-TERM Database to Depict the Californian Drought

Before devising water accounts and adapting the theory of USAGE-TERM to deal with drought, a new master database had to be created based on relevant regions. Chap. 9 discusses two master databases, one based on 70 regions in which the largest states are divided into key sub-state regions, and another based on 436 congressional districts. Section 9.3 discusses some of the decisions governing the choice of a different set of regions for a master database. In order to model the Californian drought, the 70 region master database was extended. The six sub-state regions of California were split into a further 12 regions. More specifically, the 45 counties that comprise the Rest of California region in the 70 region database were split so as to represent the counties of Butte, Colusa, Fresno, Glenn, Merced, Kern, Kings, Madera, San Joaquin, Stanislaus, Tulare and Yolo as separate bottom-up regions. The revised Rest of California region includes the remaining 33 counties.

The revised 82 region master database was aggregated in the next step. Although the data are available to represent water accounts in all Californian counties with significant agriculture, not all are represented individually in the aggregation. The aggregation represents the 12 counties listed above separately, plus two composite regions, one covering the remainder of the state and the other the remainder of the nation (Fig. 11.1). The aggregated database was updated to 2013 using the approached outlined in Sect. 9.2.3.2. Details concerning the treatment of water appear in Sect. 11.2.2.

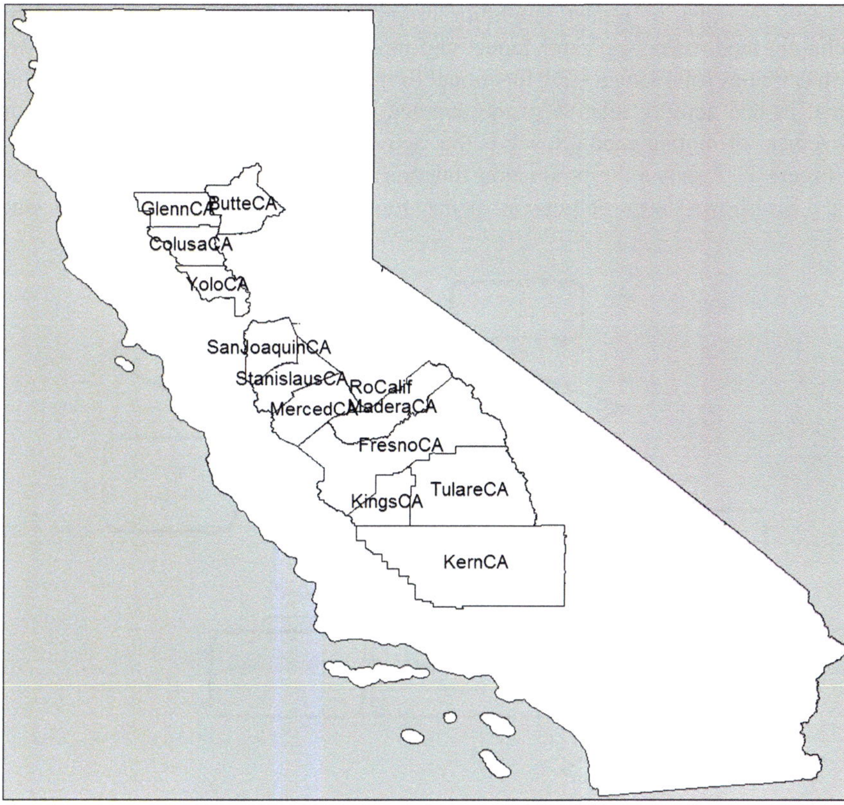

Fig. 11.1 Bottom-up Californian regions in USAGE-TERM-H_2O

11.2.1 Theoretical Modifications to USAGE-TERM

One of the key tasks in devising a model of agriculture is to reflect apparent factor mobility. A rule-of-thumb is that annual crops have greater flexibility than perennials, because a lack of water leads to fallowing in the case of annuals, and may lead to plantation destruction in the case of perennials. If market conditions are favorable, farmers may devote considerable resources to preserving plantations. It follows that there are market pressures during times of drought for perennial producers to buy water from farmers of annual crops. Rigidities such as appurtenant water rights and the absence of mature water markets will constrain water trading, and prevent the movement towards equalization of the marginal product of water across irrigators as scarcity worsens.

Following Dixon et al. (2011, 2012), agricultural land is divided into irrigable land and dry land. Irrigable land is used for either irrigated agriculture or dry-land farming. Dry land can only be used for dry-land farming. As water availability falls, either an irrigated industry switches to other irrigated activities or to dry-land activity. In order to reflect flexibility in production possibilities, farm factors including land, owner-operator inputs and mobile capital move between different farm activities following a CET functional form. For example, an increase in capital rental in one activity relative to the average of all farm activities will induce a movement of mobile capital towards that activity.

Figure 11.2 shows the production function used in farm industries. The top of Fig. 11.2 shows farm outputs as being formed from a Leontief or constant

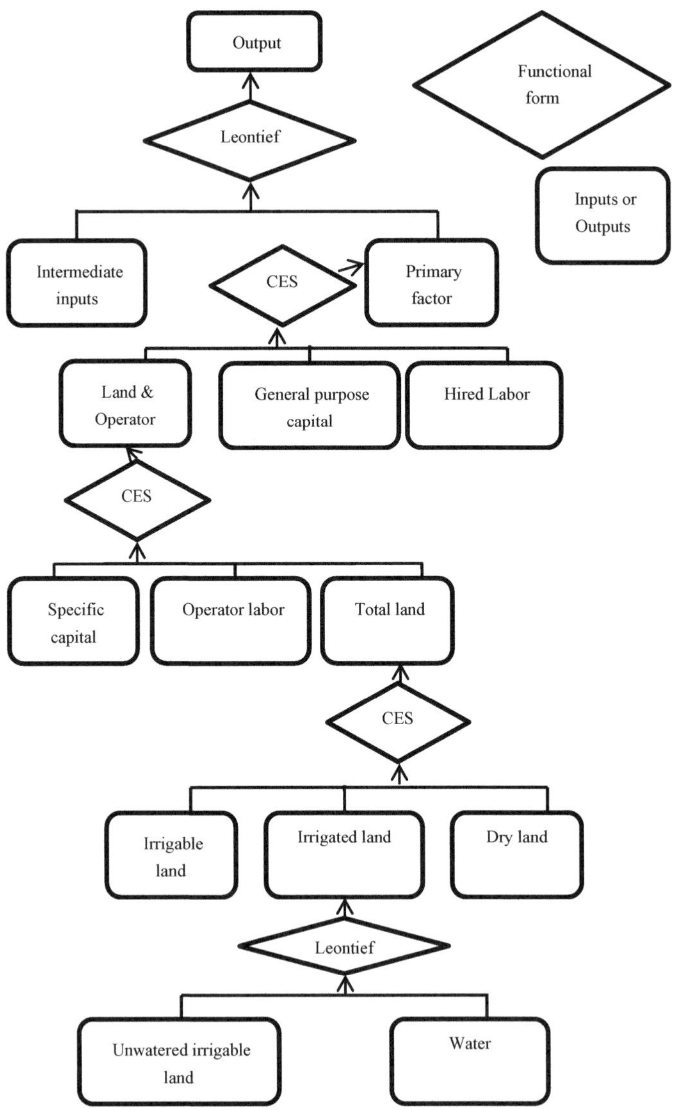

Fig. 11.2 Production function for farm industries

proportions combination of intermediate inputs and primary factors. The theory of intermediate input demands mainly follows that of a standard CGE model (Dixon et al. 1982).

The main difference between the functional form used here and that in TERM-H_2O (Dixon et al. 2011, 2012) is that the Hay and forage sectors (split into dry-land and irrigated technologies) are intermediate inputs into livestock production, rather than a substitute for irrigated land. This implies that if livestock producers in California suffer cuts in water availability, they will substitute from on-farm Hay and forage to similar inputs from other regions. A single farm may include several industries, Hay and forage and livestock among them. The on-farm use of Hay and forage is treated as a marketed input in the present theory, regardless of whether the source is own-farm or external.

Land and operator inputs are substitutable with mobile capital and labor in forming a primary factor CES composite. The land and operator formation differs from earlier theory (Dixon et al. 1982). It is a CES composite nest of specific capital (i.e., livestock herds or perennial plantations), operator labor and total land.

Land in turn is a CES composite of irrigable land (i.e., land that may be irrigated but is not at present), irrigated land and dry-land. Irrigated land is a Leontief composite of un-watered irrigable land and water. This means that subject to a given water-using technology, the volume of water applied per unit of irrigable land is constant for a particular crop. The implication of this constraint is that if water availability falls, irrigable land moves to an un-watered state. The three types of land are highly mobile in dry-land production, with a CES parameter of 10.0. In the case of irrigation industries, watered irrigable land accounts for all of the total land input.

11.2.2 Water Trading

On the assumption that the CGE database reflects a typical year, we assume that water is not scarce in the initial database. Therefore, we impose an arbitrarily low unit value on water (i.e., $50 per acre-foot). Our interest is in how much water prices increase as scarcity worsens. Since we wish to examine the impacts of hypothetical water trading, following Dixon et al. (2011, 2012), the model includes theory that enables water trading either between irrigators within a region or between irrigators in a group of regions.

In practice, in response to drought in California, farmers have had limited opportunities to sell water to other users. Since the average product of water in production of some crops is only a few hundred dollars per acre-foot, rising water scarcity will induce producers of crops with low average products of water either to switch to different irrigation activities or, assuming water is tradable between farmers, sell their water to willing buyers. USDA data provide us with a set of initial conditions for irrigation water use.[1] Optimal allocations within USAGE-TERM will change as water scarcity worsens and the marginal product of water rises. Modeled water trading volumes are likely to be much higher than those observed in actual response to drought, due to institutional constraints on water trading.

11.2.3 Groundwater, Surface Water and Rainfall

The theory of this version of USAGE-TERM includes two sources of water, namely irrigation water and rainfall. There is no theory explaining the volume of irrigation water available in each region, nor is there a distinction between surface water and groundwater. USAGE-TERM determines how a given volume of water is distributed between users.

The starting point in modifying USAGE-TERM is USDA data. From these data, we obtain the number of acres of farmland used for different types of crops, primarily in California. Data were collected for other states and the exercise could be repeated for a different watershed region. USDA also provides estimates of irrigation water required for each crop, usually at the state level. Rainfall accounts for a share of total water requirements. However, average rainfall varies between counties, from as high as 40 in. in Butte County to as low as 8 in. in Kings County. We must assign different rainfall contributions when calculating the different irrigation water requirements by region for a given crop. Table 11.1 shows average annual rainfall and the author's estimate of effective rainfall. This latter figure is relevant when calculating irrigation water requirements. For example, if an irrigation crop requires 4 feet of water per annum in California and the effective rainfall is 12 in., then irrigation must supply 3 feet of water.

There may be more detailed data available on effective rainfall by region. It may also vary by type of crop. USDA data on water requirements are statewide rather than by county. Such data reveal that Arizona, for example, has higher irrigation water requirements on average for a given crop than California. We might expect different overall water requirements in different regions of California for a given crop, given differences in rainfall and evaporation across regions. Improved data, should they emerge, can be added to the data-generation programs used in devising USAGE-TERM so as to improve the model's database.

A theme prominent during drought is that of water-saving technological change. When water is abundant, there is little economic motivation to use water more efficiently. Water saving per unit of output in USAGE-TERM is depicted in two ways. First, as shown in Fig. 11.2, water is substitutable with primary inputs. This implies that if the relative price of water increases many-fold, as is the usual case during drought, less water and more primary inputs will be used per unit of output

[1]See http://quickstats.nass.usda.gov/.

Table 11.1 Annual rainfall contribution by county

	Average (inches)	Effective (inches)
ButteCA	40	25
ColusaCA	18	10
FresnoCA	13	7
GlennCA	23	13
MercedCA	12	6
KernCA	7	1
KingsCA	8	2
TulareCA	11	5
YoloCA	32	17
SanJoaquinCA	18	10
StanislausCA	13	7
MaderaCA	12	6
RoCalif	23	13

Source: http://www.usclimatedata.com accessed 21 July 2015. Effective rainfall based on author's judgment

(endogenous water saving). The second way of ascribing changes in water requirements is exogenous. Research may lead to a particular watering regime that reduces the volume required without impacting on yields for a given crop. This could be ascribed as a shock to water-saving technological change within the model.

USDA data on crop acreage are multiplied by water requirements to provide estimates of acre-feet of water used. The volume of irrigation water used for each crop type is then calculated as the total volume used minus the volume contributed by effective rainfall.

11.2.4 Reducing California's Irrigation Water Availability by 40%

This scenario is a stylized version of drought. It does not account for differences in water availability between regions. It does not consider increased extractions of groundwater in response to reduced surface water availability or the increased costs of pumping. Water trading is permitted between irrigated sectors within a region. Trading is also permitted between Kings County and Kern County in this setting. This therefore is a hypothetical exercise in order to examine the possible impacts of water trading in response to drought.

Our a priori expectation based on the theory of USAGE-TERM is that a worsening of water scarcity will induce substitution among irrigators away from water (embedded in total land and land and operator in Fig. 11.2) towards primary factors. This means that the percentage decrease in output will be smaller than the

Table 11.2 Macroeconomic impacts on 12 Counties and terms-of-trade impacts, full intra-regional water trading (% change from base case)

12 counties	Macro results	Terms-of-trade by region	
Real consumption	−0.97	ButteCA	0.0
Real investment	−0.04	ColusaCA	2.2
Real GDP	−0.78	FresnoCA	−0.1
Employment	−0.51	GlennCA	−0.9
Real wage	0	MercedCA	−1.0
GDP deflator	−0.80	KernCA	−0.2
CPI	−0.62	KingsCA	0.3
		TulareCA	0.5
		YoloCA	−0.1
		SanJoaquinCA	0.1
		StanislausCA	−0.6
		MaderaCA	−0.3

percentage decrease in water applied. In the case of the other fruit and nuts sector in the model run, the average reduction in water intensity per unit of output across the 12 counties is 17%: total water usage falls by 30% with a 13% reduction in output. Since we do not assume any reduction in average rainfall in this scenario, the cut in irrigation water used of 40% (net sales of water to other irrigators are zero, Table 11.3) is larger than the percentage cut in total water used.[2]

A short-run setting is depicted, in which capital is fixed in quantity, although mobile farm capital can move between different farm activities. Real wages are fixed in the short term setting.

The marginal impact of water trading is to alleviate reductions in farm output arising from worsening water scarcity. A cut in water allocations of 40% may reduce farm output by between 10 and 20% without water trading, after accounting for substitution away from water. In this scenario, farm output across the 12 counties drops by only 5.4%. However, there is a substantial increase in purchases of Hay and forage inputs from interstate by the livestock sectors in the 12 counties. The change in output therefore underestimates the impact of drought on farm value-added.

In Table 11.2, we see that real GDP across the 12 counties has fallen by 0.81% relative to a base case with usual irrigation water allocations. Real consumption by households has fallen by 1%, a larger percentage than the real GDP loss due to a decline in the terms-of-trade across the region. The one county with a substantial

[2]During a prolonged drought, the early years tend to include a reduction in the rainfall contribution and a lesser reduction in the irrigation water availability. Water managers, based on the Australian experience (see Wittwer and Griffith 2011, Table 7.5), tend to impose more severe cuts in the later years of drought and maintain reduced allocations in the first recovery year.

Table 11.3 Net sales of water (thousands of acre-feet)

	HayForage	Almonds	OthFruitNut	Vegetables	OthAgri	Cotton	Grapes	Rice	Tomatoes	Total	Trading price $/ac-ft
ButteCA	3	−35	−8	0	−10	0	0	50	0	0	146
ColusaCA	6	0	−17	−6	−2	0	0	29	−11	0	130
FresnoCA	117	−248	47	23	−29	98	63	0	−70	0	405
GlennCA	21	−65	−10	−2	−3	0	0	59	0	0	208
MercedCA	180	−176	−17	−7	−17	40	3	6	−12	0	383
KernCA	114	−274	47	−3	−66	48	16	0	−11	−129	387
KingsCA	144	−46	7	−7	−5	69	0	0	−32	129	387
TulareCA	148	−42	5	−1	−97	6	−17	0	0	0	169
YoloCA	36	−18	−1	−14	−5	0	−3	18	−13	0	165
SanJoaquinCA	95	−93	35	1	−48	0	17	6	−14	0	343
StanislausCA	91	−96	5	10	−6	0	5	0	−8	0	713
MaderaCA	34	−104	27	3	0	2	41	0	−3	0	528
Total	988	−1197	120	−3	−288	263	125	168	−174	0	290

terms-of-trade[3] gain is Colusa. This is because livestock production is relatively small in Colusa. Most of the other Californian counties rely on imports of Hay and forage to maintain livestock production, the price of which rises as scarcity worsens. This has a negative impact on regional terms-of-trade. Kings County has a water trading terms-of-trade gain of 0.9%, which more than offsets a merchandise terms-of-trade loss of 0.6% in the county, resulting in an overall gain in the terms-of-trade of 0.3%.

Water trading results in a movement of water towards crops with a higher average product of water. In each region that has almond production, the industry imports water from other farm sectors. Vegetables have a relatively high average product of water, but in Fresno and Stanislaus counties, water purchases by almonds dominate, so that vegetables are a net seller rather than buyer of water in these counties.

This hypothetical scenario includes a volume of water trading that is likely to exceed actual water trading volumes in response to drought. Therefore, we may move closer to a depiction of the actual marginal impact of drought by restricting water trading.

In a second version of the scenario in which 40% of irrigation water availability is cut in each region, water trading is restricted in so far as there are no sales of water from Hay and forage to other irrigators in Fresno, Glenn, Merced or Stanislaus counties, the four largest almond-producing regions.

The restriction on trading results in a substantial terms-of-trade gain for the 12 counties. The terms-of-trade gain across the 12 counties varies from 0.2% in Yolo to 2.5% in Glenn. Among the 12 counties, almonds account for the largest share of GDP in Glenn County. Now, real consumption is 0.3% below the base case, compared with 0.97% below in the unrestricted intra-county trading scenario. At the same time, real GDP falls by 1.07%, compared with a fall of 0.81% in the unrestricted water trading scenario. Employment in this scenario falls by 0.64%, or around 12,000 jobs in the 12 counties, compared with a fall of 0.51% or around 9500 jobs in the unconstrained water trading scenario.

The prices of almonds, grapes and other fruit and nuts are between 5 and 15% higher in the constrained water trading scenario than the unconstrained trading scenario. The price hike is due to a higher water price. Comparing Tables 11.2 and 11.4, in most counties the price of water is much higher. In Merced County, for example, the trading price is $383 per acre-foot if Hay and forage water is moved to other uses, compared with $1180 per acre-foot if it is not. In reality, backdoor water trades and on-farm switches are likely to start with water being diverted from Hay and forage production to other uses. Nevertheless, comparing hypothetical full

[3]In the regional context, the terms-of-trade refer to the price index for international plus inter-regional exports divided by the corresponding international plus inter-regional imports price index, inclusive of water trading.

Table 11.4 Macroeconomic impacts on 12 counties and terms-of-trade impacts, restricted intra-regional water trading (% change from base case)

12 counties	Macro results	Terms-of-trade by region		Water trading price $/ac-ft
Real consumption	−0.30	ButteCA	1.1	140
Real investment	−0.04	ColusaCA	2.4	130
Real GDP	−1.07	FresnoCA	1.3	600
Employment	−0.64	GlennCA	2.5	255
Real wage	0	MercedCA	2.1	1080
GDP deflator	0.59	KernCA	0.7	388
CPI	−0.22	KingsCA	1.3	388
		TulareCA	0.8	165
		YoloCA	0.2	161
		SanJoaquinCA	0.6	347
		StanislausCA	1.0	1121
		MaderaCA	2.2	606

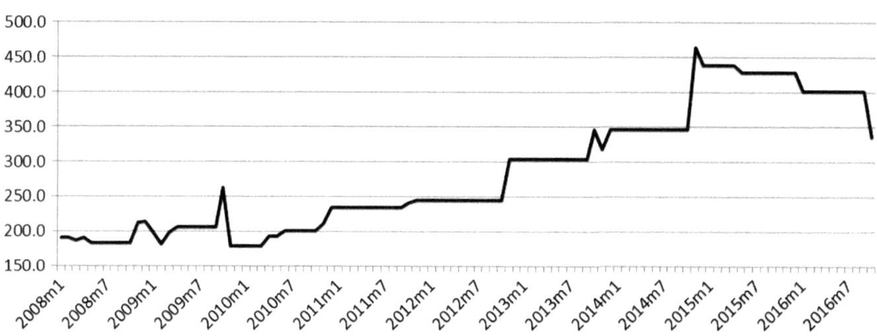

Fig. 11.3 Almond price (c/lb), January 2008 to October 2016. (*Source*: http://www.economagic.com/em-cgi/data.exe/blswp/WPU01190102 accessed 6 December 2016)

trading with the removal of Hay and forage from the set of outputs with water trading possibilities illustrates the marginal impact of more comprehensive water trading.

In the case of almonds, a combination of the Californian drought, rapid growth in global demand and a temporarily weaker US dollar contributed to a more than doubling of the observed price between late 2010 and late 2014 (Fig. 11.3). The drought-related price spike in late 2014 may have been exacerbated by the absence of a futures market for almonds.Water trading possibilities face institutional constraints. An insight from the modeling is that a liberalization of water trading would move more water into almond production and alleviate drought-induced farm output price pressures.

11.2.5 Reducing California's Surface Water Usage by 40% and Pumping to Reduce the Shortfall to 10%

In a normal year, groundwater accounts for about one-third of California's water requirements (Chappelle et al. 2015). Groundwater in theory should act as a buffer resource, with drawings rising during drought. Howitt et al. (2015) estimated that surface water usage fell by 8.7 million acre-feet and groundwater extractions increased by 6.2 million acre-feet in 2015 in California relative to a normal year, implying reduced water usage of 2.5 million acre-feet.

In this scenario, we attempt to replicate the water availability conditions reported by Howitt et al. (2015). However, we also need to account for rainfall deficits. Rainfall shocks in the scenario are based on estimates of rainfall deficits shown in Table 11.5 for July 2014 to June 2015. The shortfall of 2.5 million acre-feet is allocated among counties in proportion to annual crop water requirements of a normal year. The other shocks imposed in the scenario are to depict increased pumping costs arising from the extraction of an additional 6.2 million acre-feet of water. At $100 per acre-foot (Howitt et al. 2015), these additional costs total $620 million. In order to depict limited water trading possibilities, Hay and forage and other agriculture water in each region are not transferable to other agricultural activities.

The macroeconomic impacts of this scenario are shown in Table 11.6. Compared with the first scenario shown in Table 11.2, the real GDP outcome is similar (−0.83% compared with −0.78) but the aggregate consumption impact is smaller (−0.51 vs. −0.97%) and the employment outcome better (−0.37 vs. −0.51%) in the 12 counties.

Table 11.5 Effective rainfall deficit by county

	Average effective rain (in.)	Effective July 2014 to June 2015 (in.)	Deficit (in.)	Irrigation cuts ('000 acre-feet)
ButteCA	25	10	15	41
ColusaCA	10	9	1	79
FresnoCA	7	4	3	263
GlennCA	13	10	3	54
MercedCA	6	2	4	142
KernCA	6	1	5	182
KingsCA	2	2	0	136
TulareCA	5	1	4	117
YoloCA	17	6	11	51
SanJoaquinCA	10	3	7	116
StanislausCA	7	3	4	94
MaderaCA	6	1	5	33
Rest of Calif.	13	5	8	1191

Source: http://www.usclimate.com accessed 28 August 2015

Table 11.6 Macroeconomic impacts on 12 counties and terms-of-trade impacts, "observed" scenario (% change from base case)

12 counties	Macro results	Terms-of-trade by region		Water trading price $/ac-ft
Real consumption	−0.51	ButteCA	2.9	278
Real investment	−0.04	ColusaCA	0.7	107
Real GDP	−0.83	FresnoCA	0.3	337
Employment	−0.37	GlennCA	0.1	119
Real wage	0	MercedCA	2.1	571
GDP deflator	0.04	KernCA	0.4	259
CPI	−0.30	KingsCA	0.4	259
		TulareCA	0.8	361
		YoloCA	0.2	490
		SanJoaquinCA	0.5	452
		StanislausCA	−0.2	690
		MaderaCA	1.0	713

However, there are costs associated with groundwater extractions that are not included in this scenario. First, additional groundwater extractions have required substantial investments in new or deeper wells. Only the marginal pumping costs are included in the scenario. The other cost not modelled is the impact on sustainability: the more existing groundwater is pumped, the higher will be the costs of extracting more water. Groundwater pumping is causing land subsidence, thereby damaging property and the environment.

11.3 The Need for Water Reforms in California

There is little institutional support for water trading between farmers in California. However, given the wide difference in the average product of water of different crop types, and the tendency for perennial crops to have higher average products of water, we expect that perennial crop producers are desperate to obtain water when allocations are cut. Some producers have chosen to sink new wells at $100,000 each (Walker 2015). Others have used back door deals with farmers of annual crops to obtain water. Without institutional support, the volume of such trades remains unknown.

One of the key findings from modeling of the Californian drought is that diverting water from perennial crops to urban uses, beyond minimal necessary quantities for basic needs, is unlikely to be welfare enhancing. Microeconomic theory does not support the notion that equalizing the price of water between rural and urban users in different regions is efficient. This is because water trading so as to equalize prices will widen the gap between rentals on other factors. For example, if fixed factors include urban capital, farm capital and farm land, increasing the amount of water available for urban uses at the expense of farm uses is likely to have a small positive impact on urban capital rentals but a large negative impact on farm capital and land rentals. If, however, farmers are paid for water diverted from agriculture to urban uses, such payments may offset land and rural capital rental losses.

Regional impacts from USAGE-TERM modeling indicate that unconstrained trading between farmers in each region minimizes job losses across the Central Valley and California overall. By preventing some farm activities from trading water within the model, trade volumes shrink and perennial producers benefit from higher than otherwise output prices. These price increases in turn elevate regional terms-of-trade and thereby raise regional real aggregate consumption. However, they do so at the expense of regional and state employment. That is, the gains to producers are at the expense of equity; these gains are concentrated among farmers, with job losses worsening as output prices rise in response to water scarcity. Even among farmers, there are likely to be substantial winners, namely those who maintain access to water and benefit from higher output prices, and substantial losers. The latter will include almond farmers whose plantations have died due to deficient water availability.

We can use the finding that restricted water trading is worse for employment, at the same time as raising regional terms-of-trade to the benefit of farmers rather than households, to infer the impacts of diverting water from rural to urban users. Some diversion may have clear social benefits. During the prolonged millennium drought in Australia, rural-urban water trading between the Murray-Darling Basin and Melbourne should have obviated the need for a desalination plant. Unfortunately, the state government of the time chose to construct a pipeline for rural-urban water movements at the same time as planning a desalination plant, which has proven to be expensive (Cook 2014). Some rural-urban water trading may be advantageous during drought.

Beyond a certain point, however, it is likely that the costs to urban households of higher food prices will outweigh the benefit obtained from increased urban water volumes. The Central Valley is a sufficiently important producer of some farm outputs that it influences global prices. In effect, increasing the volume of water diverted from farm uses will reduce the volume of virtual water imports by households from farmers. Reducing water for farm uses so as to lessen the restrictions imposed on urban users is likely to raise food prices and may lessen employment.

A separate issue is that of urban water access. As wells dried in some urban areas of California during the drought, some residents were left without running water. Basic human needs take precedence over market principles in such a circumstance. But without the infrastructure to give affected urban areas access to mains water, notions of water trading are in any case irrelevant.

Almonds became a temporary scapegoat for California's water woes.[4] This came at a time, early in April 2015, when California's Governor Brown announced compulsory urban water restrictions with the intention of reducing overall urban water usage by 25% (James 2015). A common perception is that almonds require more water than other tree crops. USDA data (footnote 1) indicate that the number of feet of water required by almonds does not stand out from other crops. The perception may arise from the weight of produce per unit area arising from almond production. However, almonds have a higher value per unit weight than most other tree crops. The high average value product of water used in almond production ought to result in almond's share of total water used increasing as total water availability diminishes.

A major concern in the Central Valley is the dominance of perennial crops, including almonds, in farm production. Perennials require water every year and therefore are less flexible than annual crops, production of which can be suspended until drought conditions end. Groundwater ought to guarantee water supply. Ideally, groundwater supplies should be recharged or at worst not drawn down during years of normal rainfall. There is nothing new about proposals to improve management of California's groundwater. Howitt and M'Marete (1991) proposed a groundwater bank with the objective of lowering the costs of pumping groundwater during drought years. The authors noted that the incentives to manage groundwater were absent. As an example, it would be socially optimal for a new well to pump water only during times of exceptional water scarcity. But once a well has been constructed, the owner is likely to seek a return on the investment through pumping in normal or even wetter years, instead of viewing the well as a form of insurance.

Improved management of groundwater is unlikely to occur until all extractions are metered. The development of transparent water markets would place a value on water according to varying seasonal and market conditions.

References

Chappelle C, Hanak E, Mount J (2015) Reforming California's groundwater management. PPIC Water Policy Center. http://www.ppic.org/main/publication_show.asp?i=1106. Accessed 9 Sept 2016

Cook H (2014) $613 m for desalination plant, no water ordered. The age, March 27. http://www.theage.com.au/victoria/613m-for-desalination-plant-no-water-ordered-20140327–35k7c.html. Accessed 24 Aug 2015

Dixon P, Parmenter B, Sutton J, Vincent D (1982) ORANI: a multisectoral model of the Australian economy. Contributions to economic analysis, vol 142. North-Holland, Amsterdam

Dixon PB, Rimmer MT, Wittwer G (2012) The theory of TERM-H_2O, chapter 5. In: Wittwer G (ed) Economic modeling of water, the Australian CGE experience. Springer, Dordrecht

[4]The Huffington Post provided a light-hearted review of the short-lived "almond shaming" campaign at http://www.huffingtonpost.com/2015/04/16/in-memoriam-demonizing-almonds_n_7082966.html. Accessed 7 August 2015.

Dixon PB, Rimmer MT, Wittwer G (2011) Saving the southern Murray-Darling basin: the economic effects of a buyback of irrigation water. Econ Rec 87:153–168

Howitt R, M'Marete M (1991) Well set aside proposal: a scenario for ground water banking. Calif Agric 45(3):6–8

Howitt R, MacEwan D, Medellín-Azuara J, Lund J, Sumner, D (2015) Economic analysis of the 2015 drought. UC Davis Center for Watershed Sciences ERA Economics. https://watershed.ucdavis.edu/files/biblio/Final_Drought%20Report_08182015_Full_Report_WithAppendices.pdf. Accessed 20 Nov 2015

James I (2015) Calfornia board approves emergency water rules. http://www.usatoday.com/story/news/nation/2015/05/05/california-water-restrictions-missed-targets/26928275/. Accessed 21 July 2015

Walker T (2015) California drought: almond growers fight back over reports they are causing chronic water shortages. http://www.independent.co.uk/news/world/americas/california-drought-almond-growers-fight-back-over-reports-they-are-causing-chronic-water-shortages-10224339.html. Accessed 21 July 2015

Wittwer G, Griffith M (2011) Modelling drought and recovery in the southern Murray-Darling basin. Aust J Agric Resour Econ 49:342–359

Chapter 12
The Economic Effects of a Hypothetical Nuclear Attack on Downtown LA

Peter B. Dixon, Maureen T. Rimmer and Glyn Wittwer

Abstract The multi-regional and dynamic attributes of USAGE-TERM enhance the modelling of the impacts of a hypothetical nuclear attack. In the regional dimension in this example, the congressional district of the attack is represented separately from the rest of LA, the rest of California and rest of USA. In the period of the attack, there are immediate deaths and destruction. A recovery phase follows, in which massive public resources are devoted to restoration. This phase provides a temporary strengthening of the labor market in the rest of LA. But the direct impacts of the attack ensure that economic activity in the downtown region of the attack remains permanently below forecast after the attack. From the national perspective, the costs of the restoration phase add significantly to net foreign liabilities. This results in national aggregate consumption persisting below forecast for many years into the future.

Keywords Homeland security · Adverse events · Urban economic impacts

12.1 Introduction

One response of the US government to the terrorist attacks on September 11, 2001 was the formation of the Department of Homeland Security. Congress passed the Homeland Security Act in November 2002 and the department commenced operations in March 2003.[1] As part of its charter to secure the US from threats, the

[1]http://www.dhs.gov/creation-department-homeland-security accessed 24 February 2015.

P.B. Dixon · M.T. Rimmer · G. Wittwer (✉)
Centre of Policy Studies, Victoria University, 300 Flinders St, 3000 Melbourne, VIC, Australia
e-mail: Glyn.wittwer@vu.edu.au

G. Wittwer (ed.), *Multi-regional Dynamic General Equilibrium Modeling of the U.S. Economy*, Advances in Applied General Equilibrium Modeling,
DOI 10.1007/978-3-319-58866-7_12

department has commissioned economic modeling of hypothetical adverse events in order to assist in planning responses and quantify the resources required to respond to an adverse event.

USAGE-TERM has several attributes that make it a suitable model for such analysis. First, the 436 region version of the master database of the model can represent congressional districts individually.[2] Aggregations typically include a single congressional district in which a hypothetical event occurs, plus a region representing the rest of the city in which the attack occurs comprising a handful of congressional districts, plus a composite region covering the remainder of the state and another composite region covering the rest of the nation. Second, USAGE-TERM is dynamic, so that we can a model the timeline of a hypothetical scenario. This will include the year of the event, subsequent years in which there is clean-up and re-building phase, and later years in which there may be ongoing morbidity, health costs and deaths as a consequence of the attack.

12.2 A Hypothetical Nuclear Attack on Downtown LA

In our scenario, we assume that terrorists detonate a 1 kt nuclear device in downtown Los Angeles in California's 34th congressional district (CA-34). We aggregate USAGE-TERM to four regions, namely CA-34, rest of Los Angeles (RoLA), rest of California (RoCalif) and rest of USA. The model is also aggregated to 18 sectors (see Fig. 12.6).

The shocks and financing assumptions applied in USAGE-TERM follow.

12.2.1 *Region of Attack, Immediate Deaths and Survivors*

In the scenario, property damage and radioactive fall-out affect only part of CA-34 without direct impacts in other congressional districts. The residential population of CA-34 is about 700,000. Census data at the zip code level indicate place of employment, indicating the daytime population, as distinct from the place of residence data (i.e., reflecting the night-time population) used to devise the USAGE-TERM database. The directly impacted area has a daytime population of about 315,000 and a night-time population of around 125,000 (Heatwole et al. 2014). We assume that the detonation occurs in the daytime, resulting in an affected population of 315,000.

[2]USAGE-TERM has two master databases. The 512 sector, 70 region database was based on a split of the national USAGE database into 41 separate states plus DC. In addition, this database includes sub-state representation within California, Florida, Illinois, Michigan, Missouri, New York, Pennsylvania, Ohio and Texas. The 121 sector, congressional district based master database is most appropriate for scenarios located within city regions.

We assume that there are tens of thousands of immediate deaths, leaving an affected surviving population of 315,000 minus the number of immediate deaths. We assume that the percentage of the population killed immediately is equal across age groups. The labor supply calculations in Sect. 12.4 are based on these numbers.

12.2.2 The Shutdown, Evacuations and Impact on Labor Supply

The directly impacted area is shut down for 2 years with clean-up expenditures and repairs spread evenly between year 1 and year 2. No business is undertaken in the impact area in this period.

In the scenario, 87,250 people are evacuated from the impact area for the duration of the shutdown period. In calculating the number of evacuees we assume that the surviving night-time population of the impact area requires evacuation and the night-time population suffers the immediate death rate that applies to the day-time population.

Where do the evacuated people go and how much does it cost to accommodate them during the shutdown period? We assume that 25% of the evacuees from the impact area spend the shutdown period elsewhere in CA-34, 25% go to the rest of LA, 25% go to the rest of California and 25% go to the rest of USA.

Evacuation and subsequent accommodation expenses total $3.97 billion over the evacuation period of 2 years. This is based on an evacuation expense of $9000 per person plus accommodation expenses of $50 per day per person for 2 years [3.97b = 87,250*(9000 + 50*2*365)]. Beyond the shutdown period, we assume that the surviving evacuees who do not return to CA-34 stay in the regions to which they were evacuated. However, once the shutdown period has ceased, we do not count their accommodation expenses as an additional cost associated with the event.

Evacuations and immediate deaths in the event year reduce the labor supply in CA-34. We arrive at the modeled labor supply reduction in several steps. First, tens of thousands of the night-time population in the impact area suffer immediate death. We assume that 60% of these people were participating in the labor force. Second, a significant percentage of the daytime workers in the impact area suffer immediate death. Third, 65,438 (= 0.75*87,250) night-time residents of the impact area evacuate from CA-34. Workers in this group cease offering labor to CA-34, further reducing CA-34's labor supply by 39,263 (= 0.6*65,438). Fourth, surviving non-evacuated workers reduce their participation rate by 25% (see Sect. 12.2.4).

The 65,438 people who are evacuated to locations outside CA-34 add to labor supply in those locations. Their impact effect on labor supply in each of RoLA, RoCalif and RoUS is 9816 (= 65,438*0.6*0.75/3). This takes account of the baseline participation rate (0.6), the participation effect of the event (0.75) and our assumption that equal numbers of evacuees go to each of the three regions outside CA-34.

The impact on the labor supply is calculated from the first, second and fourth effects plus 0.25 times the third effect. In percentage terms, the reduction in labor supply is 0.070. Over time, the national labor supply effect gradually diminishes with the aging of people who were in the impact area at the time of the event (Fig. 12.14).

12.2.3 Radiation Clean-up and Decontamination Costs

We treat these costs as additional government spending, occurring for 2 years and amounting to $70 billion in each year.[3] Much of this expenditure, $60 billion a year, pays for labor drawn from the rest of LA. The remaining expenditure, $10 billion a year, is attributed to CA-34.

12.2.4 Later Deaths, Morbidity and Medical Expenditures

There are thousands of later deaths caused by cancer related to exposure to radiation, equal to around 17% of the number of immediate deaths. Section 12.5 details the calculated impact on labor supply, based on the time path of later deaths, the age profile of the affected population, baseline life expectancy for different age groups and labor force participation behavior.

We assume that the cost of medical treatment in the year of the event is several thousand dollars per affected survivor, amounting to hundreds of millions of dollars (Heatwole et al. 2014). Treatment takes place in the regions to which the evacuees have relocated. Non-cancer medical costs arising from the event gradually diminish over the next 20 years, reaching an accumulated total of $6 billion.

Beyond the shutdown period, we assume that additional medical expenditures are required to deal with cancer costs. The cumulative total is $0.33 billion (2012 dollars) after 20 years. This may seem a low cost but recall that most of the cancer deaths (and therefore associated expense) occur more than 20 years after the adverse event.

We assume that health expenditures are half covered by public spending and half by private spending. In a national emergency, there may be a case for increasing the public contribution. However, those who are able to afford private health spending may prefer to pay their own expenses rather than wait for public provision.

[3]The US Domestic Nuclear Detection Office provided a spreadsheet of estimated consequences of a nuclear attack to the National Center for Risk and Economic Analysis of Terrorism Events (CREATE), University of Southern California. Some numbers have been confidentialized and replaced by qualitative statements referring to an order of magnitude.

12.2.5 Capital Destruction and Aversion Behaviour in Labor Market

18% of CA-34's capital, valued at $16 billion is destroyed in the attack. Following the nuclear attack, we assume that workers will require elevated wages to induce them to take jobs in the region (CA-34) in which the event took place, even after the measurable danger from radiation has passed. Similarly, some goods and services produced in CA-34 may suffer stigmatization in the market place.

The labor-market issue is handled via the equation specifying labor supply to CA-34 (Sect. 12.5). We set a shift variable in this equation to give a degree of aversion to working in CA-34 consistent with a return of labor supply at any given wage to only 80% of its pre-event level following the 2-year shutdown. For subsequent years we maintain the initial aversion level in the first simulation, while allowing it to fall over time in the second simulation.

12.3 The Results

Figures 12.1, 12.2, 12.3, 12.4, 12.5, 12.6, 12.7, 12.8, 12.9, 12.10, 12.11, 12.12, 12.13, 12.14 show results for the four regions (CA-34, rest of Los Angeles, rest of California and rest of USA) and for the nation from two simulations. All of the results are deviations from a no-incident baseline. For example, Fig. 12.1 shows that the incident (nuclear attack in downtown Los Angeles) causes labor supply in CA-34 to be 37% less in 2012 than forecast. The difference between the two simulations is that aversion behavior (Sect. 12.5) is maintained throughout simulation 1 but diminishes gradually in simulation 2.

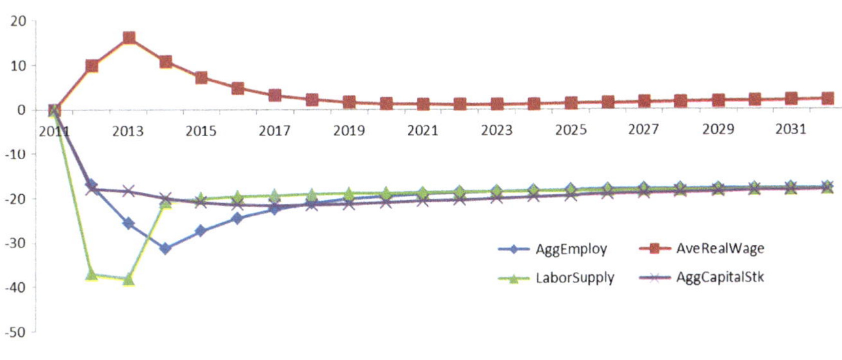

Fig. 12.1 Impacts on labor market and capital in CA-34, no recovery in aversion (% deviation from base)

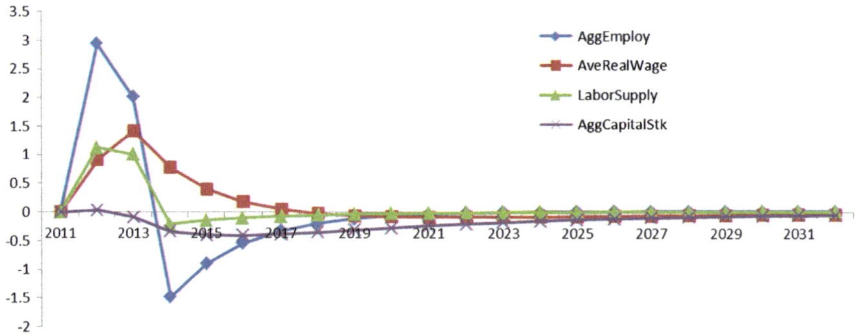

Fig. 12.2 Impacts on labor market and capital in Rest of LA, no recovery in aversion (% deviation from base)

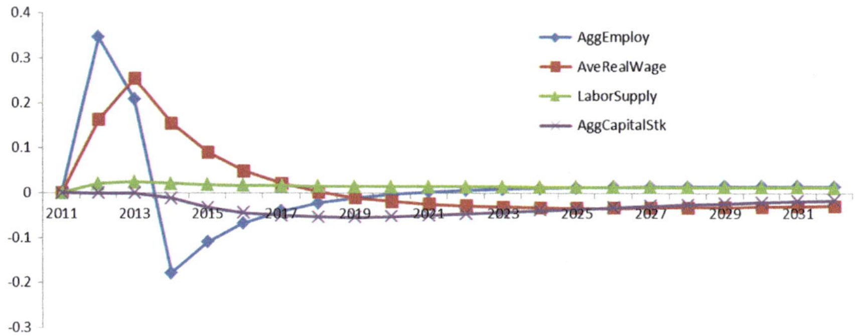

Fig. 12.3 Impacts on labor market and capital in Rest of California, no recovery in aversion (% deviation from base)

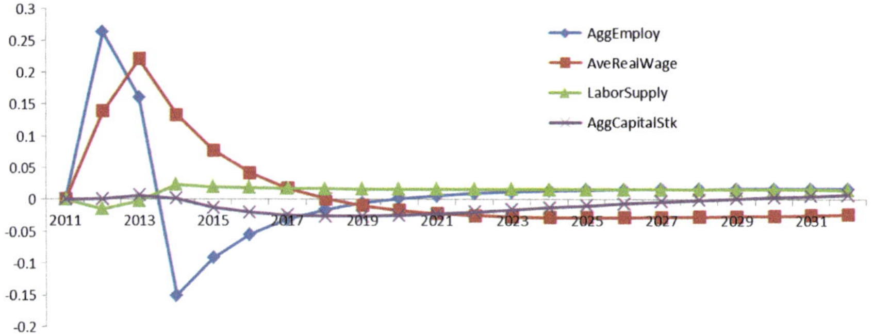

Fig. 12.4 Impacts on labor market and capital in Rest of USA, no recovery in aversion (% deviation from base)

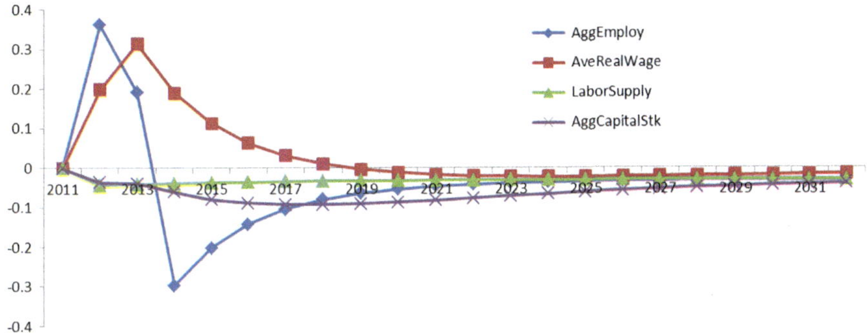

Fig. 12.5 Impacts on national labor market and capital, no recovery in aversion (% deviation from base)

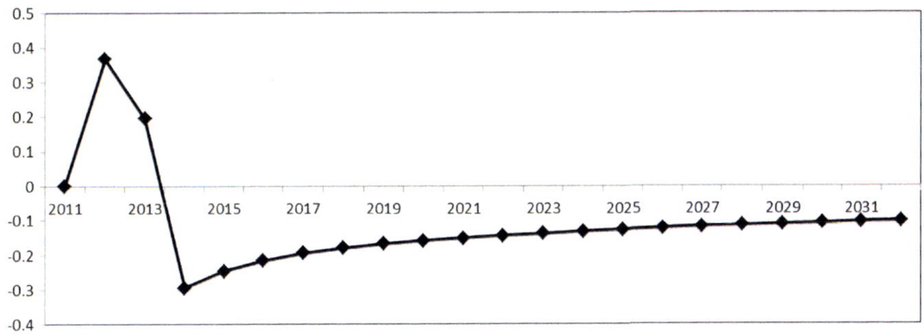

Fig. 12.6 Impacts on national aggregate consumption, no recovery in aversion (% deviation from base)

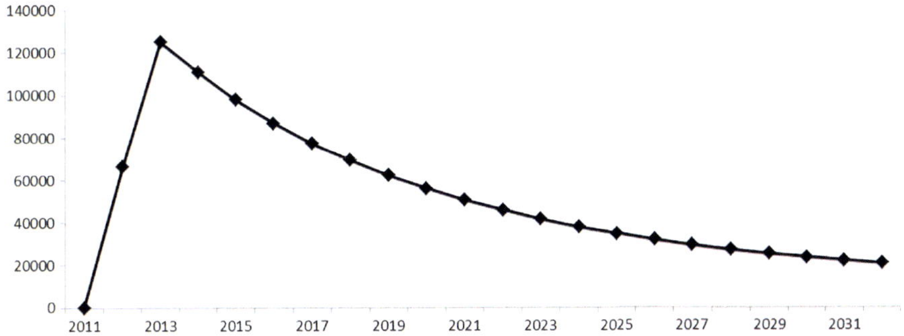

Fig. 12.7 Impacts on net foreign liabilities, no recovery in aversion ($m 2012 deviation from base)

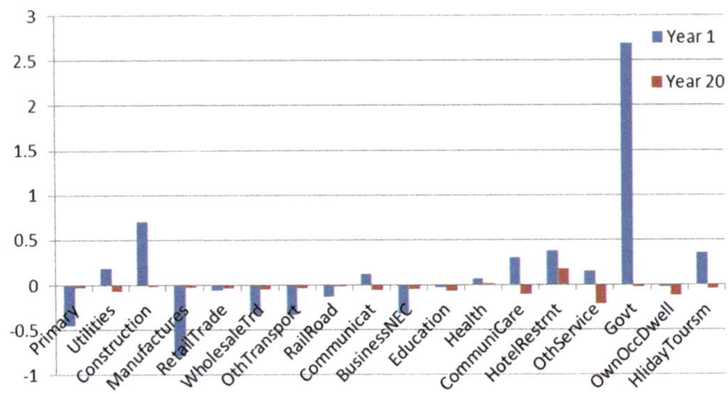

Fig. 12.8 Impacts on national industry output, no recovery in aversion (% deviation from base)

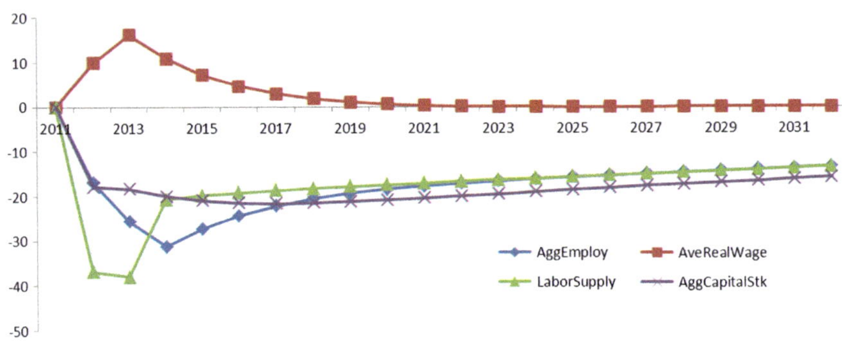

Fig. 12.9 Impacts on labor market and capital in CA-34, recovery in aversion (% deviation from base)

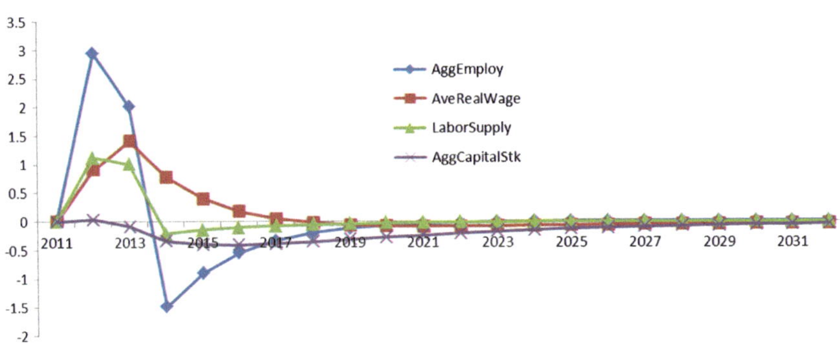

Fig. 12.10 Impacts on labor market and capital in Rest of LA, recovery in aversion (% deviation from base)

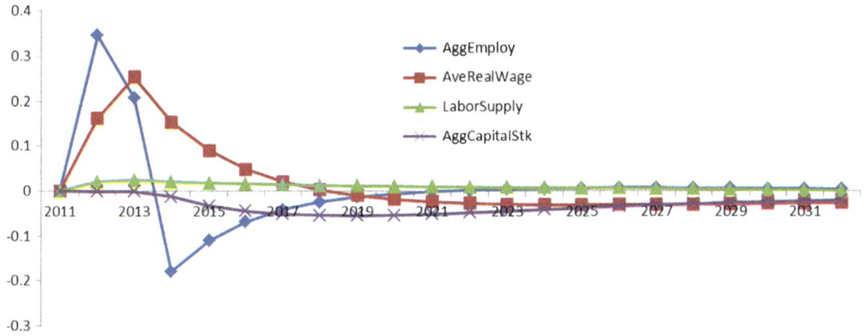

Fig. 12.11 Impacts on labor market and capital in Rest of California, recovery in aversion (% deviation from base)

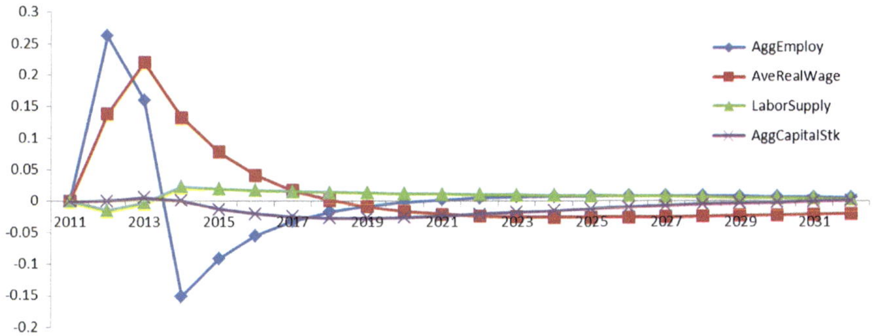

Fig. 12.12 Impacts on labor market and capital in Rest of USA, recovery in aversion (% deviation from base)

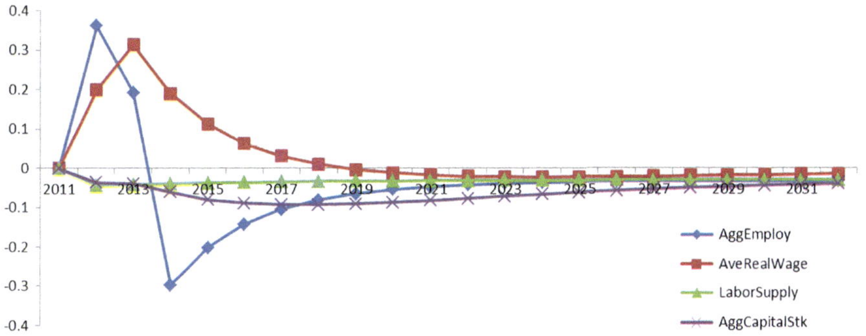

Fig. 12.13 Impacts on national labor market and capital, recovery in aversion (% deviation from base)

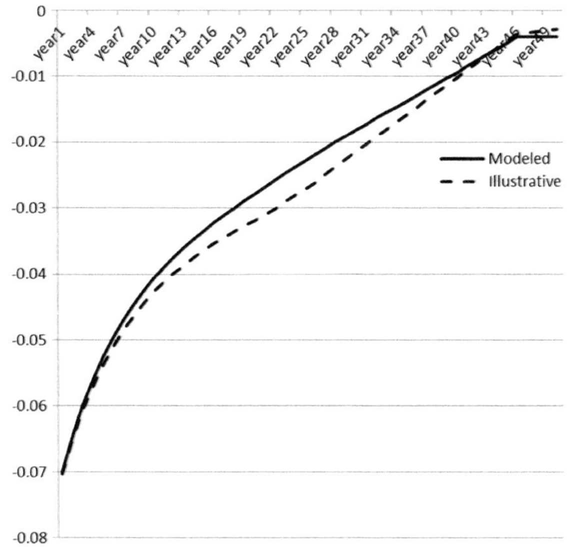

Fig. 12.14 National labor market, illustrative v. modeled deviation from forecast

12.3.1 First Simulation

Apart from the short-run reduction in labor supply (imposed as a shock as detailed in Sect. 12.2.2), the main short-run economic effects in CA-34 of the incident shown in Fig. 12.2 are: a reduction in available capital of 18% (Sect. 12.2.5); a sharp increase in wage rates to overcome labor shortages caused by the evacuation (supply reducing) and the clean-up (demand increasing); and a reduction in employment of about 20%, implying a considerable tightening of the CA-34 labor market in light of the 37% reduction in labor supply.

In the long term, CA-34 stays permanently depressed in the incident simulation, with employment, capital stocks and labor supply all remaining about 20% below their baseline levels. Why 20%? In the long run, CA-34 must produce goods and services that are competitive with those produced in the rest of USA. Consequently, CA-34 cannot sustain high wage rates relative to those in the rest of the nation. With CA-34 wage rates eventually returning to near their baseline levels (reflecting those in the rest of USA), the aversion assumption outlined in Sect. 12.2.5 means that labor supply to CA-34 is reduced in the incident simulation by 20% relative to the baseline. With labor supply reduced by 20%, the rest of the CA-34 economy is also reduced by 20%.

In the rest of Los Angeles, increased clean-up expenditures raise employment above forecast in 2012 and 2013 (Fig. 12.2). $60 billion out of $70 billion of clean-up services is supplied in each of these years from this region. Increased demands for health services and accommodation also contribute to employment growth. In 2013, employment is subdued by rising wages, which were 1% above forecast in 2012 and 1.4% above forecast in 2013. Since real wages persist above forecast once the clean-up has finished, employment falls to 1.5% below forecast in 2014. Increased demands by government and households in these 2 years crowd out other final expenditures, including investment. Therefore, for several years, aggregate fall slightly below forecast before eventually recovering to near forecast levels.

The proportional impact of the incident on the rest of California in 2012 and 2013 is much smaller than that on the rest of Los Angeles region (Fig. 12.3). For example, aggregate employment in 2012 rises 0.35% above forecast in the region, compared with 3% in the Rest of Los Angeles. This is because additional demands in the Rest of California are limited to the health and accommodation needs of CA-34 evacuees. Unlike the Rest of Los Angeles, the Rest of California does not make any direct contribution to the clean-up effort in CA-34. Real wage increases in CA-34 and the Rest of Los Angeles during the clean-up force up wages in the rest of the state and nation, though by smaller percentages. Since real wages adjust sluggishly, they also persist above forecast in the Rest of California and the Rest of USA (Fig. 12.4) when the clean-up ends, so that employment in these regions falls below forecast in 2014.

In the Rest of LA, Rest of California and Rest of USA, employment persists below forecast for several years until real wages have fallen sufficiently to enable labor demand to match labor supply. Once full wages adjustment has taken place, each of these regions has slightly larger employment than in the baseline, due to persistent labor market aversion in CA-34 and a consequent permanent exodus of workers from the affected region relative to forecast.

Figures 12.6, 12.7, 12.8 refer to the national effects of the incident. In the short run, the incident boosts national employment, wage rates and consumption (Figs. 12.6, 12.7). However, in the long run, the incident leaves the USA economically poorer as it pays off incident-related debt (Fig. 12.7). Consumption, a reasonable indicator of economic welfare, is still 0.1% below forecast 20 years after the event (Fig. 12.6).

Figure 12.8 shows that the incident causes a sharp short-run increase in output of government activities. The construction industry also shows a significant national gain. By contrast, trade related industries (primary and manufactures) contract, reflecting higher costs as real wages rise. In the long run, the incident causes all industries other than health and hotels/restaurants to be smaller than in the baseline.

12.3.2 Second Simulation

The results for the second simulation are in Figs. 12.9, 12.10, 12.11, 12.12, 12.13. In this simulation, labor-market aversion in CA-34 gradually dissipates allowing labor supply to increase. Nevertheless there is still considerable aversion remaining in 2032 leaving CA-34 labor supply about 15% below baseline despite wage rates being at their baseline level.

With much of the labor-market aversion remaining, CA-34 continues in a depressed state throughout the simulation period. In 2032, labor supply, employment and capital are around or below 85% of their pre-event levels (Fig. 12.10). The long-term outcome for CA-34 is only moderately better in the second simulation than the first.

In the rest of LA, rest of California and rest of USA, long-run employment rises by a smaller proportion above forecast than in the first simulation, because more workers return to CA-34 than in the first simulation. However, the differences between the effects of the two scenarios outside CA-34 are minor.

12.4 Appendix: Labor Force Effects in Our Illustrative Application

Ideally, we want two paths for the labor force: a baseline without the incident and a "policy" path with the incident. To work out the gap between the two paths, we need to trace out what the incident-affected people would have done in the labor force with and without the incident.

12.4.1 Baseline Path

For the baseline, we assume that incident-affected people have the same age profile and workforce participation rates as the rest of the US population. Then we can age them and figure out how many of them would be participating in the workforce in each future year. More technically, we can calculate the proportion of the affected people currently (i.e., in the incident year, or year t = 0) aged *a* who will be in the workforce in year *t* by multiplying the following probabilities:

1. Probability of a person currently aged *a* surviving to year *t*, $pr_{1b}(a,t)$;
2. Probability of a person currently aged *a* who survives to year t being between 20 and 64 in year *t*, $pr_{2b}(a,t)$;
3. Probability of a person currently aged *a* who survives to year t participating in the workforce (participation rate for work-age people) in year *t*, $pr_{3b}(a,t)$.

This gives the proportion of people currently aged *a* who are in the workforce in year *t* as:

$$\mathrm{pr}_b(a,t) = \mathrm{pr}_{1b}(a,t) * \mathrm{pr}_{2b}(a,t) * \mathrm{pr}_{3b}(a,t) \tag{12.1}$$

Probability 1 is readily calculable from http://www.ssa.gov/oact/STATS/Table4c6.html.

Probability 2 is either 0 or 1. Probability 3 can be calculated from population and workforce statistics.

Having calculated $pr_b(a,t)$, we can calculate

$$pr_b(\bullet, t) = \sum_a S(a) * pr_b(a, t) \tag{12.2}$$

where $pr_b(\bullet,t)$ is the *baseline* proportion of people in the affected group (the people either killed or evacuated due to the incident) who are in the workforce in year t and $S(a)$ is the share of these people with current age a.

12.4.2 Incident Path

Probabilities 1 and 3 are affected by the incident. There are tens of thousands of immediate deaths and then delayed incident-related deaths over the next 50 years. Participation rates are also reduced due to morbidity. Some incident-related deaths in year t will involve people who would no longer have been in the workforce in the baseline. If, however, people no longer in the workforce suffered morbidity during work-age years that led a premature exit from the workforce, the impact on labor supply occurs several years before death.

To calculate labor force numbers on the incident path, we start by defining

DD(a,t) as cumulative delayed deaths that have occurred up to year t for people who were initially aged a; and

N_b(a,t) as the number of people in the affected group that were aged a at the time of the incident and survived to year t in the baseline.

On the incident path, the probability of a person aged a surviving to year t is given by

$$pr_{1i}(a, t) = pr_{1b}(a, t) * pr_{survive} * (1 - [\mathrm{DD}\,(\mathrm{a, t}) \,/\, [\mathrm{N}_b(\mathrm{a, t}) * pr_{survive}]) \tag{12.3}$$

where $pr_{survive}$ is the probability of a person in the affected group surviving beyond the year of the incident.

The adjusted participation rate in year t of a person initially aged a is given by

$$pr_{3i}(a, t) = pr_{3b}(a, t) * \mathrm{mf}\,(\mathrm{a, t}) \tag{12.4}$$

where mf (a,t) is the morbidity factor applying in year t to people aged a at the time of the incident. The morbidity factor takes account of reductions in workforce participation associated with incident-related illnesses. It lies between 0 and 1.0 (1.0 implies no morbidity-related reduction in participation).

We assumed initially that mf(a,t) was given by

$$\begin{aligned} &\mathrm{mf}\,(\mathrm{a},1) = \mathrm{mf\_}(1),\\ &\mathrm{mf}\,(\mathrm{a},2) = \mathrm{mf\_}(2),\\ &\mathrm{mf}\,(\mathrm{a},3) = \mathrm{mf\_}(3),\\ &\mathrm{mf}\,(\mathrm{a},\mathrm{t}) = \mathrm{mf\_}(\mathrm{t}) * \left[1 - \frac{\mathrm{D}\,(\mathrm{a},\mathrm{t}+3)}{\mathrm{N_i}(\mathrm{a},\mathrm{t})} * 0.75 - \frac{\mathrm{D}\,(\mathrm{a},\mathrm{t}+2)}{\mathrm{N_i}(\mathrm{a},\mathrm{t})} * 0.5 - \frac{\mathrm{D}\,(\mathrm{a},\mathrm{t}+1)}{\mathrm{N_i}(\mathrm{a},\mathrm{t})} * 0.25\right]\\ &\text{for } \mathrm{t} > 3 \end{aligned} \tag{12.5}$$

where

mf_(t) is the morbidity factor for survivors of the incident, which is 0.75 in the year of the incident and tends towards 1.0 over the next 20 years;

N_i(a,t) is the number of people in the affected group that were aged a and survived to year t in the incident scenario; and

D(a,t + n) is the number of delayed deaths in year $t + n$ of people initially aged a, given by

$$\mathrm{D}\,(\mathrm{a},\mathrm{t}+\mathrm{n}) = \mathrm{DD}\,(\mathrm{a},\mathrm{t}+\mathrm{n}) - \mathrm{DD}\,(\mathrm{a},\mathrm{t}+\mathrm{n}-1). \tag{12.6}$$

In (12.5), we assume that health problems associated with the incident reduce the participation rate of people in each age group by 25% (relative to the baseline participation rate for the group) in the year of the incident. Beyond that, we assume a movement towards the full participation rate except for people facing incident-related delayed death within 3 years. For these people, the participation rate is reduced by 25% 3 years before death, 50% 2 years before death and 75% a year before death.

Table 12.1 shows the estimated timeline of estimated cancer deaths and injuries arising from the incident, based on an index set to year 13 estimates. Morbidity arising from fatal cancers has been included in (12.6). Morbidity arising from non-fatal cancer injuries has not been included at this stage.

At this stage we can calculate

$$\mathrm{pr}_i(a,t) = \mathrm{pr}_{1i}(a,t) * \mathrm{pr}_{2i}(a,t) * \mathrm{pr}_{3i}(a,t) \tag{12.7}$$

where $pr_i(a,t)$ is the proportion of people currently aged a who are in the workforce in year t in the incident scenario.

From here we obtain $pr_i(\bullet,t)$, the *incident* proportion of people in the affected group who are in the workforce in year t, as

$$\mathrm{pr}_i(\bullet,t) = \sum\nolimits_a \mathrm{S}(a) * \mathrm{pr}_i(a,t). \tag{12.8}$$

Finally, we calculate the incident-induced percentage change in the national labor force (natlabsup) in year t as

Table 12.1 Index of incident-related cancer deaths and injuries (year 13 = 1.0)

Year	All cancer deaths & injuries	Year	All cancer deaths & injuries
1	0.06	26	1.90
2	0.22	27	2.12
3	0.54	28	2.35
4	0.84	29	2.61
5	1.07	30	2.89
6	1.19	31	3.19
7	1.24	32	3.50
8	1.24	33	3.83
9	1.20	34	4.17
10	1.15	35	4.51
11	1.10	36	4.85
12	1.04	37	5.19
13	1	38	5.52
14	0.96	39	5.84
15	0.94	40	6.15
16	0.94	41	6.44
17	0.95	42	6.70
18	0.98	43	6.95
19	1.02	44	7.17
20	1.09	45	7.39
21	1.17	46	7.57
22	1.27	47	7.74
23	1.40	48	7.89
24	1.54	49	8.03
25	1.71	50	8.15

Source: Based on Preston et al. (2007)

$$\text{natlabsup}\,(\text{t}) = 100 * \text{N}_b(\bullet, \text{t}) * [\text{pr}_i(\bullet, t) - \text{pr}_b(\bullet, t)] \,/\, \text{LABSUP}_b(\text{t}) \tag{12.9}$$

where

$\text{LABSUP}_b(\text{t})$ is the baseline workforce number in year t and
$\underline{\text{N}_b}(\bullet,\text{t})$ is the number of incident-affected people who survive to year t in the baseline

12.4.3 Illustrative Calculation

Assume that the incident takes place at the beginning of year 0.

Assume there are 75 age groups, 0–74.

Assume that the affected population is N.

Assume that there are initially N/75 people in each age group.

Assume that the baseline participation rate for people in age groups 20–64 is 0.75. For other age groups, it is 0.

Assume that people die at the end of their 74th year. Hence, $pr_{1b}(a,t) = 1.0$ if a + t = < 75. If a + t > 75, then $pr_{1b}(a,t) = 0$.

Assume $pr_{survive} = 0.7$.

Assume that the fraction of delayed deaths to surviving affected population is spread evenly over the years 1 to 25.

Thus, $D(a,t) = \sum_t D(a,t)/25$ for $1 \leq t \leq 25$.

$$DD(a, t) = \left(\sum_t D(a, t)/25\right) * t \text{ for } t \leq 25.$$

The above stylized assumptions were initially used to calculate the baseline and impact workforce participation levels for the affected population. The delayed deaths have now been modified to follow the time profile provided by CREATE. The difference between the baseline and impact national labor supply for each year, calculated in Eq. (12.9), has been ascribed to USAGE-TERM in the incident scenario. Figure 12.14 shows the deviation in the illustrative application from base compared with the modeled deviation from base for the incident. Most of the difference between the respective deviations arises from differences in the timing of delayed deaths. The modeled application follows the timeline of Table 12.1 whereas the illustrative application outlined above assumes that deaths are spread evenly over the 20 years following the incident.

12.5 Appendix: Technical Note on Labor Supply

We assume that U.S. workers decide their supply of labor to region q [LS(q) for all q] to maximize

$$\begin{aligned} &\text{CES}\,(\text{LS}\,(q)A\,(q),\ \text{for all } q) \\ &\text{subject to } \sum_q \text{LS}\,(q) = \text{LS} \end{aligned} \tag{12.10}$$

where LS is total labor supply and A(q) is a variable, to be discussed shortly, reflecting the desirability of working in region q. By writing the constraint as

$$\sum_q [\text{LS}\,(q) * A\,(q)] * \frac{1}{A\,(q)} = \text{LS} \tag{12.11}$$

we can reduce the regional labor allocation problem to a standard CES optimization in which LS(q)*A(q) plays the role of a quantity variable [X(q)] and 1/A(q) plays the role of a price variable [P(q)]. Then we find that

$$\mathrm{ls}\,(q) + a\,(q) = \mathrm{ls} + \sum_{q} S\,(q) * a\,(q) + \sigma * \left[a\,(q) - \sum_{r} S\,(r) * a\,(r) \right] \tag{12.12}$$

where

lowercase symbols refer to percentage changes in variables whose levels are denoted by the corresponding uppercase symbols;

σ is the substitution parameter in the CES function; and
S(q) is the share of the economy's labor that is devoted to region q.

We specify A(q) according to

$$A\,(q) = W\,(q) * ER\,(q) * PR\,(q) \tag{12.13}$$

where

W(q) is the real wage rate in region q;
ER(q) is the employment rate in region q, that is employment divided by labor supply; and
PR(q) is a variable reflecting preferences for working in region q.

In percentage change form we have

$$a\,(q) = w\,(q) + er\,(q) + pr\,(q). \tag{12.14}$$

We interpret W(q)*ER(q) as the expected real wage of a worker seeking employment in region q. We do not restrict ER to values less than one. We interpret values greater than one as meaning that workers can expect to receive overtime opportunities. Variable PR can be used to introduce aversion. The parameter σ in the simulations described in Sect. 2 is set at 1.5. This implies that a 1% increase in wages in region q relative to the average for the economy generates a 0.5% increase in labor supply to region q.

References

Heatwole N, Rose A, Dixon P, Rimmer M, Wittwer G, Wei D (2014) Modeling the temporal and spatial consequences of nuclear terrorism events. Final report to the US. Domestic Nuclear Detection Office (DNDO) by the National Center For Risk And Economic Analysis of Terrorism Events (CREATE), University of Southern California

Preston DL, Ron E, Tokuoka S, Funamoto S, Nishi N, Soda M, Mabuchi K, Kodama K (2007) Solid cancer incidence in atomic bomb survivors: 1958–1998. Radiat Res 168:1–64

Erratum to: Tourism and Transport in a CGE Model and an Illustrative Application

Glyn Wittwer

Erratum to: Chapter 6 in: G. Wittwer (ed.), *Multi-regional Dynamic General Equilibrium Modeling of the U.S. Economy*, Advances in Applied General Equilibrium Modeling, https://doi.org/10.1007/978-3-319-58866-7_6

The original version of the book was inadvertently published with author's incorrect explanatory text in Section 6.2.3. The author provided a new explanatory text "In the case of……demand overall:" which has been included after Eq. 6.10. Also, the last three paragraphs of the section have been replaced by the new text "The second type of shock……is 1.5%." The erratum chapter and the book have been updated with the changes.

The updated online version of this chapter can be found at https://doi.org/10.1007/978-3-319-58866-7_6

G. Wittwer (ed.), *Multi-regional Dynamic General Equilibrium Modeling of the U.S. Economy*, Advances in Applied General Equilibrium Modeling,
https://doi.org/10.1007/978-3-319-58866-7_13

About the Authors

Prof. Peter B. Dixon had his PhD awarded by Harvard University in 1972 and his thesis was subsequently published in the *Contributions to Economic Analysis* series of North Holland. After woring at the International Monetary Fund and the Reserve Bank of Australia, Dixon joined the IMPACT Project in 1975 under the direction of Professor A.A. Powell. With Powell, he was the joint recipient of the 1983 Research Medal of the Royal Society of Victoria given in recognition of the outstanding contribution of the IMPACT Project to social science research in Australia over the preceding 5 years. He was elected a Fellow of the Academy of Social Sciences in Australia in 1982; awarded the Distinguished Fellowship of the Economic Society of Australia in 2003; appointed Sir John Monash Distinguished Professor by Monash University in 2006; and appointed Officer in the Order of Australia (AO) in 2014.

Dixon is known internationally for his work in computable general equilibrium modelling. Together with colleagues at the IMPACT Project and the Centre of Policy Studies, he created the ORANI model and its dynamic successor, MONASH. These models have been prominent in the Australian economic debate for 35 years and have been used as templates for the development of other models throughout the world. He is the principal author of the ORANI and MONASH books published in the North Holland *Contributions* series in 1982 and 2002. In recent years he has led the development of the USAGE model of the U.S. which is being used by the U. S. International Trade Commission and the Departments of Agriculture, Commerce and Homeland Security.

Dixon's publication list contains about 220 articles and 8 books, including three North Holland Contributions monographs. He edited with Dale Jorgenson Elsevier's *Handbook of Computable General Equilibrium Modeling* (2013).

In 2014 Dixon took up his present position as Professor in the Centre of Policy Studies at Victoria University Australia.

Dr. Janine Dixon is a Senior Research Fellow at the Centre of Policy Studies (CoPS) at Victoria University. She works mainly with the Vic-Uni, VURM and TERM models of the Australian economy, undertaking economic consultations for various public and private sector clients in Australia and internationally.

G. Wittwer (ed.), *Multi-regional Dynamic General Equilibrium Modeling of the U.S. Economy*, Advances in Applied General Equilibrium Modeling,
DOI 10.1007/978-3-319-58866-7

Janine is responsible for the Victoria University Employment Forecasting (VUEF) project. As part of this project she has worked on the development of detailed "baseline" forecasts of the Australian economy and labour market, which are regularly updated to reflect changing economic conditions.

Janine is a member of the Economic Society of Australia's National Economic Panel, a regular panellist on the Melbourne Economic Forum, and a member of the expert panel advising NSW's Centre for Economic Development. In 2016 Janine was awarded a Vice-Chancellor's citation for Excellence in Engagement.

Prior to joining CoPS in 2007 Janine worked at the Australian Bureau of Statistics (1997–2002) where she was the manager of various surveys of the service industries in Australia. Dr Dixon has a PhD from the University of Dublin, Trinity College (2006) and a Bachelor of Economics with First Class Honours from Monash University (1997).

Prof. Mark Horridge is an expert on CGE databases and software. He has helped to develop CGE databases for Albania, Australia, Brazil, China, Finland, Indonesia, Jersey, Kazakhstan, New Caledonia, New Zealand, Philippines, South Africa, Taiwan, Thailand and Vietnam. He is the Director of GEMPACK software, a specialist CGE package used by over 400 organisations in over 70 countries. He is primarily responsible for developing a number of GEMPACK tools. He is the creator of the TERM model and its predecessor MMRF, and also contributed to the development of the dynamic MONASH model. He has developed a unified database that underlies these Australian models. Professor Horridge has developed much teaching material for short CGE courses, and is in high demand as an instructor as these courses around the world. For many years he has also instructed at the GTAP short courses.

Prof. Maureen T. Rimmer is the author and co-author of about 75 scholarly published articles, appearing in matematics and economics journals and edited volumes. Her main area of expertise is model development and application. She is the co-author of numerous consultancy reports from the Centre of Policy Studies. With Peter Dixon she is the co-developer of the MONASH model of the Australian economy and the co-author of the MONASH book which was published in 2002 in North-Holland's *Contributions to Economic Analysis*. In the last fifteen years she has been a key contributor to the development and documentation of USAGE. This is a 500-industry, dynamic model of the U.S. economy, with facilities for generating results for the 50 States and 700 occupations. The model is used in Washington by the U.S. International Trade Commission and the U.S. Departments of Commerce, Homeland Security, Agriculture and Transportation. Professor Rimmer has made major contributions in applications of the model to key policy areas such as: the replacement of imported crude oil with domestically produced biofuels; legalization of unauthorized immigrants; analysis of the 2008–2009 U.S. recession with and without the Obama stimulus package; and the effects of terrorism events on the U.S. economy.

Prof. John Madden is a Professor in the Centre of Policy Studies (CoPS) at Victoria University. Past positions include: Deputy Director of CoPS and Director of the Centre for Regional Economic Analysis. He is a past President of the Pacific Regional Science Conference Organisation.

In the 1980s, John developed FEDERAL, one of the first large-scale multiregional computable general equilibrium models. In recent years he constructed dynamic fiscal CGE models for the Malaysian Government and the Florida Legislature. His applied modelling work includes studies on fiscal federalism, tax policy, microeconomic reform, labour markets, transport policy, higher education, health policy, major industrial projects, and mega-events.

Prof. Glyn Wittwer is a regional dynamic CGE modeling expert. He has played a major role with Mark Horridge in developing databases for TERM versions in several countries. He edited the Springer volume *Economic Modeling of Water* (2012) and contributed the majority of chapters in the volume. He has extensive consulting experience. His list of projects includes dynamic, multi-regional CGE modeling in Australia, China and the United States. These includes modeling of the impacts of major dam and transport projects, drought and water trading, flood, hypothetical plant disease scenarios, productivity scenarios, wine tax scenarios, major mine construction projects and industry closures.

Index

G. Wittwer (ed.), *Multi-regional Dynamic General Equilibrium Modeling of the U.S. Economy*, Advances in Applied General Equilibrium Modeling,
DOI 10.1007/978-3-319-58866-7